CLAUDIO MARCELLO COSTA

doctorcosta

Tears and triumph: my life in the Clinica Mobile

FUCINA

First published in Italy by Fucina Srl
Via Ennio 8, 20137 Milan – Italy
Tel. (+39) 02.55189946 Fax (+39) 02.55181329
Web site: www.fucinaeditore.it
E-mail: info@fucinaeditore.it

Translated by Centro Traduzioni Imolese di Masi & C.
Via Melloni 7/c, 40026 Imola (BO) – Italy
Tel. (+39) 0542.35342 Fax (+39) 0542.35606
Web site: www.centrotraduzioni.com
E-mail: cti@centrotraduzioni.com

ISBN 88-88269-03-7

CONTENTS

Shel
Vanguard
8
27
MOTOBI
11

This book is dedicated to Checco Costa, the man who created the Imola race track to honour the skill and courage of motorcycle racers. This book is published exactly 50 years after the opening of that circuit.

PREFACE

When a book is written the writer is generally convinced he's being original, narrating something unique. To quote from Saint-Exupéry's *The Little Prince*, "that is your rose, your reward for the love and commitment with which you nurtured it". Similarly, this story is *my* story.

After a lifetime's dedication to the sport of motorcycling, I felt the need to put that story into print. It tells of my family, my father Checco and the riders that I have met and treated. In this book they have all been brought together in an attempt to understand just what it means for a man to face risk and face it alone. Moreover, I have also tried to analyse the age-old conflict between the individual and society: a clash that reaches its peak on the battleground of the motorcycle race track – one of the last arenas where a man can test himself to the limit.

It is a nostalgic story, full of both the joy of victory and the pain of the accidents and injuries that mould these modern-day knights we know as motorcycle riders, these heroes: to me, they are the best friends I have. While autobiographical, this work is also a study of man when he endures the extreme consequences of what he does and is face-to-face with himself. It is also a romantic attempt to accept death as part of life.

In writing this book I have been influenced not only by my father's and my own experiences, but by the classical education – encouraged by my mother and my aunts Dirce and Dida – received at the Benvenuto Rambaldi Grammar School of Imola, my friends, my first "love" and of course, "my" riders too.

A less direct but equally important stimulus has come from a maestro that I have never actually met: Aldo Carotenuto, Professor of Psychology at the University of Rome. His works have given me the confidence to take a close look at myself and provided me with the inspiring words that sparked my desire to write this book: "Injuries sometimes allow you to take a unique view of the world". My experience in treating injured riders has convinced me of the truthfulness and wisdom of this statement. The Danish philosopher Søren Kirkegaard confessed that he only ever read works by the condemned or persons who had been exposed to great danger: I feel more than sure than Søren would put this book on his reading list, as it deals not only with the obvious perils of the race track but was largely written after escaping from the shadow of a serious illness that hit me at the end of the year 2000. Fortunately, my friend Gianluca entrusted me to the skills of his cousin, Dr. Diego Ettore Cuzzocrea and I was subsequently cured, as confirmed by Doctors Ariele Saragoni, Michele Lazzari and Roberto Rossi.

This book also owes its existence to friends who have made words their livelihood. The journalist Ezio Pirazzini provided me with a goldmine of advice, secrets and stories he had been telling me since my childhood. Luca Delli Carri's book *Gli indisciplinati*, five stories of young racers, offered me lasting inspiration: it is with Luca that I put together not only the final chapter of this book (Faith) but a lasting friendship too.

I would like to express special thanks to Maria Teresa Sembianti and Gianfranco Morsiani who were the first to read this work, and Steve Davies, Claudia Cherici, David James and Alda Zanelli for translating the text into English.

PART ONE

My story

1. *Checco Costa*

The centaurs of ancient Greece were half man, half horse: led by their guide, Chiron, they would roam woods and mountain slopes in total freedom to give us the myths of history: "the while they raced along the brink, as when their game they hunted in the world of men" (Dante, *Inferno*, Canto 12, verses 55-57).

Populating many a tale told to grammar-school pupils, these creatures have fired the imagination of generations of students – and provided welcome relief from school studies.

Checco Costa was fascinated by such stories. They suggested to him the idea of re-creating the atmosphere of ancient Greece with its centaurs. Driven by enthusiasm and a vivid imagination he embarked on a project that would allow these "centaurs" – in their modern day incarnation as motorcycle riders – to roam once more, this time over the hills surrounding his home town of Imola. His efforts were to transform that dream into reality when, back in 1949, he organised the first motocross races – almost unheard of in Italy at that time – around the Acque Minerali park.

In fairness, the idea of creating a race track in Imola was not just Checco Costa's: it was shared by a group of motorcycle enthusiasts which included, in addition to its "core" members, Graziano Golinelli, Ugo Montevecchi, Alfredo Campagnoli and – by sheer weight of likeableness – Gualtiero Vighi.

One summer night in 1947, as they strolled along Via Romeo Galli, a country lane linking the Acque Minerali park with the bridge over the Santerno river, these pioneers sketched out a provisional circuit: along Via dei Colli, a link to the Tosa and Piratello corners, then back along Via Romeo Galli. As such, the entire route was less than 4 Km long and some 6 m wide.

But this was not the ideal that Checco Costa had imagined. Like all so-called dreamers he envisaged something unique: the simple plan drawn by his friends was not enough. He began to examine the question in greater depth, applying a mix of zeal and clear-cut thinking that would give rise to the definitive layout of the Imola race track.

A keen naturalist and an expert in agricultural sciences (some varieties of corn still bear his name), Checco Costa's knowledge of the track area was unsurpassed. As a child he used to spend summer holidays on the Rivazza farm with his brother Luigi (a talented painter who still lives in Imola), surrounded by nature and suffused with that special innocence children believe is eternal.

A love of motorcycles, the unique opportunities offered by the Castellaccio park and the short circuit sketched together with his friends came together to fire Checco's imagination: that summer night, in a park lit only by a wispy moonlight, the idea for a definitive circuit some 5 km long and 9 m wide that would one day become the famed Imola race track was born.

Francesco Costa (left), agriculture graduate: some grain varieties still bear his name.

This frail yet exciting idea was welcomed, nurtured and developed by many, but the circuit's founding father was clearly Checco Costa.

Checco Costa also designed the track corners, establishing their radius and giving them a special "lemniscate" form. He made sure that the tarmac was laid under the supervision of the Istituto Sperimentale Stradale (Experimental Road Institution) of the Italian Touring Club. Luck was had in that "Romita Act", a law in force at the time, was thought by the land surveyor Campagnoli likely to help the project gain official approval. Silvana, Checco's wife, happened to know the Minister the Act was named after, as he was a close friend of her father's. Checco's wife, Silvana was excep-

Francesco and Silvana Costa in the 1940's.

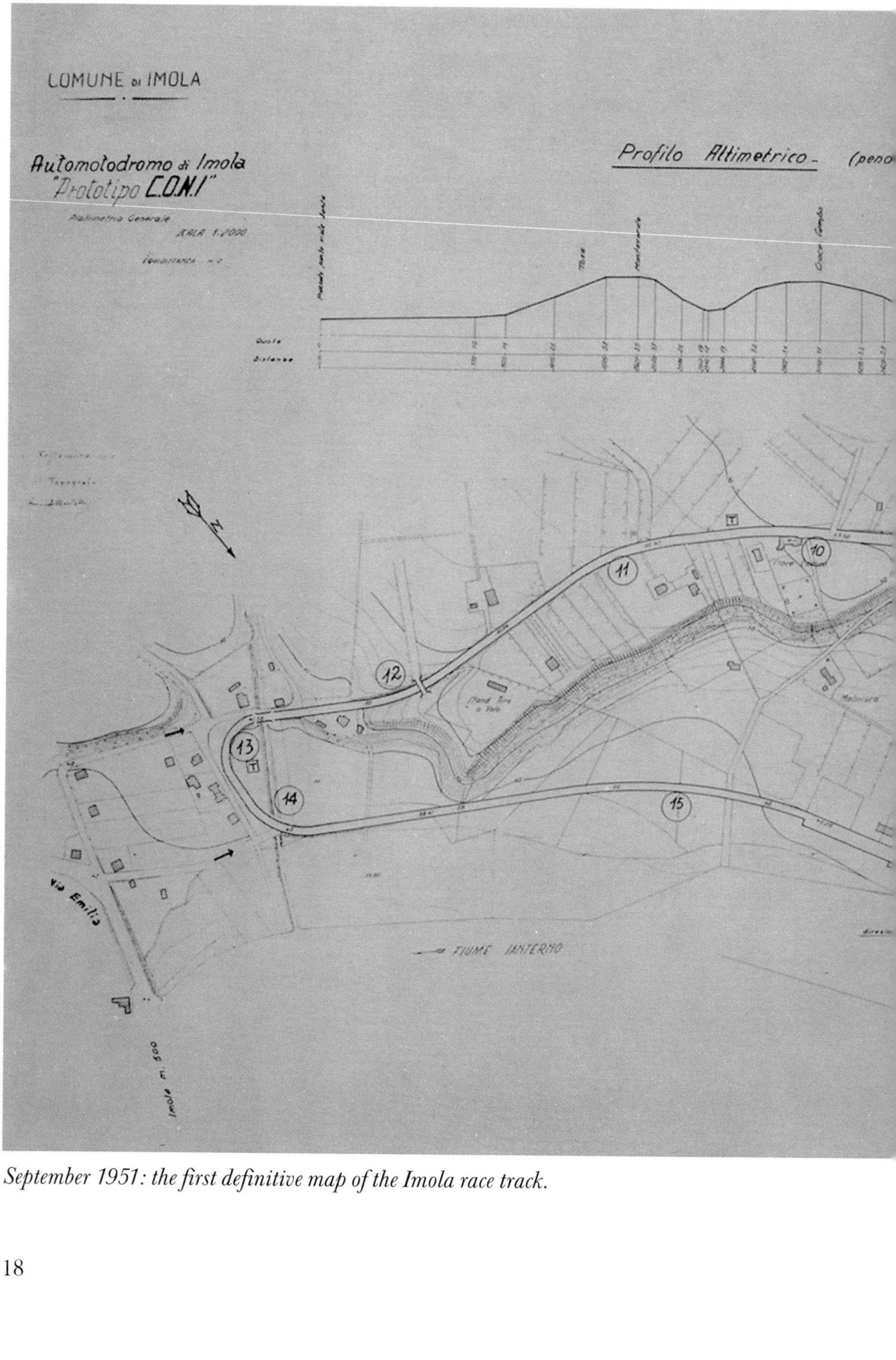

September 1951: the first definitive map of the Imola race track.

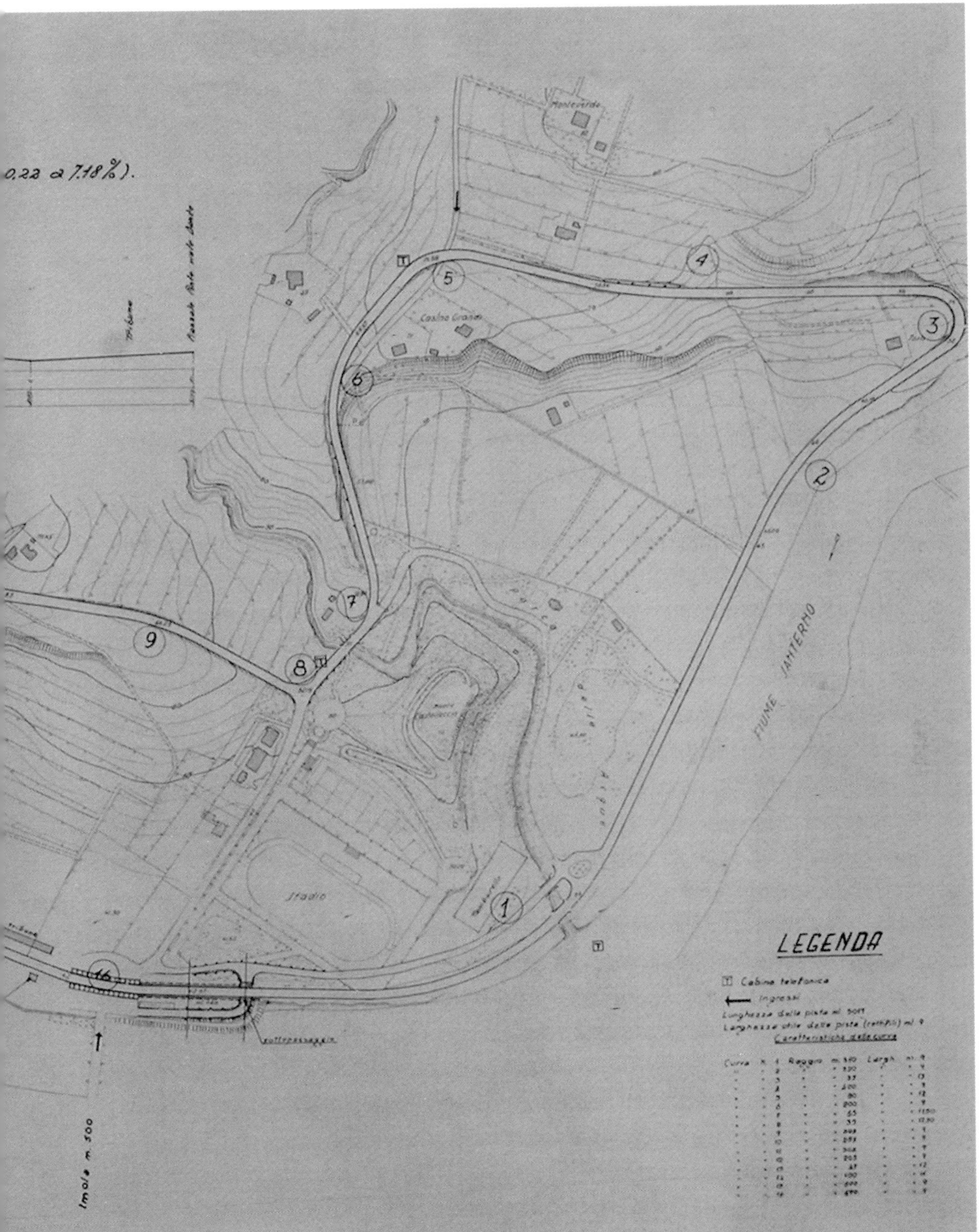
0,22 a 7,18%).
Monteverde
Casino Grande
Stadio
FIUME JANTERMO
LEGENDA
Cabina telefonica
Ingressi
Lunghezza della pista ml 5011
Larghezza utile della pista (rettifili) ml 9
Caratteristiche delle curve
sottopassaggio
Imola m 500

tionally beautiful; but it was not this that made her unique. While she may still not be aware of it, her face was the reflection of Checco's "anima", the feminine side of a man who had left the world and its needs behind to live in a quasi-Franciscan mysticism, closer to the mystery of nature and the sources of genius and creativity.

ESTI (The Imola Sport and Tourism Body) was founded on November 25, 1947, Tommaso Maffei Alberti being appointed chairman. After submitting the initial project to the President of the Italian Motorcycling Federation, Emanuele Bianchi, the final project was submitted to CONI (the Italian Olympic Committee). It was approved and works soon began. It should also be pointed out that the then Mayor of Imola, Amedeo Tabanelli, enthusiastically embraced the idea of a circuit immediately and assured the support of the local government. This impeccable conduct was adopted by his successor, Veraldo Vespignani.

The first strike of the pickaxe was dealt by CONI Chairman Giulio Onesti on March 6th, 1950. On October 18th-19th 1952, technical and sports tests were effected on the circuit in the presence of FMI Chairman Emanuele Bianchi, ESTI Chairman Tommaso Maffei Alberti, the Chairman of the Imola "Moto Club", Checco Costa, Enzo Ferrari, the Mayor of Imola, Veraldo Vespignani and even the Bishop of Imola, Benigno Carrara. At the opening ceremony the Italian tricolour tape was cut by Alberto Ascari in a Ferrari and Umberto Masetti on a four-cylinder Gilera.

By this time Ferrari was already a worldwide sporting legend and the rivalry between Gilera and Guzzi was delighting motorcycling fans all over Italy, especially the passionate enthusiasts of the Romagna: that day they assembled at Imola en masse in what was to be a stirring, emotional occasion.

Today, this circuit, this theatre of speed, is still there, winning the acclaim of those that love it and, ultimately, even those who suffer it or even hate it.

The disputes, the environmental controversies, the complaints by land owners, have all gradually died down. Because just by being human, we are the very expression of conflict: we are born to die! Only by accepting that conflict and ambiguity can we hope to, perhaps, one day, find an explanation as to why we were born to this world at all.

So, driven by genius and creativity, Checco Costa began to "write" the history of "his" circuit, a legacy left not just to Italy but the world.

On April 25th, 1953, he organised a race valid for the Italian championship. On that very first day of its long history, the crowds flocked to

October 18th, 1952: inauguration of the Imola race track. Checco Costa is second on the left.

The event's "Godfathers": Alberto Ascari (left) and Umberto Masetti in the Ferrari.

the Imola race track. Emilio Mendogni, a slightly-built yet big-hearted youngster entered the history books as the track's first-ever winner: riding a 125 cc Morini, his command of bike and track won him a spectacular victory. In the 500 cc class Alfredo Milani triumphed on his Gilera.

The following year, Checco Costa created one of motorcycling's most prestigious events, the Shell Gold Cup. Since it was vital that this race not be confused with other competitions – not even with World Championship races – he offered up a total of ITL 12 million (about 6,000 Euro) in prize money, an astounding sum for 1954. The only thing that could stop the event being a hands-down success was rain. And, needless to say, it bucketed down, not just at the first edition but at all too many others too. Consequently, Checco Costa faced financial disaster: creditors and bailiffs came knocking on his door and he was forced to weather the storm alone.

But Checco Costa was a not a man to be easily deterred: despite his sequestered furniture and numerous other difficulties, nothing seemed capable of denting this motorcycling patriarch's peace of mind. His confidence and trust in the world and the future remained intact.

It was a confidence that would prove to be justified. In April 1957, the stream of spectators became a tide. The epic battles between the rider-heroes of the riverside Santerno circuit were magical and unforgettable. A chapter unique in the history of motorcycling – one unrivalled to this day – was unfolding. Checco Costa became the "prophet" of a new era of motorcycle racing, later winning even further acclaim by "importing" the Daytona formula associated with the classic race in Florida.

Enthusiasm for traditional motorbike racing was beginning to wane by then, and Checco thought that the introduction of the Superbike "monsters", spiced up by duels between European and "New World" racers, would provide the crowds with just the thrills they were seeking: he opened up Europe to a whole generation of then unheard-of American racers.

After eighteen editions of the Shell Gold Cup, 1972 saw the beginning of the roll of honour for the "Daytona of Europe", the Imola 200 Mile Race. This competition was to endure until 1985 when the chequered flag was taken by a triumphant Eddie Lawson in front of Randy Mamola.

The undisputed "kings" of the Imola 200, though, were Giacomo Agostini and Kenny Roberts, true aficionados of the River Santerno circuit, Imola and Checco Costa.

Another thrilling International event, full of tension and competitive

April 25th, 1953: the first-ever Imola motorcycle race gets under way.

Emilio Mendogni on his Morini 125: the Imola race track's first-ever winner.

spirit, was the Grand Prix of Nations, in which motorcycling fans flocked to see the best international bike racers compete as national teams. In 1978 and 1979 the race was given an even more original flavour when talented riders from the United States, Italy, Great Britain and France battled it out against a "rest-of-the-world" team.

Checco was a brilliant organiser. His generosity and concern ensured that

Imola and its swarms of motorcycling fans.

the riders received only the best medical assistance. Right from the very first editions of the Gold Cup, he insisted on having only the best doctors. It is with enormous respect and nostalgia that I mention just two of them, Dr. Luigi Lincei and Dr. Adriano Mondini.

He put together an efficient – and enthusiastic – team of trackside marshals: Sante Bendanti, Giuseppe Cavina, Benso Sabbioni, Livio Zanelli,

Checco Costa unveils the Gold Cup which would symbolise an entire era of motorcycling.

Imola, April, many years ago: Checco Costa, the speeding motorcycles, the rain.

Alieto Martelli, Graziano Valli, Dulio Gavanelli, Filiberto Buscaroli and Luigi Carmonini. Some of these names form the core of the Santerno Moto Club (named after Checco Costa). He formed an alliance with Ermete Amadesi who, with the invaluable support of his two daughters Patrizia and Rossella, headed – and still heads – the CEA Group, famous the world over for its fire-fighting prowess.

The combination of simple ideas and solid commitment saw Imola, starting in 1949, produce over 40 years of motorcycle racing history: 23 Gold Cups, twelve editions of the Imola 200, 9 Motorcycle World Championship events, 5 European Championship Motocross races, 10 World Championship Motocross events.

It is a history that owes its existence to Checco Costa, and one that continues to be written thanks to the efforts of his younger son Carlo – the official circuit commentator – and his older son Claudio, who, ever since childhood, has shared his father's passion for these "centaurs". In creating the Clinica Mobile, Claudio has become not only the riders' doctor, but their friend too.

Giacomo Agostini and Kenny Roberts at Imola.

Barry Sheene and Kenny Roberts chat in the Imola pit lane.

Auguste Mingels, winner of many of the motocross events organised by Checco Costa.

Marcel Meunier, a keen favourite with the Imola fans.

Motocross at Imola in the 1950's: the centaurs ride again.

2. *Claudio Costa*

The following pages are an attempt to narrate a lifetime of events for which mere words may prove inadequate. It is an attempt to confide emotions that others may understand, but never feel. And no matter how much passion I might put into the telling of my story I fear that these written words will still have a hollow ring to them. To list the events of a story is easy: communicating the depth of experience that they entail is much more arduous; yet it is a story that I feel compelled to tell. In viewing the wealth of images projected onto the screen of my memory I feel that the time has come to describe and explain just where the acclaimed Clinica Mobile came from – and what it means to me.

In writing of the Clinica Mobile and how it came into being it is impossible for me to ignore that distant childhood in which I was blissfully

Dr. Costa as a child, when he believed that only good things could happen.

unaware that life does not last forever. I remember my father: he was my dream, my law, my destiny. I have no idea what I would have achieved without him, but I do know that I would have achieved it through my own labours: although it was virtually decided for me that my career would be in medicine, the success of the Clinica Mobile has given me enormous satisfaction.

The world of the Clinica Mobile has become my world, a refuge in which to shield myself from self-doubt. The Clinica Mobile is founded on an alliance between doctor and patient: a pact based on trust, a whole new dimension where medicine as science is ousted by love. The love of he who loves his heroes and the love the hero reserves for only his most trusted allies.

The Clinica Mobile for the riders, the riders for the Clinica Mobile. In this almost sacred atmosphere the riders' most heartfelt desire is to recover from fractures, injuries and illness and do so free from the dogmatic rules of science, the rules of "common sense" and that arrogant genetic programming which, to conserve the species, paralyses, crushes and freezes the individual.

"DNA feels nothing and knows nothing: DNA simply exists and all living beings cannot but dance to its music.

The universe that we contemplate shows only cruel indifference, no comforting design or finality. In this world of selfish genes, of blind physical forces and genetic replication, some human beings suffer, others less so: there is no sense to be made of all this, no reason, no justice.

We are evolution's children and as such we have to live our lives in a universe that is totally indifferent to our suffering. All that remains is the freedom to be successful or fail in that which we have chosen" (from concepts by Stephen Jay Gould and Richard Dawkins).

Yet it is only when man turns his attention towards the immensity of his inner world, when he hears its music, that he finds the harmony that lets him write his song, decide his destiny and thus cancel the absurdity of indifference's suffering and cruelty.

Legends and fairy tales are packed with the stuff of heroes. In the words of Aldo Carotenuto, "the hero, who, after his astonishing exploits, receives invaluable riches, a vast kingdom and the love of a beautiful girl, is actually no more than a courageous man who has challenged life's

30 — THE AUSTRALIAN www.news.com.au Monday October 5 1998 — 30

SPEED WEEKEND

Cheer for a champion: Michael Doohan proudly shows off his prize to the crowd after winning the Australian 500cc Grand Prix yesterday

Picture: AFP

● **Victory prize:** World champion Michael Doohan sits with the Australian flag (above) after his win. Doohan (below) shows the style that got him across the line first

Pictures: ROY HAVERKAMP, DARREN TINDALE

Doctor-patient relationship gives life a new dimension

A WORLD champion in a truly global sport becomes many things. To the throng of Australians at Phillip Island and many points beyond yesterday, Michael Doohan is Greg Norman with five United States majors golf tournaments, Wayne Carey with five football premierships and as many Brownlow Medals, or cricketer Stephen Waugh 500 not out batting against Curtly Ambrose without a protector.

He's an incomparable hero in a sport in which the dangers are as close as the blurred tarmac and always potentially fatal.

But to Dr Claudio Costa, motorcycling's permanent medical attache-cum-resident miracle worker and a man whose birthplace, education and workplace offer him many heroes from the past to the present, Doohan is far more about life than the ubiquitous threat of death.

He's a towering inspiration, a template for his daily existence and for his other patients.

"I am the doctor of his health, but he is the doctor of my life," Costa said yesterday while restoring life and limb to the endless array of limping riders at Phillip Island's mobile clinic.

The two men, the working-class Australian boy turned world champion bike rider and the well-dressed, cultured Italian doctor, have formed the most intimate of bonds since Costa saved Doohan's leg and with it his now stellar career after a crippling fall in the 1992 Dutch Grand Prix.

Doohan has often spoken of his deep gratitude to Costa, dedicating his win in the doctor's home town of Imola this year to the "team in the paddock" who support him. At other times, he has called Costa "a great man". Each time, the moment of recognition has given the 57-year-old doctor a lump in the throat. Only now, though, has Costa 'fessed up about the depth of his feeling for Doohan.

Clearly, it goes beyond the normal boundaries of patient and doctor. "From the medical point of view, sure I have helped Mick," Costa said. "But from the human point of view we help each other and maybe he teaches me how to get over the problems of life.

"In a risky sport like motorcycling, you can overcome problems to be a better man, you can do that in life."

Dutch doctors wanted to amputate Doohan's leg when it became infected after the accident in 1992.

"He was so close to losing the leg, I had to find the strength to save it," Costa said.

A keen fan of motorcycle racing, Costa knew the sport couldn't afford to lose the young Australian. However, he was prevented by Dutch laws from treating Doohan in the Netherlands.

Horrified at Doohan's treatment and eventually ejected from the hospital by the local doctors for showing his revulsion, Costa effectively kidnapped the rider in a private jet and took him to Italy.

Costa strapped the good leg to the bad, swapping blood between the two limbs as part of urgent, remedial therapy. Even now, Doohan doesn't have full use of his leg but can still ride bikes. For both men, that was all that was needed.

In 1994, after intense rehabilitation, Doohan began his sequence of unbeaten 500cc championship wins. Unlike Norman or other world champions from the land down under, global fame hasn't given him an American accent, let alone taught him to speak fluent Italian.

So he and Costa have developed a private patois. "We have our own unique language that is quite magic," the Italian said. "Don't forget, the child can communicate with its mother without speaking, only with its eyes."

And what are those eyes saying about a fifth successive world title? "The exchange will be one of paradise reached."

Doohan is not the only Australian rider to have been helped by Costa. His healing hands were allowing Garry McCoy to ride his Yamaha yesterday, even though a smashed leg won't let him walk for another three and a half months.

And in 1989, the year in which Wayne Gardner won the first grand prix at Phillip Island, the rider was restored to health by Costa after a fall. But it is Doohan with whom Costa has forged the most potent bond.

"I help all the riders in the same way," Costa said. "But because the injury to Mick happened in 1992, a very deep friendship has been born. This is why we are very close at the moment. I love him."

Much good has come out of that 1992 incident. The rules have been changed to allow Costa to practise medicine in every country which hosts a grand prix. And his dedication to his profession and the sport he has loved since he was a bambino have been richly vindicated.

Even when it includes the provision of a private jet, a spot of kidnapping and the odd minor miracle, the doctor can only do so much. It then befalls the patient to show the mental strength and courage to build on the chances provided.

Every time he leans gracefully into a corner or roars down a straight and takes another chequered flag, Doohan takes all these little homilies about the grasping of opportunity into celestial dimensions.

Little wonder his doctor loves him.

Thanks doc: Doohan with Dr Claudio Costa, the man who saved his legs and career, on the podium after the race

Picture: GEORGE SAL

Doctor-patient relationship gives life a new dimension

A world champion in a truly global sport becomes many things. To the throng of Australians at Phillip Island and many points beyond yesterday, Michael Doohan is Greg Norman with five United States majors golf tournaments, Wayne Carey with five football premierships and as many Brownlow Medals, or cricketer Stephen Waugh 500 not out batting against Curtly Ambrose without a protector.

He's an incomparable hero in a sport in which the dangers are as close as the blurred tarmac and always potentially fatal.

But to Dr Claudio Costa, motorcycling's permanent medical attache-cum-resident miracle worker and a man whose birthplace, education and workplace offer him many heroes from the past to the present, Doohan is far more about life than the ubiquitous threat of death.

He's towering inspiration, a template for his daily existence and for his other patients.

"I am the doctor of his health, but he is the doctor of my life," Costa said yesterday while restoring life and limb to the endless array of limping riders at Phillip Island's Clinica Mobile.

The two men, the working-class Australian boy turned world champion bike rider and the well-dressed, cultured Italian doctor, have formed the most intimate of bonds since Costa saved Doohan's leg and with it his now stellar career after a crippling fall in the 1992 Dutch Grand Prix.

Doohan has often spoken of his deep gratitude to Costa, dedicating his win in the doctor's home town of Imola this year to the "team in the paddock" who support him. At other times, he has called Costa "a great man". Each time, the moment of recognition has given the 57-year-old doctor a lump in the throat. Only now, though, has Costa fessed up about the depth of his feeling for Doohan.

Clearly, it goes beyond the normal boundaries of patient and doctor. "From the medical point of view, sure I have helped Mick," Costa said. "But from the human point of view we help each other and maybe he teaches me how to get over the problems of life.

"In a risky sport like motorcycling, you can overcome problems to be a better man, you can do that in life."

Dutch doctors wanted to amputate Doohan's leg when it became infected after the accident in 1992.

"He was so close to losing the leg, I had to find the strength to save it," Costa said.

A keen fan of motorcycle racing, Costa knew the sport couldn't afford to lose the young Australian. However, he was prevented by Dutch laws from treating Doohan in the Netherlands.

Horrified at Doohan's treatment and eventually ejected from the hospital by the local doctors for showing his revulsion, Costa effectively kidnapped the rider in a private jet and took him to Italy.

Costa strapped the good leg to the bad, swapping blood between the two limbs as part of urgent, remedial therapy. Even now, Doohan doesn't have full use of his leg but can still ride bikes. For both men, that was all that was needed.

In 1994, after intense rehabilitation, Doohan began his sequence of unbeaten 500cc championship wins. Unlike Norman or other world champions from the land down under, global fame hasn't given him an American accent, let alone taught him to speak fluent Italian.

So he and Costa have developed a private patois. "We have our own unique language that is quite magic," the Italian said. "Don't forget, the child can communicate with its mother without speaking, only with its eyes."

And what are those eyes saying about a fifth successive world title? "The exchange will be one of paradise reached."

Doohan is not the only Australian rider to have been helped by Costa. His healing hands were allowing Garry McCoy to ride his Yamaha yesterday, even though a smashed leg won't let him walk for another three and a half months.

And in 1989, the year in which Wayne Gardner won the first grand prix at Phillip Island, the rider was restored to health by Costa after a fall. But it is Doohan with whom Costa has forged the most potent bond.

"I help all the riders in the same way," Costa said. "But because the injury to Mick happened in 1992, a very deep friendship has been born. This is why we are very close at the moment. I love him."

Much good has come out of that 1992 incident. The rules have been changed to allow Costa to practise medicine in every country which hosts a grand prix. And his dedication to his profession and the sport he has loved since he was a bambino have been richly vindicated.

Even when it includes the provision of a private jet, a spot of kidnapping and the odd minor miracle, the doctor can only do so much. It then befalls the patient to show the mental strength and courage to build on the chances provided.

Every time he leans gracefully into a corner or roars down a straight and takes another chequered flag, Doohan takes all those little homilies about the grasping of opportunity into celestial dimensions.

Little wonder his doctor loves him.

(The Australian, October 5th 1998)

difficulties in the name of his values. Thus he enters the enchanted forest, challenges its ghosts and spectres, draws his sword once more even though already injured. And just when fate seems to be tormenting him something happens, someone runs to his aid, allowing him to complete his mission". Risk-taking is nothing less than the desire to transform the impossible into the possible: to throw oneself into the fray is the only way to capture that magic key that grants entry to the castle where true existence resides.

Yet in reality, men do not feel immortal nor live the fleeting moment as if it were eternal. Besieged by consumerism, slaves to a "fashion" that sows an interior death as real as any biological one, they have become brittle masks, invisible to themselves and the world. Those, instead, who attempt to cut through life's fog and discover the truth about themselves and have the courage to accept the absurd ambivalence of the human condition, wear no mask and are visible to the world. Like our fairy-tale hero, only he who accepts the risk of the dragon's flames can hope to succeed in his quest. At the Clinica Mobile we often witness, as on the day of Epiphany, a marvellous transformation: the heartfelt desire to recover illuminates an immense, mysterious world hidden in the mind of the injured rider, and an irrational will fulfils it, drawing on energies until then unknown.

Pain mutates from the unbearable to the acceptable and then softens to become an almost welcome companion; suffering feeds the bud of hope that can bloom into that most beautiful of flowers – courage. Yet courage is never alone: it is always accompanied by fear, a fear that some are able to use to drive themselves onwards and upwards.

The heroes of world championship motorcycling – like ordinary people injured in the everyday accidents of road and motorway – will have encountered this dimension. The tears that stain their faces are not the tears of resignation; instead, they shine with a nostalgia that should be marvelled at. A nostalgia that recalls long-past yet never forgotten moments of joy, which remind the sufferer that happiness is inside us and, perhaps, in our future. Injuries and tears are the ambassadors of a happiness to come; a happiness that lasts forever yet lasts only a moment as it does in dreams. Injuries and tears are the building blocks of the bridges that carry the sufferer over the abyss into the kingdom of future achievement. To witness this resurrection is nothing less than astonishing: it is an event that carries a message of hope not only for the world of motorcycling but the world of sport and the world as a whole. Perhaps the Paradise from which we were ejected – sad, tearful and demoralized, afraid to look back, our minds full of suffering and darkness yet equally full of stupendous sentiments such as love, trust and hope – has not been lost. At the Clinica Mobile, this "bridge-building" is witnessed almost daily and the immensity of these events is humbling. In these moments our work becomes the art of creating an altar at which human determination can be worshipped.

To aspire to something: perhaps this is the meaning of a life, even if that something is unattainable. The sheer force of wanting, the letting loose of an irrational "folly" hidden from the dim light of reason, the freeing of the gods that live in all of us and the discovery of the Dionysian divinity that lives in each human heart can drive us towards even the unattainable. Of course, there is a risk that such marvellous sentiments will expose the rider to a dangerous sense of omnipotence or invincibility. But when he puts on his helmet and lowers the visor he makes a gesture that is humbly human, a clear acknowledgement of his finite, human condition.

The crash helmet symbolises that fabric which cloaks and dresses a life truly lived.

Young people – and all too often their older counterparts – do not wear crash helmets willingly. Upbringing and advertising combine to associate the image of the helmetless rider with coolness and bravado. Youngsters, in not wearing their crash helmet, cushion themselves with a sense of invulnerability and invincibility, and in this fog of delusion they sadly forget their real nature, just like "old" riders who go helmetless to ward off the spectre of the coming, inevitable end. In letting the wind race through their hair they hope to mitigate the unease they carry in their hearts: a terrible illusion. Feelings of omnipotence and invulnerability are, by definition, inhuman: rather than cancelling the error, they compound it tragically. To assume a front of invincibility is to fall into a cycle that begins with belligerent arrogance and flows inexorably into violence, war and – ultimately – the apocalypse. Young people should be made aware of this "attitude trap". In escaping from the fog of illusory immunity they have everything to gain. Yet to do so is extremely difficult as the values which reveal that immunity for the hollow fraud it is are stolen from them daily by a society that has slipped into darkness and decadence. Every day, young people are alienated from reality, truth and authenticity: the ensuing slide into discomfort encrusts their minds in ice. Now, separating us from the imagination and play of childhood, there stands a cold wall built from rules built of arid mediocrity. A frozen lake covers the genius and creativity of the young, hardening their hearts and minds. The result? A world of frozen sentiment.

The creation of youth was, perhaps, God's finest work. Why put it at risk? For all we know, when God created the Earth, on the sixth day he created youth. On the afternoon of the same day – perhaps a little "tired" from his efforts – he created adults... and here the result left something to be desired. The Guardian Angels of youth return to the heavens daily to sing the Lord's praises: their colleagues who safeguard the adults are a little more perplexed. Angels may be celestial and all-knowing yet they still fail to understand – and sometimes remain dumbfounded – as to why adults suffocate the almost divine spirit of youth in the name of power, progress and technology.

And what is power, if not a monster that tramples on the fervid minds of the young, separating them from their play and snatching away nature's whispered truths to deliver them into a future full of false promises without hope?

Yet I have enormous trust in the young and know that their boundless imagination will soon carry them to a new existence that, despite having the same merits and flaws as this one, will be unaffected and closer to real life. To reach this "paradise" they will ride a metaphorical "motorbike" providing them not only with unlimited freedom but psychological strength with which to oppose the ruin of false promises and thus conquer true freedom of spirit.

The motorbike: a perfect modern-day version of the natural, animal half of our mythological centaur, a vehicle-cum-guide on which youngsters will escape from the prison of the world and crack the ice that freezes their emotions.

I see the motorbike as the perfect metaphor of unsuppressible desire, the means by which identity is conquered and youths can finally enter into a dimension that coincides with their destiny. My trust in the young remains undaunted. Soon they will set aside the cloak of invulnerability thrown over them by stupidity, lower the visor of their crash helmets and, on completing this symbolic gesture, join the human race and zoom off along its track to live a life as it should be lived.

Nothing is more marvellous than a youth who appears before us as an adult, who rides the meaning of life itself, fully accepting the ambivalence of the human condition, the joy and the pain. A youth who – like Peter Pan – has retained the marvellous gifts of childhood.

Only then will the Guardian Angels of men find the tranquillity of those that watch over youths. But they still won't be without their doubts. How is it that men manage to redeem themselves from pain and suffering by facing challenges of almost mythological proportion? How do these mere humans find greatness – and even happiness – by overcoming an ordeal to reach a goal? Is it not, perhaps, that this redemption is the most marvellous work of all "Creation"?

For us at the Clinica Mobile, this is the very essence of what it means to be a motorcycle rider. Helmeted youths imbued with life, real life, hurtling through the wind of challenge, their fingertips tantalisingly close to God's in a fresco of speed equal in magnificence to that of Michelangelo's Sistine Chapel.

The symbols air-brushed onto the racers' crash-helmets recall those etched onto the shields of medieval jousters. The very mirror of man's age-old desire to change reality, those symbols are a source of magic and superstition that makes it easier to push the rock of existence up the hill. It is almost as if the mythological Sisyphus, forced by the gods to roll a rock to a mountain peak only to crash unavoidably back down into the valley with it – were happy to have been assigned this absurd, arduous task. Warding off ill-luck gives the illusion of dominating life's uncertainties. Hence every rider treasures his crash helmet as if it were a part of him – and loves it as if it were his strongest shield. It is his and his alone – not only to protect his head but to banish the doubts that weaken the spirit.

Magic and astrology have no basis in fact. Yet despite their irrationality, they are an essential part of our imagination as they bolster the illusion that a sometimes absurd, disheartening reality can be dominated. The ritual of superstition is a key part of what it means to be human – and thus a key part of every rider's psyche. The doctors of the Clinica Mobile are no exception to this rule: especially in the midst of injured "centaurs".

"Centaur: half-man, half horse. Apollo's splendid light of reason and the immense natural 'folly' of Dionysus". These words were written on 1st May 1997 on the inauguration of the fourth Clinica Mobile. Today, that phrase is still to be found on the blackboard in this small hospital: in the hearts of those that work at the Clinica Mobile it is an indelible message, a maxim that, while it does not exclude fatality, liberates men from slavery and grants them the energy needed to find true freedom of spirit and a sense of wonder. It is a message that poets and artists have conveyed repeatedly over the centuries.

Steven Spielberg's World War Two epic, Saving Private Ryan, illustrates the point. The story is based on the eternal conflict between society and the individual. After three of the Ryan brothers die in various theatres of war, the American High Command decides to bring the fourth brother – still fighting somewhere in Normandy – back home to his mother. Yet this last Ryan refuses the offer, preferring to continue to fight. It is a battle between a species seeking to save itself and the free will of the individual who desires self-determination and wishes to follow a path that will one day allow him to say "I have led a good life". Compassionately, America wants the sole surviving Ryan to stop fighting and return home for the good of the "species"; yet despite the evident risks, he decides to fulfil an irrepressible desire to carry on with the war. The "common sense" of society versus the "sense" of the individual whose individuality pushes him to lead his life, seek out his talents, achieve his own goals.

Even the platoon sent to save Ryan cannot but acknowledge the spirit behind his "insane" decision, the subtle truth underlying his "recklessness". Their understanding, their recognition of the magic that motivates Ryan's self-determination ultimately costs them their lives.

In the end the "species" is saved – at the others' expense – via the extreme violence of war as graphically illustrated in the first part of Spielberg's film.

Outside the context of war, the only battle that will save the individual is the fight to achieve all his wishes; in taking up that fight he will find true respect for others, understand the meaning of diversity and perhaps help humankind save itself from cruelty, violence and indifference.

A similar story is endured by Goethe's Doctor Faust, who, in order to understand his own meaning, sells his soul to the devil. At the end of this disturbing literary classic, Faust, despite carrying this abominable pact with Mephistopheles to its conclusion, is saved.

The Clinica Mobile "of the Centaurs" is the cradle of that insuppressable human desire to be oneself, a desire that is the essence of the ugly duckling that risks drowning to become a beautiful swan, the Cinderella who sweeps aside her misery by challenging the cruel restrictions imposed by her family, the hero who wishes to heal his wounds and defeat the woes of the world.

Like Achilles and Siegfried, the bulk of mythological characters are blighted by a wound that never heals, "a rent that offers them an original view of the world" as Aldo Carotenuto wrote. He that cries out against these heroic efforts, he who would burn the myth of Nuvolari and his disciples is a nonentity, a sick decadent who has failed to intuit the true meaning of life; he is a powerless slave, a stifled nobody who lives in the complex of his own neuroses. He holds the misleading conviction that "common sense", rules, the arid mediocrity of the daily, prejudice, power, technology and idle chatter are truths. Backbiting is an awful pastime, because, in the words of Perls "if you hate anything which is outside yourself, that thing is yourself, no matter how difficult that might be to accept... you hate yourself yet think it's me you hate".

The greatest drama of existence is to ignore truth, one's own personal desires, background, legends. Every day choices are imposed on us by "others", choices that are, mostly, sterile or damaging; they load us up with inexistent needs and a diluted philosophy of passive survival. These "others" see an injured man who attempts to recover and make the most of what this unique life has to offer him as something scandalous. I honestly cannot decide whether this is a genuine blindness to the fascination of courage, or the envy of those unable to walk life's true path.

Yet the reader should not be misled into thinking that the staff at the Clinica Mobile have some "superior" ability to perceive the riders' courage with absolute clarity; on the contrary, we are sometimes quite perplexed. The point is that we do not feel envy and we do not shout "scandal": to do so would be to shout against ourselves: it would be a shout that inexorably condemns us to slavery, making us powerless prisoners in a cavern of "non sense".

To resist that condemnation is to become a hero. That resistance has opened up a fantastic destiny for the staff of the Clinica Mobile: to help the heroes of world championship motorcycling, the riders who cloak themselves in a life suspended between dreams and reality.

The conviction that I should dedicate my life to these riders was sentimentally and emotionally reinforced by two life-changing experiences, the first of which occurred during the second edition of the Shell Gold Cup on 11th April 1955 and the other during the fourth edition of the same race on 22nd April 1957.

During the first of the above-mentioned races Ray Amm, debuting on an MV Agusta, died after skidding off at the Rivazza on the 22nd lap, while tailing Ken Kavanagh (who went on to win the race) riding a Guzzi. A few days before the race Ray Amm had been a dinner guest at my home and I had realised that, despite his fame as a fearless, death-defying motorcycle rider, he was an unassuming, kind man with a passion for the opera. That this "hard man" of motorcycling should be so ambivalent and tender was a source of great fascination to me: when he died I felt that a part of me had died too. That day, devastated by grief, I felt an overriding desire to possess the omnipotence that would resurrect him.

That first episode was to be reinforced by the second: on that day, in 1957, I distinctly remember disobeying my father who had ordered me to

Imola, 7th April 1955: Ray Amm and a very youthful Claudio Costa.

keep a safe distance from the race track. To get closer I hid behind some straw bales that had been stacked up against a pine tree at the Acque Minerali corner. As Duke rode his Gilera 500 cc into the curve he lost control and crashed right in front of me. In a flash I was on the track and managed to drag Duke to safety. I then ran back to get the bike out of the way of the oncoming riders. This "perfect" rescue was immortalised by a nearby photographer. The next day my father saw the photo of that amateur rescuer (hidden under the "disguise" of an adult's hat) on the sports pages of the Resto del Carlino: he punished me severely – yet predicted that on becoming a doctor my life's mission would be doing just that – saving riders.

These experiences helped me enter a magical world that I would never again leave. Never again would I abandon that inexhaustible source of experience which reinforces my conviction that "life is there to be lived". Only once did I meditate leaving this "home" that my father's vivid imagination had handed me; it was a Sunday, on 20th May 1973 at Monza.

At 3 in the afternoon, at the first corner (there were no chicanes back then) Jarno Saarinen and Renzo Pasolini died in a terrible accident that toppled a total of seventeen riders. Despite the efforts made by Dr. Giancarlo Caroli – a skilled trackside medic our team had specially called in for the event – these two riders could not be saved. Not even the fact that we had managed to resuscitate Walter Villa and Victor Palomo was able to console us. That day, the tears that ran down my face as I hugged Saarinen's gentle wife seemed to flow without end, and through them I caught a blurred glimpse of the unforgettable moments that had marked my friendship with the two dead riders. My grief-stricken mind was filled with memories, the most insistent of which were linked to events that had occurred some two months previously, at a time when nothing seemed to hint at such a terrible future. On the eve of the second edition of the Imola 200, Renzo Pasolini was running a fever and had a terribly sore throat. Just before the race, despite all the treatment he'd received, his chances of being on the starting grid were practically zero. Yet his will to race was so great that despite being almost delirious with fever, he mounted his Harley Davidson Superbike and, lap by lap, to the applause of the crowd, steadily rose up through the ranks of riders. Suddenly, he pulled off the track to enter the pits. Taking off his helmet to reveal a bright red fever-struck face, he said "I stopped 'cause something strange was going

Imola, 22nd April 1957: Geoff Duke falls at the Acque Minerali corner…

…and a young Claudio Costa performs his first trackside rescue.

on: at the start I had twelve riders in front of me, and after overtaking several of them there still seemed to be loads to overtake. I just couldn't figure it at all, and it was only towards the end that I realised I was practically delirious and was – quite literally – seeing triple. For every rider in front of me, I saw three. Three times twelve is a lot of competition even for me, so I thought I'd best get back for some serious treatment".

On 25th March 1973, an International Race had been organised by the Costa-Ronci-Tempesta triumvirate and family friend Pietro Dalpozzo. In the 350 cc category Jarno Saarinen was battling it out in the rain with Giacomo Agostini; as he came into the Tamburello, one of motorcycling's most thrilling – and dangerous – corners, he fell heavily. The apprehension was great; Jarno arrived at the small trackside hospital conscious and calm, more than anything dismayed at having fallen. As he stripped off his mud-covered leathers he put us at ease, convinced that his injuries were superficial. However, the translator Giovanni Fantazzini – one of my father's most faithful followers and beautifully fluent in German (even more fluent than in Italian according to some) – said that the Finnish rider's right knee was beginning to trouble him. I examined him again. Unable to find anything wrong, I suggested he apply plenty of ice to the knee as it could swell. It was not a suggestion based on clinical diagnosis: it was, rather, made out of a sense of concern for someone who I thought of as a legend. In the evening, as we were having supper at the Hotel Molino Rosso, a worried Giovanni Fantazzini urged me to take another look at Jarno Saarinen in his hotel room. I found him lying on the bed, his wife Soili sitting next to him looking thoughtful. There was a lot of ice packed around his knee. Smiling, he started talking in German, Giovanni translating: "Doctorcosta", (all in one breath, a habit that, years later, would be Mick Doohan's too) he began, "you told me that this knee would have swollen and now that you've been proved right you're going to have to do something about it because I want to race on 1st April at Misano, 8th April at Modena, 15th April at the Imola 200 and 22nd April during the 'first ever' World Championship race in France at Le Castellet". The knee was horribly swollen, full of liquid which was most likely blood. I took him to the casualty Department at the Istituto Ortopedico Rizzoli of Bologna where I had worked in my graduation year, 1967. Consulting with my maestro, Prof. Alessandro Dal Monte, I removed a large quantity of blood from his knee. We immobilised the joint in a lightweight support.

Renzo Pasolini.

Jarno Saarinen holds off Giacomo Agostini.

I already knew riders were strange and "mad", but it was only then that I became fully aware that riders have something magical about them which keeps them outside the prison of rules. I now know that man's most lucid, vivid moments are lived when he is at his "craziest", anchored to reality as if in a dream, where pain is no longer just a useless worry but a kind of gift – of infinite value. I now know the worst madness is that of those who declare their sanity yet immediately retire to their lair to lick their wounds: those that see protection in only the still waters of tranquillity. They fail to realise that stagnant waters offer a poor spectacle compared to the tumultuous crash of the mountain stream, the waterfall.

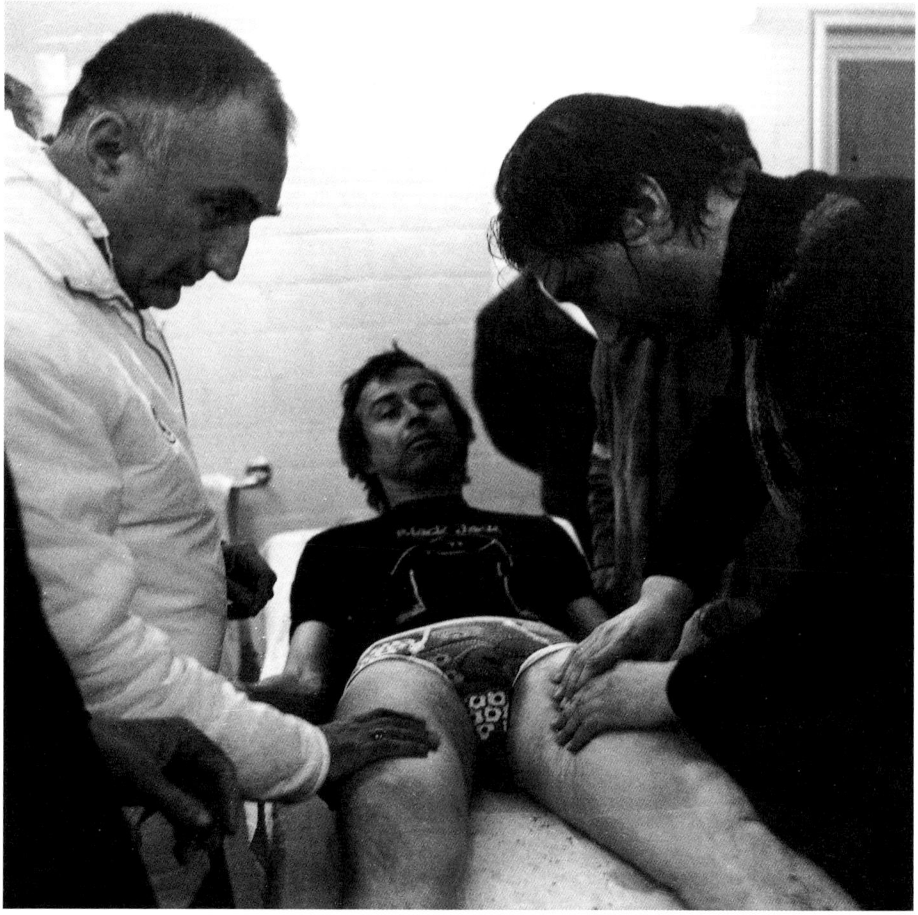

March 25th 1973: Claudio Costa (right) examines Saarinen after his crash at the Tamburello.

Feeling somewhat excited, I told Jarno – who I admired greatly – that "in five days the support can come off and on 1st April you'll be racing at Misano". On pronouncing these words I immediately felt a twinge of unease as I knew I was pushing my luck – and his: yet the look of happiness that suffused Saarinen's face instantly banished any doubts.

The next day Saarinen left for Holland to see the new 500 cc Yamaha and meet the managers of this famed motorcycle manufacturer. Concerned for their protégée, they offered him the services of top-level doctors. Jarno politely refused, as he already had a doctor – "doctorcosta" – and that he intended to hang on to him as long as he lived. The immense pri-

A smile illuminates the steely gaze of Jarno Saarinen.

de and joy I felt on hearing these words was enhanced by a gift that Jarno gave me: today, it is one of my most treasured possessions. I was blissfully unaware that the cup from which I had gulped down happiness would soon offer up the appalling grief of Monza.

As promised, after five days I freed Jarno' knee; together, we decided it would be best to skip the Misano race on 1st April and return to competition on 7th April at the City of Modena Grand Prix. The coincidence that this was also my father's birthday bolstered my belief that Saarinen would return to racing on that day. (Fascinating superstition? Yes! The warding off of bad luck helps men to change the absurdity of life, remember?). On Friday 6th April we moved from Imola, where Jarno was staying for treatment, to the Donatello Hotel in Modena. That day we had decided not to do any track trials so as to prolong treatment of the knee. In the hotel room I played the role of both masseur and doctor and as I spent more and more time with Jarno I felt growing friendship and affection for him. I began to realise that happiness is an inhabitant of the human interior, and is freed only when we do something with love, when we

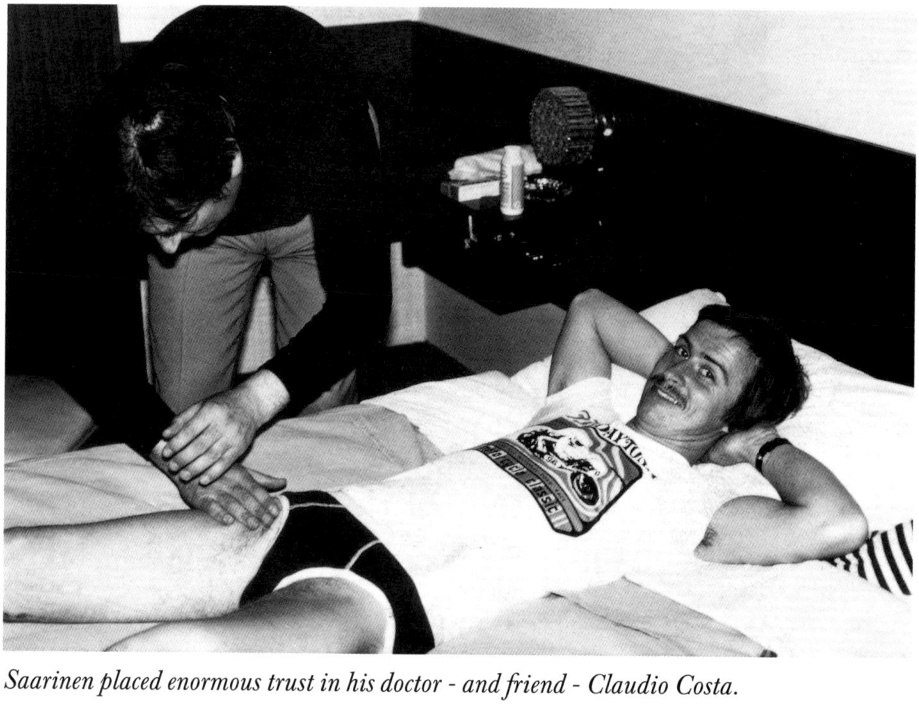

Saarinen placed enormous trust in his doctor - and friend - Claudio Costa.

create or invent, when we master an art or strike up an alliance with others to dispel the fear and solitude of the unknown.

On Saturday 7th April Jarno rode 10 laps (five to qualify for the 250 cc race and another five for the 350 cc class). When race day, Sunday 8th April, came, we were both very excited – perhaps me more than him. The arrangement was thus: he would run through the first race cautiously to get the feel of things and then give it everything in the second. Jarno was true to his word: during the first race he put his knee through its paces, content to find that it was working well. I was probably as happy as he was in this regard, but it was a happiness dulled by anxiety: "What if, in the second race he throws caution to the wind, and compromises his recovery?" Doubts multiplied. An ever-more insistent voice was shouting at me to advise Jarno against competing in the second race. In the end I went over to him and stammered that I thought he'd best wait another week, for his own good. I will never forget his crushed look of disappointment nor his disturbing reply. The joy had left the scene altogether. I was accused of having betrayed the one true moral in the world. I had been deviated towards that irrepressible need to save the species – to the detriment of that noble mission to help a human being respect his individuality, his inclination and his innate talent. Jarno's words would prove unforgettable, words that still guide me through life's uncertainties: "If you want to keep on being my doctor, providing me with proper treatment won't be enough. Because you'll have to abandon any reservation you might feel in letting me return to racing as soon as I'm able. Give me the truth about my condition and after that any responsibility is mine and mine alone". Soon afterwards he mounted his bike and went on to win that second race, then the Imola 200 and then all the 250 cc and 500 cc races in the World Championship for the next 42 days until he died on the track at Monza.

During that appallingly sad night I cried like a child, blaming myself over and over again for not having encased him in plaster for 2 months, envious, for once, of those who hide in the quagmire of indecision. That night I dreamt of my father who had, in the morning, received reassurance from Jarno that he would be competing in three races (a combined 250, 350 and 500cc event) on 30th September at the Imola-held Shell Gold Cup. The smiling, serene features of my father cheered me. I saw that the face of the disappointed Jarno who has listened to my cautious advice at Modena was no worse than the one that I had seen after his death at

Monza. The loss of a life well lived is, no matter how sad, a natural fatality. To lose a life without living it is, though, a mortal sin.

So I continued working in the world of motorcycling and since then I have always taken sides with those who try to live their life to the full rather than those that try to run from it. Every time I help a rider get back in the saddle it is Jarno's smiling face that encourages me. Jarno taught me that we can choose to be men and that joy is drunk from the same cup that contains grief.

On 12th May 1979, again at the Tamburello corner, Virginio Ferrari was saved by my close friend Dr. Giuseppe Russo thanks to prompt resuscitation: Ferrari's lightning recovery soon presented me with another dilemma. The following morning he said he wanted to race as he "felt fine", and tests seemed to confirm this. Yet the world was not interested. The instinct to protect the species cancelled out the truth of the moment, that Virginio Ferrari was all right. That which was real and concrete was ignored. Virginio Ferrari had come close to death on the Saturday, but had been saved by Beppe Russo: this is a fact. The day after, the rider felt fine, an opinion confirmed by clinical and instrumental tests. That too is a fact. In the end, Virginio Ferrari not only competed in the race, he nearly won it too, losing out by just a short margin to Kenny Roberts in the final sprint and equalling Robert's fastest lap. These are, simply and truthfully, the facts of that weekend. The newspapers wrote that it was madness to let riders compete under such circumstances and that the doctors who permitted such "recklessness" were a disgrace to their profession: it wasn't the truth, but that's how the events were reported in the papers.

We feel that our contribution to medicine is a new, creative one, free from the restrictions of dogma. We dealt with Virginio Ferrari's situation from a completely new viewpoint, and in doing so completely ignored prejudice in the name of truth and humanity. Consequently, we were accused of negligence by those who hide behind a wall of platitudes, false beliefs and outdated dogma, those who, rather than face reality prefer to shy from it. To ignore that reality means to hide behind the mask that society offers us when it takes us into its fold. It is a mask that these "people" will never remove, as to do so would reveal their small-minded ugliness and fragile, sick personalities, whole lives spent vegetating in the grip of their neuroses. All they are doing is marking time: waiting for an end that may well derive from the violence and wars triggered by their own anger at not

Monza, 20th May 1973: Jarno Saarinen signs his last autograph on Carlo Costa's shoulder.

Monza, five minutes before the tragedy. Soili, Jarno's wife, smiles at him for the last time.

having conquered their own destiny. These "people" have sacrificed their spirit on the false alter of inexistent needs. They are the lifeless slaves of modernity, a crowd of mental amputees in whom the divine spark is extinguished forever. Huddling in the mass through fear of the unknown, inebriated by the fleeting gratification of consumerism, arrogant with power and technology, they have tragically abandoned the truth: abandoned that creative child-like genius that lives in all of us and accepts the worst traits of human character just as it exalts the finest.

The Clinica Mobile provides concrete help for those in need: our sense of responsibility can only be enhanced by respecting the truth – and that youth who resides in the heart of every motorcyclist. This is no easy commitment, yet in motorcycling there is no other way: truth has characterised its entire history, from the feats of the great Nuvolari up to the present day. It is a history of men who have chosen their own way forward, who have tried to honour their ideals and had the courage to suffer for their success. Motorcycling is a marvellous theatre, where the spark of aspiration ignites the fuel of talent to give us incredible feats of speed and control.

Their audacity spreads to the trackside stands and fields where it intermingles with the curiosity, enthusiasm, and anticipation provided by the spectators. For the latter, packed together like grains of sand on a beach, these races are a heartfelt experience, enjoyed from a side of the safety fence that I visited only as a child (when I used to disobey my father, who preferred to have me in the pits where he could see me). The cheering of the crowd is a comforting cheer, free from the explosive violence which all too often mars other sports. Encamped on the hills and meadows that line the world's race tracks, these fans light fires not only to keep warm or cook food: they also light the flame of a humanity – with all its merits and defects – that has gathered to witness an event. An almost knightly competition in which the knights are motorcycle riders: when their visors are lowered and the joust begins, the crowd is a key participant. It is an almost mystical participation in which the crowd discovers a human alliance that banishes violence altogether, almost as if it were sub-consciously aware that life can only be truly lived in the presence of death.

To forget this is to open the Pandora's box of human misery and leave the way open to that inexplicable violence which taints those who belie-

Virginio Ferrari, a friend forever.

Virginio puts his Yamaha through its paces.

ve in the reality of power, technology, "globalisation" and "homogenisation" (words nauseating in themselves).

The windswept motorcyclist escapes from this false reality to discover the beauty and richness of instinct, the sensation that reality is made all the more real by a two-way ambiguity. It is this natural, true and vital dimension that they take onto the race track; it lights the fire that warms the cold night and illuminates a theatre where there is no violence, only humanity, clamour and enthusiasm. The fact that I have never ridden a motorcycle gnaws at me terribly! And how I "envy" the spectators on the other side of the safety fence! Maybe, one day, I'll join them: but for the time being I intend to stick with my riders, certain that I will be able to help them fulfil their wishes.

The riders are not, of course, completely free to make their own decisions. They are subject to stringent medical examinations by the health services in the event's host country. It is not the doctors of the Clinica Mobile who decide whether riders can or cannot compete after accident or illness, because our concepts of health and illness are not founded on so-called "common sense" but, rather, on the reality of subjective responses, free from preconception.

Unsurprisingly, riders often prove to be particularly persuasive with these doctors, mysteriously convincing even the most sceptical to authorise their plans to get back on the track.

A life based on free will makes it easier for them to bear the broken bones and the tears. In the words of Dante Alighieri "Love moves all, even the stars and the sun". The rider's love is a love that Dante would understand immediately.

It is the only effective response to anguish and pain. Almost magically, a love of motorcycling frees the energy imprisoned in the heart and switches on that natural light which is the foundation of every soul. Love can help one accept life's absurdities and smooth the sea of suffering into one of life's greatest sensations: that of existing happily for one's dreams, thus transforming the punishment of pain into a gift.

In today's world only very few of us ever glimpse this magical transformation, this hidden and hard-to-accept truth. In Greek mythology Cassandra always spoke the truth yet after spurning Apollo she was punished cruelly when he ordered that no-one must ever believe her again. In today's world, perhaps, people refuse to believe the truth because looking at it involves too much sacrifice. It is just too much effort to give harmony to all those faces, all the secret meanings behind events. Science helps us avoid this effort, taking us even further away from the sublime truth that lives in men's hearts. The technology that springs from science brings with it the hatchet that amputates the truth. And to amputate it is to kill it: but most men would die before bringing themselves to believe Cassandra.

But not so the riders: they return to the race track with a speed and trust that says they believe in her, and that she is the Mobile Clinic's one true goddess...

3. *Clinica Mobile 1*

On April 23rd, 1972 the first 200 mile race (the "Imola 200") was held in Imola: the Daytona of Europe.

That first thrilling race, organised by Checco Costa, was won by Paul Smart on a Ducati. As Chairman of the local "Moto Club", my father insisted on having only the best possible medical services for this top level event, services much more advanced than those that had been seen at other national and international events. This vital task was entrusted to me and successfully undertaken with the help of Dr. Giancarlo Caroli, a capable emergency and intensive care medic at the Istituto Rizzoli of Bologna.

For the very first time, the theatre of motorcycling was to have an emergency doctor – a key specialist capable of drawing an injured rider back from the brink of death. The riders were so pleased with this enthusiastic new team of medical staff that they insisted on them being present at every race in the World Championship. So began the story of the Clinica Mobile. For

The sticker publicising the first ever Imola 200.

Paul Smart wins the first Imola 200 on a Ducati.

Presentation of the Imola 200: from left, Enzo Ferrari, Carlo, Claudio and Checco Costa.

five years (1972-1976) Dr. Claudio Costa and his team, equipped with First Aid bags, followed the World Championship. But the level of service was still far from perfect: "motorcycling medicine" was still a rather primitive affair at the time, human resources and equipment being so scarce that riders often had to help each other after crashes.

In 1976 it was decided that a Clinica Mobile should be created, a little "travelling hospital" staffed by specialised doctors who would take care of riders before, during and after races. Even non-riders working at Motorcycling Grand Prix events were able to benefit from its services.

The first Clinica Mobile was founded thanks to the generosity of the Moto Club Santerno of Imola and Gino Amisano, the owner of AGV Helmets. The Clinic was dedicated to all motorcycle racers.

On February 3rd, 1977, on the little island of Bendor, near the Paul Ricard circuit of Le Castellet, the Clinica Mobile was presented to the press. On that same day Checco Costa twinned his splendid Imola 200 with the same named French race organised by Moto Journal.

This mini mobile hospital put in its first day of active service on May 1st,

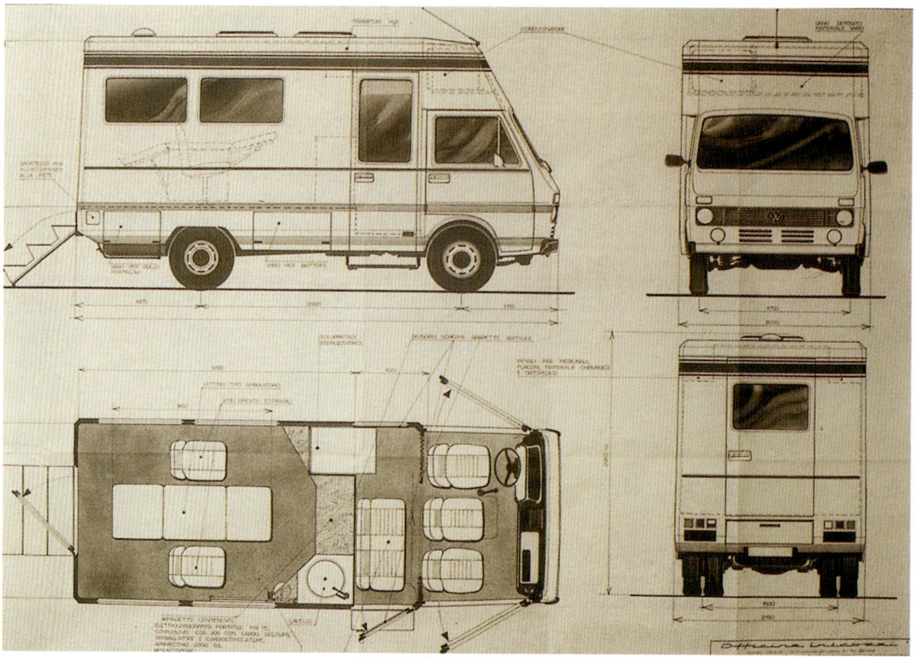

The original blueprints for the first Clinica Mobile.

Disdain at improvised rescues like this one brought about the idea of the Clinica Mobile.

Marco Lucchinelli kneels to help an injured Franco Uncini.

The first Clinica Mobile carries the name of the Santerno Moto Club, its biggest backer.

Giancarlo Caroli, Claudio Costa and Beppe Russo "launch" the first Clinica Mobile.

Claudio Costa (left) invites his father, Checco (right), to see the new clinic.

Claudio Costa and the Clinica Mobile's first driver, Ruggero Dal Fiume.

1977 at Salzburgring (Austria). It was to be a baptism of fire. In the 250cc class, 5 riders – Uncini, Ceccotto, Braun, Fernandez and Stadelman – crashed together on the fastest and most dangerous corner of the whole circuit (Fahrerlager corner). All five received terrible injuries: sadly, those of the German rider, Stadelman, were to prove fatal.

The Clinica Mobile doctors rushed to the scene of the disaster. Franco Uncini was no longer breathing but was saved by prompt resuscitation. Vital aid was also administered to Ceccotto, Fernandez and Braun.

In saving a man's life the Clinica Mobile had shown – on its very first day – that its role in the world of motorcycling was indispensable.

That year 178 riders were treated and 1287 treatment sessions provided. Out of those 178, the rescue of Philippe Coulon at Anderstorp in Sweden was to arouse the greatest emotion. This Swiss rider was saved by the swift response of the Clinica Mobile's doctors and its cutting-edge equipment, his treatment being completed by the Swedish doctors in hospital. Ever since, Philippe Coulon and the Swiss journalists have referred to the Clinica Mobile as "Bon Dieu".

October 1976: Michel Rougerie's terrible fall.

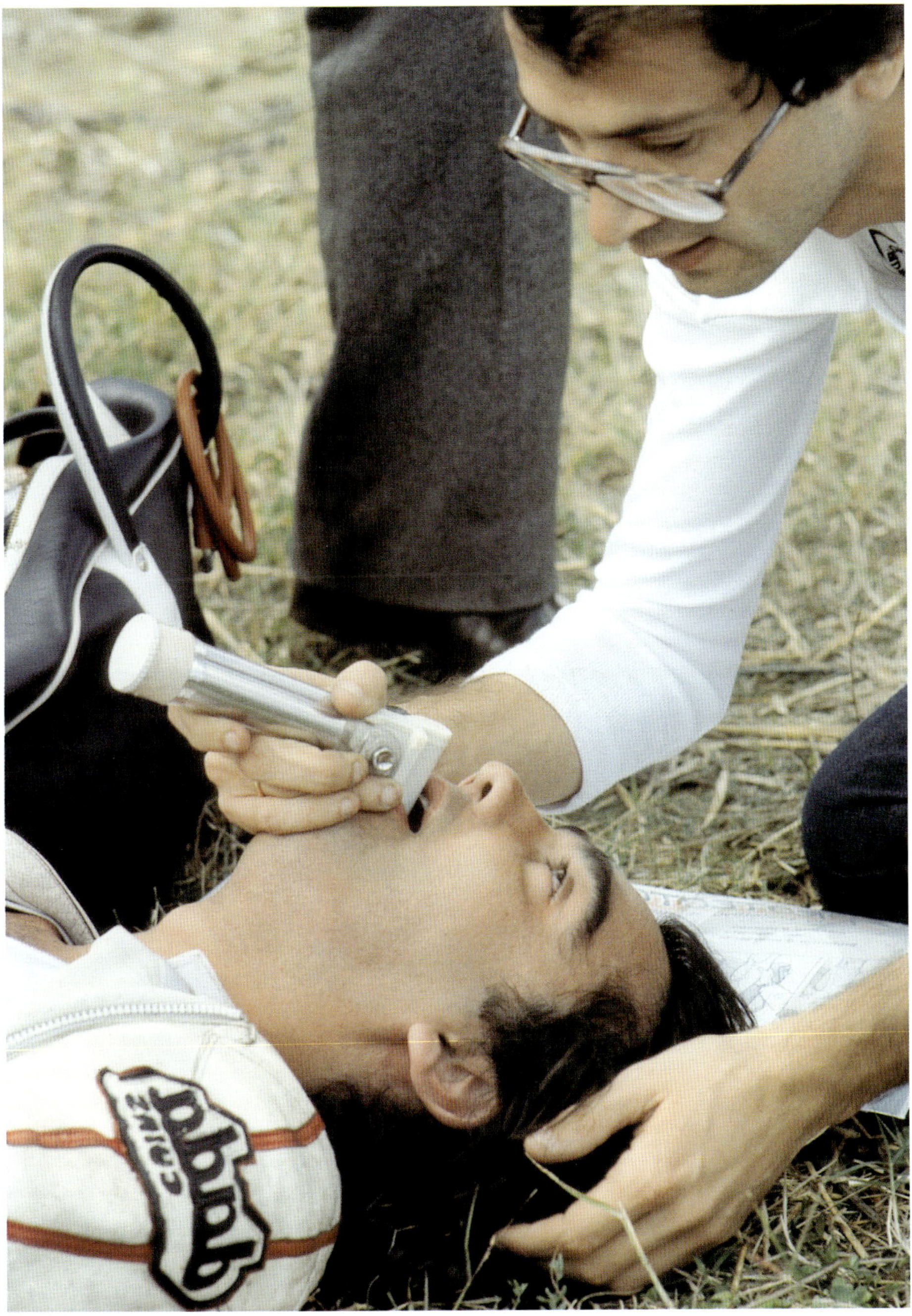

Emergency doctor and anaesthetist Arturo Parilli saves Rougerie's life.

4. *Clinica Mobile 2*

The second Clinica Mobile was created in 1981 with the aid of the Italian Motorcycling Federation, and above all, with the help of its President, Francesco Zerbi. He was right behind the idea from the word go, demonstrating a boundless humanity and an enormous sense of responsibility for a world that he would soon lead both politically and sportingly.

In times of difficulty President Zerbi came to our aid frequently: I found him fascinating, not so much because he had helped us but because a sort of elective affinity had developed between my "madness" and his own "aristocratic" philosophies. Dozens of critical moments saw him champion our cause, and he defended me tooth and nail on many an occasion. Now that those battles are over, I count him as one of my closest friends.

Francesco Zerbi with Claudio Costa.

Between 1981 and 1987, the daily workload in the Clinica Mobile 2 increased considerably, with individual consultations totalling more than 3000 and some 300 injured riders receiving treatment each year.

In 1982, during the Imola 200, Graziano Rossi crashed out at the Tosa. The emergency medic assigned to that corner, Carlo Cozza, immediately began artificial respiration and cardiac massage. Transported to the Clinica Mobile, Rossi was returned to the world of the living... and was soon able to continue fathering one little Valentino (who, even back then, was a frequent visitor to the pits – albeit in his mum's arms).

In June 1983, during the Dutch Grand Prix at Assen, Franco Uncini was run over by Wayne Gardner and suffered terrible head injuries. For one long month, he drifted between life and death, first at the Groningen hospital in Holland, and then at the Istituto Rizzoli in Bologna: after a long battle, he walked out of the latter on his own two feet, cured. Franco's recovery was as complete as it was sudden: as I watched over him during the night he simply began to give, after recognising me, a detailed description of all the corners on the Imola race track.

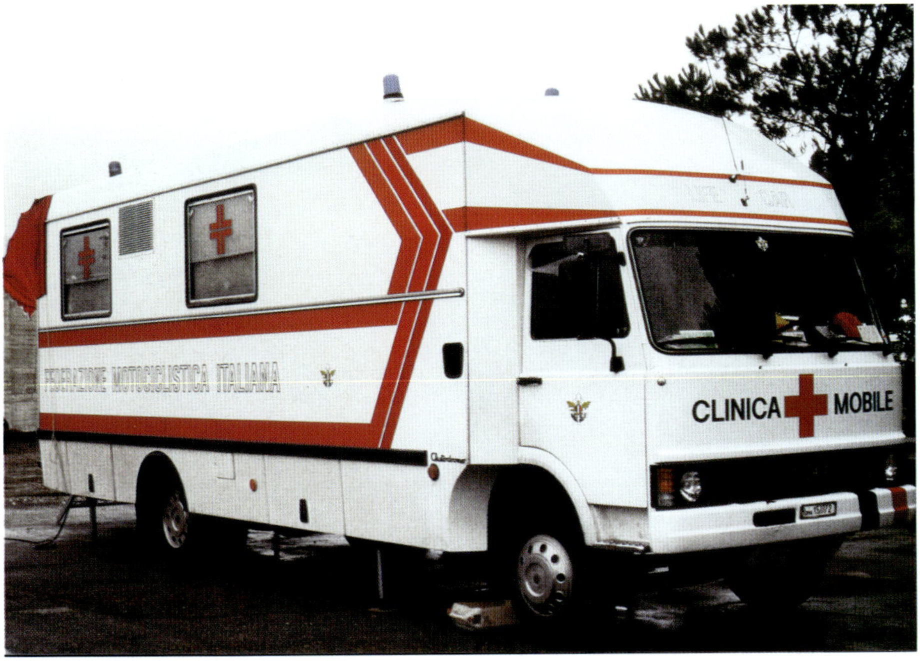

1981: the second Clinica Mobile arrives.

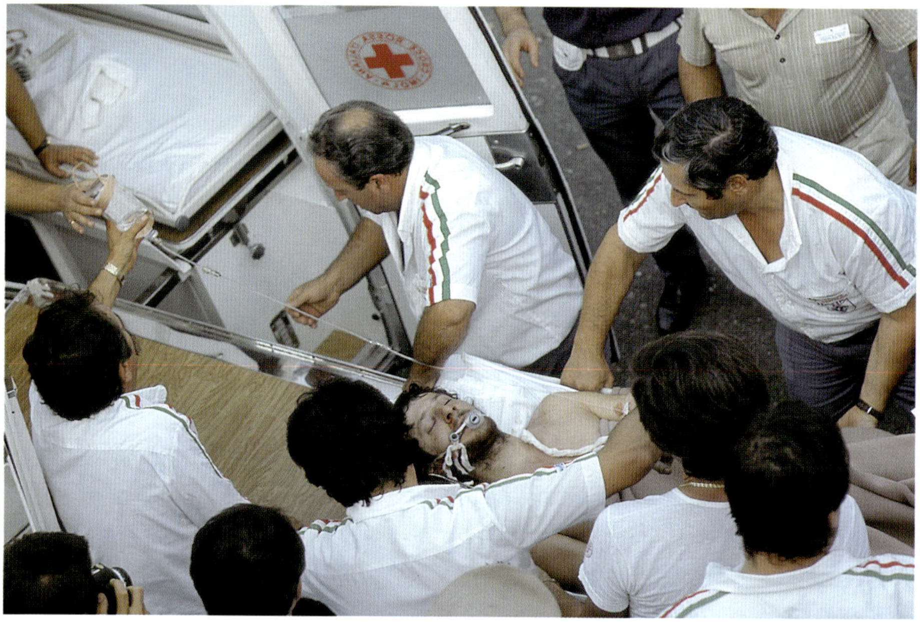

The 1982 Imola 200: Graziano Rossi fights for his life…

…while Valentino and mother, unaware of the accident, smile at the paddocks.

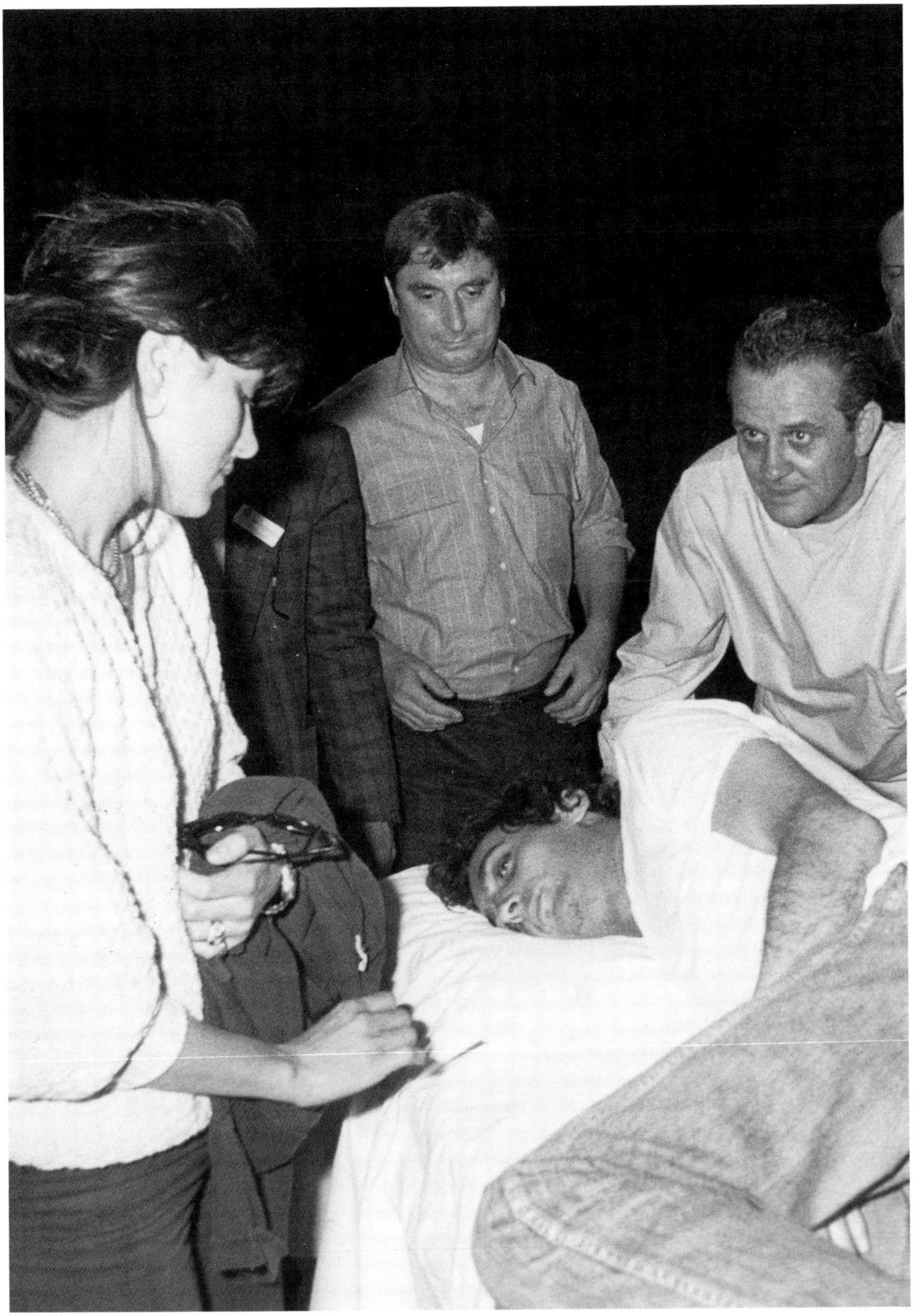

After the accident at Assen in 1983: Franco Uncini arrives at Bologna airport.

5. *Clinica Mobile 3*

On May 21st, 1988 the third Clinica Mobile made its debut, being unveiled at the "Dino and Enzo Ferrari" circuit of Imola on the eve of the Italian race valid for that year's Motorcycling World Championship.

In what was to be an exhilarating and moving day the new clinic was, with the cutting of the Italian tri-colour tape, "christened" by the following "godfathers": Giacomo Agostini, Kenny Roberts, Franco Uncini and Francesco Zerbi (then Chairman of the Italian Motorcycling Federation).

Yet the Clinic's true "inaugurator" on that day was world champion Wayne Gardner, treated for multiple fractures sustained a few days previously. Unbelievably, next day's race saw him finish second: crying with happiness – and pain – he generously donated his 2nd place prize money to the Clinica.

Rome, 1988: the third Clinica Mobile gets a veritable baptism.

Imola race track, 21st May 1988: inauguration of the third Clinica Mobile.

Pope John Paul II blesses the clinic.

IN HONOREM PRINCIPIS A
LIFE TIR
CLINICA

Thus began the 3rd Clinica Mobile's mission to help all riders. Before leaving on its tour of the remaining 1988 World Championship races, the 3rd Clinica Mobile stopped in Rome for yet another baptism, this time from Pope John Paul II who paid a memorable visit with his prelates.

The 3rd Clinica Mobile consisted of 5 rooms with three beds. Its staff would take on an incredibly high work load, with some 4000 individual forms of treatment being administered every year.

In 1989, at Hockenheim, in a terrible accident that was to cost Ivan Palazzese his life, the Italian rider Fabio Barchitta was saved from certain paralysis and enjoys a clean bill of health to this day.

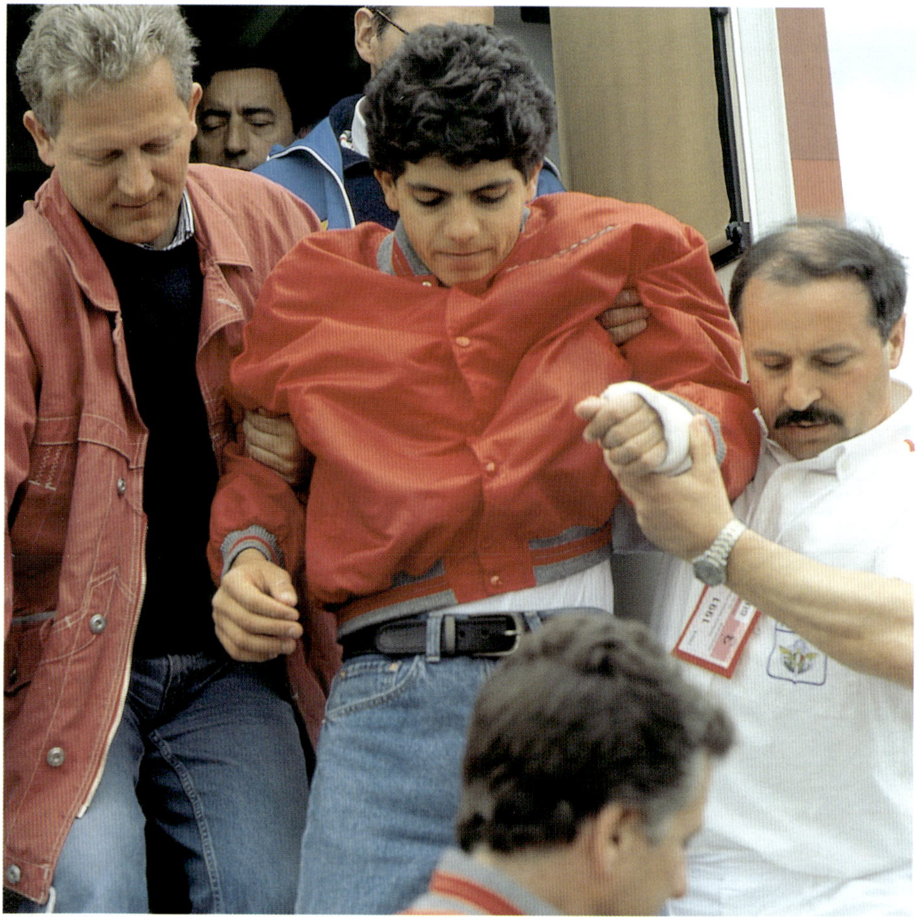

A "repaired" Alex Barros exits the Clinica Mobile.

A later accident in Yugoslavia involving Reinold Roth would so upset and frighten the Yugoslav doctors that they quickly carried him to the Clinica Mobile, the circuit's only viable medical facility.

He was brought to the clinic in a state of near-death, still wearing his close-fitting leathers and helmet: resuscitation procedures were begun immediately and although we were able to save him from death, we were unable to restore him to the life he had known. His body, mind and lifestyle still bear the scars of that accident: although alive, his injuries mean that he now has the self-sufficiency of a child and as such he is lovingly looked after by his family.

Hockenheim. May 1989: an anxious Virginio Ferrari helps Ivan Palazzese.

In May 1993, at Hockenheim, Corrado Catalano received terrible head injuries and was urgently admitted to the Mannheim hospital where he was operated on by the skilled Dr. Adrian Wolf. Although he resumed a normal life just a few months afterwards, he would never return to racing.

Over 4000 injections, examinations, medications and therapy sessions adds up to a lot of patients: many riders became frequent visitors to the Clinica. Hence a cosy hospitality tent was set up next to the Clinica Mobile truck, providing food for both Clinica personnel and the riders. The food served up by Pietro, Franco, Luigi, Bruno and Antonio – excellent drivers turned impromptu cooks – is prepared with a kindness and affection bordering

Nakano toasts the new Clinica Mobile "canteen", open to all...

on the motherly, a symbolic reminder of the nourishment taken as infants.

The third Clinica Mobile was able to continue its work thanks to the help of the President of the Italian Motorcycling Federation (FMI), Paolo Sesti. In thinking of the FMI I cannot help but recall my years as Federal Doctor from 1976 to 1996. During those years Federation members warmed me with their esteem and sincere, welcoming, smiles. I soon got to know a growing number of those who work there – Massimino, Pallino, Bruno, Mario, Claudia, Sandra, Maria Pia, Giuliana, Marzia and Anna Maria to name but a few – and became a close friend of Vincenzo Mazzi, the Federation's Secretary General during those unforgettable years.

...and a smiling Valentino Rossi joins him.

6. *Clinica Mobile 4*

In 1996, in the course of 15 Grand Prix races (with 199 competitors including wild cards) there were 579 on-track falls. Physiotherapy (massage, rehabilitation, use of laser and ultrasound treatment, magnetotherapy, electrotherapy and electroanalgesia) accounted for over 2000 of the total 7000 doctor-patient appointments that year.

For these reasons the setting up of a 4th Clinica Mobile with 5 beds rather than 3 became necessary. The number of physiotherapy specialists working in the Clinica Mobile also rose.

The announcement of this plan and the first contacts with the truck engineering specialists, Franzisella of Varese (suppliers to the Ferrari F1 Racing Team), were made late in 1996 at Eastern Creek, in Australia, but not

Claudio Costa informs Doohan, Schwantz and Rainey of plans for a fourth Clinica Mobile.

Jerez, 1st May 1997: Mick Doohan christens the fourth Clinica Mobile with champagne.

A special guest: King Juan Carlos of Spain accompanied by Carmelo Ezpeleta (left).

before Dr. Costa had announced the plan to Mick Doohan, Kevin Schwantz and Wayne Rainey.

This all-new Clinica Mobile was officially presented on May 1st, 1997 at Jerez de la Frontera, in Spain. This time its "godfather" was to be Mick Doohan, the rider with the closest ties to the Clinica Mobile and Dr. Costa.

That day the Clinica Mobile also had a high-ranking visitor in the form of King Juan Carlos of Spain, accompanied by Carmelo Ezpeleta, the President of Dorna.

On meeting the King, a very tense Dr. Costa addressed him with these words: "Your Majesty, in this clinic we shall attempt to turn suffering into happiness, yet we will not always succeed, while I know that you will constantly succeed in bringing happiness to Spain and the world".

Later on, in Jerez, the following message was written on the Clinic's blackboard:

DEDICATED TO ALL MOTORCYCLE RIDERS
TO THE WORLD CHAMPIONSHIP HEROES,
TO THE CENTAURS WHO LIVE REAL LIVES
ILLUMINATED BY THE IMMENSE FOLLY OF DIONYSUS
AND THE SPLENDID LIGHT OF APOLLO'S REASON

These oracle-like words are still to be found on the mobile hospital's wall.

Journalists, mechanics, specialised personnel, team managers, workers, technicians, organisers, craftsmen – just about anyone – can, in the unfortunate event it might be necessary, seek help and consolation in the Clinica Mobile (24 hrs a day since 1997) just as one would in the casualty department of any good hospital.

Yet most of all, the riders want the Clinica Mobile because they feel it's theirs and always has been.

Motorcycle riders race against the limits imposed on them by nature – and in doing so run the risk of injury and death. Every year riders are involved in some 500 falls during warm-up, qualification and competition. As they lean into the corners at seemingly impossible angles they challenge not only each other but the very laws of physics: that they often slide off the edge of possibility should come as no surprise.

Jerez, 1st May 1997: Claudio Costa shows King Juan Carlos around the clinic.

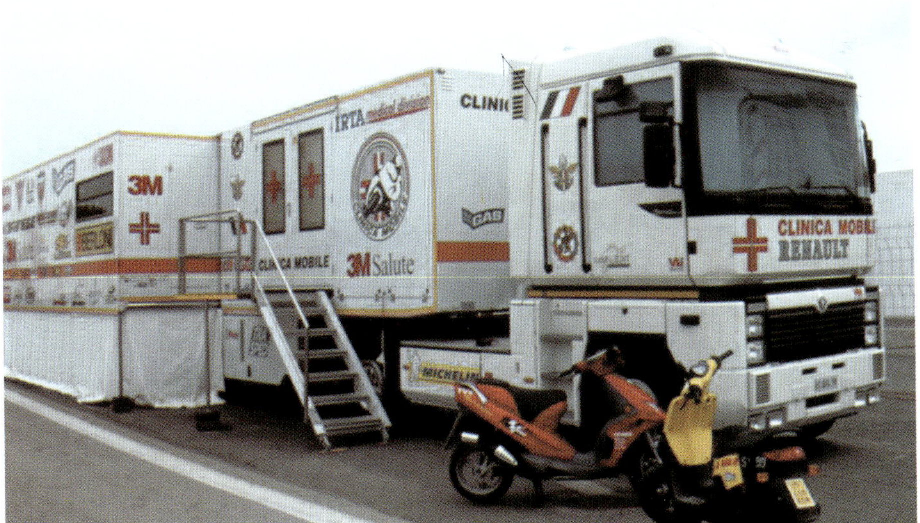

Clinica Mobile 4: an enormous 57 square metres.

Motorcyclists challenging the laws of physics, as successfully demonstrated by Randy Mamola…

…and Mick Doohan followed by Alex Barros and Max Biaggi.

But sometimes the law bites back. Mamola takes his punishment at Spa-Francorchamps...

...as do this sidecar driver and passenger, despite their more stable three-wheeled steed.

Kenny Roberts Jr.

Valentino Rossi homes in on Roberts with Checa and Biaggi close behind.

Kenny Roberts Sr.

Loris Capirossi.

Centrifugal force gets the better of Max Biaggi at Mugello in 2000.

Ambulances will only rarely transfer a rider to a nearby city hospital (perhaps 4 or 5 times a year): it is a statistic which shows the bulk of riders' injuries are resolved in the Clinica Mobile, which provides treatment for everything and anything which is non-urgent, from small and medium-entity trauma to fractures that can be reduced and set in Scotch-cast.

More serious, "urgent" cases are treated in the Emergency Rooms that form a compulsory part of every World Motorcycling Championship race track medical centres. Our role is to support the local doctors and hospitals: very badly injured riders are only treated directly by the Clinica Mobile where absolutely necessary.

During race events at Imola the Clinica Mobile is stationed near the circuit's Medical Centre (since 2000 this has also been standard practice for Formula 1 races). Close collaboration with the doctors of the local health authority (ASL Imola) plays a vital role, as the latter provides personnel and equipment vital to competitors' safety. The heads of this alliance are the untiring Dr. Mauro Vivoli and Dr. Guglielmo Vicenzi, chief consultant at the Imola General Hospital orthopaedic unit. Their continued commitment and professionalism have resulted in the "repair" of many a racer.

Just about every rider in the World Championship has had reason to visit "his" mobile hospital at one time or another. And if, in that race for real life that takes him so close to death, he should fall, it is in the Clinica Mobile that he will rise again: medical science, of course, will play its part, yet it is those inner resources that are in all of us – and which are the very heart of every motorcyclist – that ensure recovery.

Rather than sapping the rider's will, then, injuries can act as the catalyst for an amazing comeback: and as if by magic, man is transformed to heights that transcend the mere mortal.

We at the Clinica Mobile are both witnesses and accomplices to this marvellous metamorphosis: like Epiphany itself, it is a birth – or rather a rebirth – that shapes the very essence of our humanity.

That humanity – symbolised by the courage of these modern-day "centaurs" – is something that shall always be needed and that is why I believe and know that the fourth Clinica Mobile will be followed by a fifth, and many more after it.

PART TWO
Heroes

What happens inside the Clinica Mobile is extremely difficult to narrate as events there are woven with a subtle, emotive thread. Love, joy, hope, pain and torment are, quite literally, indescribable. The nights spent in foreign, and sometimes hostile, hospitals, waiting for dreams and hopes to solidify into reality and the long hours spent in operating theatres all over the world – where, behind the cold formality of the surgeon's mask and smock there often hides an envy for the way we work – were an appalling torment. Yet these events experienced in the Clinica Mobile, where so many riders have miraculously risen from injury and illness, are etched on my memory indelibly. Those memories compel me to tell a story of true heroism, the epic struggle between desire and pain, the endless conflict between individual freedom and the prison of society.

The following pages offer a glimpse into the lives of some of the most successful riders I have had the honour to treat.

7. *Anonymous*

In a far-off country a motorcycle “joust” with a great many competitors was held. One of these, despite the protection offered by his helmet, sustained severe injuries and fell into a deep sleep. In ancient times, loved ones would watch over this person not only in the hope that he would soon wake but that he would also, as he opened his hand to reveal a palmful of pomegranate seeds (for the ancients these seeds represented the inestimable riches of the afterlife), explain to them the mysteries of life and death.

This injured “knight” had succumbed to the sleep we call coma. So we helicoptered him and his nest of life-sustaining tubes to a hospital as fast as we could. Even as we arrived, his vital signs began to improve, not only as a result of the medical treatment he was getting but also because of the love of those helping him.

In Stephen Spielberg’s sci-fi classic, E.T. the alien becomes ill: the world’s scientists race to save him with mobile hospitals, sophisticated instrumentation, medical machinery, top doctors, tubing, medicines – all to no avail. In the end the poignant love of his friend, an innocent earth child yet to be contaminated by the science and laws of adulthood, miraculously saves him with a caress. Love is a marvel that can move mountains: yet many choose to avoid this divine capacity. Love is a perfect medicine, yet no hospital stores it and no doctor prescribes it.

Our injured rider was admitted to hospital: for patients in his condition there were private rooms with a connecting resuscitation area. It was probably the best room in the hospital. To the relief of those keeping vigil his condition improved steadily during the night: his reawakening seemed imminent. In the cold, dim light of the room the tension of the preceding hours began to melt away. Then, suddenly, we felt something soft and undefined brushing over our feet and ankles. Peering down into the half-light we saw a cat with six kittens exit from underneath the bed. After a few moments indecision we called a member of staff and jokingly asked him if this really was the best room in the hospital. His candid reply was “Of course it is. The others are full of mice”. His response didn’t surprise us: the marbled waiting rooms of modern airports and even the best restaurants are populated by these creatures. We thus accepted the cats without qualm, not least of all because they seemed to symbolise the forces of nature defending us. That same nature which healed our knight, our rider who happily returned to racing.

The absence of names and surnames enhances the fascination and mystery of this story. I consider myself lucky to be the keeper of many such memories. Some are extremely moving.

Once we ran to the bedside of a severely injured rider, re-igniting hope in his loved ones and the thousands of fans at home: Giancarlo Falappa was near death in a hospital in Albacete, in Spain. I had managed to reach him together with Dr. Corbascio thanks to the generosity of Claudio Castiglioni, Chairman of Ducati, who had granted us use of his private aircraft. After examining him hope was kindled anew as our words revealed an underlying trust.

Other stories are known only to me and the nameless heroes I have treated, those countless riders whose bedsides we visited with a message of solidarity and the promise of a quick recovery – even where hope seemed to fade. These wounded riders were not mentioned on TV nor cited in any newspaper, but they are heroes nonetheless, their authenticity perhaps enhanced by their anonymity.

The events described in this book shall have to represent the many I am unable to mention and I hope that in singing the praises of just a few riders I have in some way honoured them all.

Countless racers go unmentioned in this book. In the hope that they understand they have not been forgotten, the time has come to narrate some legends and name their protagonists. I also hope that love, the significance of which escapes any easy definition, emerges from these stories and spreads to embrace all the riders I have known and treated and every motorcyclist I have ever met. Love conquers all – and I hope its meaning shines through in these stories.

8. Ago – Giacomo Agostini

Fear of the unknown, the anxiety of doubt and the pain of life's absurdities are the forerunners of superstition, astrology and magic – concepts which I believe were hard-wired into the human mind as soon as it was created. Life's violence and anger is often counterbalanced by an accompanying sense of the sacred, mystery, magic and superstition; the latter has played a key role in every epoch of human history, ancient Egypt being a case in point. Even today, superstitions abound. One should not ask whether these beliefs are true or not, but simply hope that they can have an influence on reality. Their attraction is far too strong for them to be weakened by scientific explanation: one way or another, the mystery of our existence needs "priests" to reveal its mea-

Giacomo Agostini roars past on his MV Agusta.

ning. Spiritual belief can ease the world's pain: yet superstition helps you believe you can avoid it. Personally, I have no particular spiritual beliefs, and that may well explain why I'm superstitious. There are more superstitious people out there than you might think and in competitive motorcycling, where risk exasperates uncertainty, there are plenty… perhaps all of them!

My father was a maestro of superstition. He used it artfully to resolve dozens of problems. If, for example, while arranging straw bales around the Imola track prior to a race, one of them should fall, he would leave it there to protect that precise point.

In 1974 Giacomo Agostini switched teams, leaving MV Agusta for Yamaha. Pino Allievi was the only journalist to get wind of this historic transfer: in reading the news in *La Gazzetta dello Sport* the day before the official announcement, I realised I was soon to become the doctor of the most successful motorcyclist of all time. Yet the joy was dampened by the fact that my father didn't want me to fly, and flying was the only way of getting to Daytona in Florida. So I took Giacomo to one side and told him to ask for my father's approval. I also advised him to tell my father that I was the only doctor capable of saving him from the heat of Florida and I would also be the lucky charm that would grant him victory in Daytona, further world titles and the podium of other prestige races. The ploy worked, and just as Jarno Saarinen had introduced me to Europe, Giacomo Agostini introduced me to the world.

To watch him roar up the hairpin bends of San Luca in Bologna with a class equalled only by speed was unforgettable. I thought my heart would burst as I watched him speed around Lesmo at Monza in 1963 on the 250 cc Morini. A British journalist enthusiastically described him thus: "No-one can beat Agostini's panache, no-one will ever be able to catch him. The show he puts on is pure theatre: to see him racing round on his bike is to witness a proud, noble knight of olde, shining armour replaced with a skin of leather".

At Imola on 3rd September 1972, the race was cancelled by rain. Showing a concern that I found touching, he went over to my father – then under enormous financial pressure – to reassure him that he wouldn't be asking for his fee. That day, Giacomo's kindness brought my father to tears: the tears dried when, at the next event, my father honoured Ago's fee as if he had raced.

A special friendship was thus born: years later it would be reinforced when Giacomo abandoned his vacation in Sardinia to attend my father's funeral at the Cappuccini church and pay his respects to "our" Checco, who had given so much to so many.

Even as a child Giacomo Agostini knew that his bike is the key to his happiness.

9. *Mike the Bike – Mike Hailwood*

Mike the Bike: it is only fitting that this rhyming pseudonym should come from a land that produced the works of William Shakespeare and the spirited prose of George Bernard Shaw. And while God may indeed save the Queen, he also seems to keep his eye out for her heroes.

Undoubtedly the rider most able in firing the enthusiasm and imagination of a whole generation of motorcycling fans, Mike had a chameleon-like capacity to adapt to just about any bike no matter how good or bad it might be. He had all the qualities that make a man great.

Arturo Magni once asked him, just as he was dismounting from his MV Agusta, if the bike was working all right. "Arthur, it's perfect" came the reply. Filled with pride Arturo – then manager of the Cascina Costa team – went to inspect the bike and was horrified to see that the Mike had spent the last few laps riding round on a flat tyre.

A famed hell-raiser, he would dance and sing all night long, generally giving the candle a thorough burning at both ends (unlike his rival Giacomo Agostini who always went to bed early and was forever serious and duty-bound).

The duel between these two engrossed the world and resulted in one of the most fascinating chapters in motorcycle racing: all that was needed to keep the championship alive was a mix of Mike and Giacomo Agostini (with a little help from Dionysus and Apollo).

On the track, Mike Hailwood took more risks than Agostini. Like the mysterious knight in Ingmar Bergman's classic film *The Seventh Seal* he played a brazen game of chess with Death. His game was so sharp, so refined he might well have been the winner in the match against the Grim Reaper.

Years after he had left racing, perhaps irritated by his effrontery, Death threw a heavy truck across his path as he drove to the chip shop to get something to eat for his children. As he lay in the wreckage, not even Mike's last breath could cancel his smile, his scornful rebuke at Death for having cheated in order to win.

Isle of Man: Mike Hailwood, motorcycling and TT legend.

10. *The Saintly Sinner – Phil Read*

Phil Read was a cocktail of craziness, open-mindedness, "wickedness", talent, likableness, unlikableness and cunning.

Once, during one of the many races organised by my father he seriously injured his little finger in a fall at the Acque Minerali corner. Lesions of the little finger are a common occurrence among motorcycle riders and are sometimes serious enough to necessitate amputation. Therefore, when I succeeded in saving his finger, I felt so small amount of pride. On meeting him at the next race I half-expected at least a few words of gratitude from him. Holding up his scarred, deformed little finger for all to see he blurted out "Look what Dr. Costa's done to me!" My rising embarrassment was immediately quashed by Phil's raucous laughter and his subsequent, sincere thanks. Afterwards, like two comics, we would repeat this "sketch" when-ever we ran into each other.

The world often fails to accept that even where a doctor does a "good job" there is a limit to what can be done and invalidity is sometimes inescapable. Phil Read was one of the few people to take this fact in his stride and recognise that even a job well done sometimes has imperfect results. It was almost as if he intuited beauty in everything, even the inevitability of his own death: it was as if he appreciated humanity for its defects.

To be fair, Phil Read had plenty of defects of his own. That's why, among the Italians at least, the "good guys" ended up calling him "Barbed Wire" and sometimes found his foul play almost unbearable.

Even his Sports Director, Arturo Magni (right-hand man to Count Agusta, the genius who inhabited the pits assigned to the legendary MV), would refer to him as "that son of a bitch". Arturo, despite his poor eyesight, could read a race like a book and predict what was about to happen. Many a time he would tell me of Phil's extravagances yet sing the praises of his greatness.

Once he confided how Read had duped us after we had practically forced him to spend a night in hospital at Modena (he had hit his head very hard during winter practice). Knowing that this British rider detested hospitals (as do most riders), we had confiscated his clothing to prevent his "escape": later on, realising he had been tricked, Read sequestered his girlfriend's fur coat and went out to dine in a Modena restaurant with his beautiful – albeit cold – girlfriend, completely naked apart from the coat.

His intolerance of hospitals was well known: we were sometimes forced to carry out minor surgery in hotel rooms that had been transformed into impromptu operating theatres. There was no Clinica back then and these troublesome stop-gap solutions may well have played a sub-conscious role in the ideas that led to its later establishment.

In the words of Oscar Wilde, "There is only one difference between a saint and a sinner: a saint has a past and a sinner has a future". I have no doubt that Phil Read would have agreed with him.

Phil Read on the magical MV Agusta

11. *King Kenny – Kenny Roberts*

An Imola 200 without the participation of American motorcyclists would have been unthinkable. In the wake of such heroes as Tom Emde and Kel Carruthers there soon came another rider who would come to stand for an entire epoch of motorcycle racing and draw a vast following. This was

Enzo Ferrari receives an award from Checco Costa at the Molino Rosso in Imola in 1974.

back in 1974, at the third edition of the Imola 200, inaugurated by my father with the warm congratulations of another racing legend, Enzo Ferrari.

I met Kenny Roberts just before the race at the Molino Rosso hotel, where he was driving his manager, Danilo, up the wall with pranks worthy of the most playful undergraduate. The reason behind my meeting him is quite simple: as he was being driven back along the Via Selice by Barry Sheene he thought it might be fun to yank the car's handbrake: they immediately skidded off into the roadside canal. Thankfully, rather than having to treat them, the rescue largely consisted of having to dry them out. In the following years I would often cure their injuries too.

King Kenny shows his class.

Kenny Roberts was a constant participant in the races organised by Checco Costa and became one of his closest friends. Even today, this American ex-racer never misses an opportunity to talk of him. For Kenny, Imola was the gateway to Europe and the Californian from Modesto won so many races there he soon earned, in addition to the epithet "King Kenny", the nickname "the Martian". In 1983, after winning three world titles he announced his retirement. Yet the following year he was unable to resist making a brief comeback in what would be the last race of his career: the Imola 200, the race that had made him one of the gods of motorcycling. Despite a cracked vertebra he ran the race… and won it.

In the 90's, when we were in California for the World Championship, Kenny hosted me for a day at his ranch near Modesto. I accepted his invitation enthusiastically, despite the fact that Clint Eastwood, Mayor of Carmel, had invited us to a welcome reception at Laguna Seca on the same day. Although a great fan of cinema, motorcycle riders are my life and so Franco Villani and I went to visit Kenny.

There follows an extract from an interview for the book *The Imola Race Track*:

"Imola was my first European experience: Checco Costa had brought me over to race in the 1974 Imola 200. It was a close-run thing between me and Agostini and I especially remember the silence of the crowd as I took the lead. Instead, when I stopped to refuel and Agostini leapt ahead the crowd went wild, and when he eventually won the race I found their enthusiasm, quite frankly, frightening!

Imola occupies a special place in my memories, mostly because of the people. Once, in town, I inadvertently entered a one-way street from the wrong end: a policeman stopped me, recognised me and halted all the traffic to let me through! The last time I went there I decided to have a meal at my favourite restaurant, the Molino Rosso; the waiters hadn't changed and they dumbfounded me by remembering what my favourite dishes were!

Checco Costa was the first to bring me to Europe. We became great friends, and he always gave me a warm welcome. He would have done anything for his riders. Imola's one of those places you always look forward to going to. When we raced at Imola it was just great to be there! The welcome reserved for the riders at the historic races organised by Checco Costa was much better than anything we got at the Grand Prix events. We all loved Checco: there was, quite simply, no-one like him at all. He was always

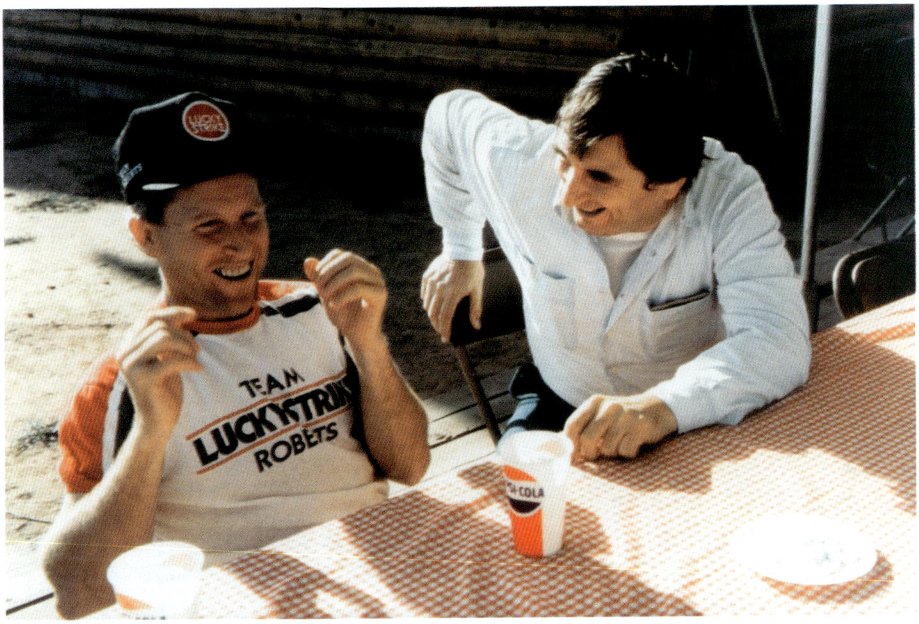

Kenny Roberts plays host to Dr. Costa at his ranch in Modesto, California.

Imola, 1978: Barry Sheene, Checco Costa, Kenny Roberts.

cheerful. In 1984 I came out of retirement to race at Imola for him: I wouldn't have done it for anyone else. Imola means a lot to me. It was my first European race and my last GP. Imola's my second home."

Kenny stayed in racing to work as a team manager and pave the way for his sons' motorcycling careers. In 2000, Kenny Roberts Jr won the Championship with Suzuki, a team skilfully managed by a perspicacious Garry Taylor.

Garry Taylor: a man, a manager.

As for Kenny Roberts Jr, I'm sure he was born with the racer's DNA – and equally sure that it was his father who taught him how to use it.

I've never enjoyed making comparisons. I've never sought out the differences or affinities between this or that champion. I believe every rider is in a class of his own, just as I'm convinced that every man is a unique, one-off entity. There's only one thing the champions have in common: greatness.

Kenny Roberts Junior: a man, a rider.

12. *Sheeney – Barry Sheene*

Barry Sheene had so many accidents that, for the staff at the Clinica Mobile, he became a sort of walking encyclopaedia of traumatology. To describe our first meeting I have to go back to the 60's when I was a student at the Faculty of Medicine and Surgery at the University of Bologna. Spellbound by its historic lecture halls, its goliardic tradition and the lectures of *maestri* such as Olivo, Pupilli, Favilli and Rizzoli and proud of the skeleton I had been given for anatomical studies, I was delighted to meet Dr. Luigi Lincei, the doctor who had, together with Dr. Adriano Mondini, been chosen by my father as chief medic at the Imola circuit back in 1953. Back then, Luigi was the most famous sports doctor in the world, not only for his unquestionable medical skills but also because he was doctor, friend and confidant to a

Fausto Coppi with his close friend and medic, Dr. Lincei.

living legend, the Italian cyclist Fausto Coppi. Often quite overcome with emotion, he told me many a story about the *campionissimo*: for example, Coppi was often a guest at Luigi's home for medical treatment, a situation which helped Coppi arrange secret meetings with his lover, the Dama Bianca, a transgression much frowned on back then. Luigi was outraged when Coppi was prosecuted for adultery and scoffed at the priggishness behind it all. He would mock the evidence used at his trial (police officers had surprised Coppi in his villa together with the Dama Bianca and observed that both sides of the double bed were still warm) and sincerely believed that many of society's ills derived from unjust demonization and denial of the sexual instinct: the persecution of such free-living individuals angered him greatly.

Luigi took me on as assistant at the Imola race track medical centre and taught me the ins and outs of sports medicine while the university taught me traditional medicine. One of my first jobs was to draw up the list of blood groups (these are still stored in the current Clinica Mobile): just recording the riders' blood pressure prior to the race was a source of enthusiasm and pride.

One day, on the eve of one of many races spent in the Imola race track casualty rooms, Luigi and I were going through the riders' routine pre-qualification medical examinations, then compulsory. After a while it was the turn of a cheerful, smiling lad with all the air of a musketeer – Barry Sheene. Rebuking us angrily and insulting us because we wanted to examine him, he yelled "Examine me! An exceptional, fantastic, man, the world's best?!". Surprised and amused, I promised him that I would just register his blood group and let his hale and hearty appearance stand in lieu of a proper check-up. As soon as he heard this he hugged me and said I was the first likeable doctor he'd ever met. Encouraged by this undeserved praise I set about explaining to him – with the help of family friend and Motoclub Santerno Imola interpreter Giancarlo Gavalotti –that the Imola circuit was a toughie, full of subtle perils. A mocking smile spread across his face before he replied "I'm the best in the world and I'm not afraid of Imola. I'm going to start off fast and go straight for the track record". His war cry over, he picked up his gear and left, leaving me quite speechless. A few minutes later I decided to radio the doctors stationed at the Tamburello and Tosa corners and advised them to keep an eye on n° 7. I told them that there was a good chance that this "hot-head" would fall. After the start of the qualifying session the medics at the Tamburello and Tosa (then the first corners of the circuit and free from chicanes) called back. "Claudio", they laughed, "you were

Barry Sheene rides the tiger of his own restlessness.

FORWARD TRUST
2
SUZUKI
MICHELIN
TEXACO
7

wrong there! N° 7 has gone through safely and what's more, he looks like champion material!".

Shortly afterwards he was brought in on an ambulance gurney, his collar bone broken and a drip-feed spiralling out of his arm, by the doctor stationed at the Piratella corner (Antonio Di Nino, today a gifted lecturer at the University of Bologna). As he lay on the medical centre bed his blue eyes sought me out and, through the interpreter Galavotti, he said "I'm not quite so fantastic, am I". I took care of him. In the coming years I would also defend him, as his doctor, from the frequent injuries he would wreak on himself and, as his friend, from the extravagances that he would invent in race paddocks and hotels (once at Le Mans he threw his entire room's contents out into the street, TV included, because the din from alcohol-fuelled guests in the room below was keeping him awake). At Salzburg he appeared nude on the hotel balcony in the company of his equally naked future wife, Stefy. Yet his shortcomings could not erase his charm. On the contrary, they seemed to be the source of his strength. Human yet hell-raising, he fascinated everyone.

In March 1975 he fell during the warm-up while powering his Suzuki at over 300 kmh along the banking at the Daytona oval, and rolled over and over, unconscious, for what seemed like forever. No one at the Medical Centre made a move so I ran to his aid. To my utter relief, he regained consciousness a few moments after I reached him: ignoring the numerous fractures he had sustained, he whispered "I want to race – if not here at the Daytona, at Salzburg, the World Championship...". I took no notice of what he was saying as he had broken so many bones that some of the fractures were simply forgotten about as they weren't priority. I spent two days at the hospital in Daytona: his femur was operated on, and I was convinced that the other fractures would heal more or less of their own accord. As he had predicted, 50 days later he went to Salzburg, and despite the fact that he was still limping around on crutches, took part in the qualifying sessions. As the required push-start was still beyond him, he asked if he could begin the race from the back of the grid already mounted with a helping push from a trusted mechanic. The rule book refused him, unaware that the bud of such a magnificently courageous start would have blossomed into one of man's most beautiful flowers: the flower that springs from pain and desire, the lotus flower that springs from mud. In being so exacting the race judges failed to realise that rules are like a trap for running water, transforming it first into a stagnant pond and then a quagmire.

12+1. *El Niño – Angel Nieto*

I met Angel Nieto back in Imola in 1972, at the end of the World Championship 50 cc race. By dragging him into my ambulance, parked nearby, I may well have saved his life: not that he needed any medical treatment, it was just imperative that I get him away from a violent brawl that had flared up between him and the Dutch riders Huberts and De Vries.

On the track he was a devil, beating everyone and even Lucifer himself. Fantastically skilled, astute, many times World Champion and superstitious to the point that he would number the titles he had won by saying "12 + 1": that way he avoided pronouncing the dreaded 13.

To digress: just why are we so afraid of this number? Thousands of years ago, when the world was more matriarchal and life's rhythms, rites and times

Caracas 1977: Nieto (left) listens in as Dr. Costa whispers to Barry Sheene.

were set by the moon, there was an incredible custom. In order to reign, the elected Queen could, in Spring, choose a husband, but at the end of the lunar year (i.e. at the end of the thirteenth month, a lunar month lasting just 28 days), this husband was solemnly sacrificed. This tragic ritual explains the fear of the number 13 (especially on the part of men). No wonder even superstitious women often have no qualms with the number 13!

Pablo Nieto.

The nickname affectionately given to this Spanish rider was El Niño. His sons Angel Nieto Junior and Pablo Nieto were to inherit their father's passion for motorcycling and he was also uncle to one Alfonso Gonzales, known simply in racing circles as Fonsi.

Motorcycling owes much to El Niño: rather than having a son who followed in the family motorcycling tradition, he decided to create a whole family.

Angel Nieto junior.

14. *Geronimo – Giuseppe Elementi*

Elementi's nickname embodies his "mad" passion for motorcycling perfectly. Like many others, he fell dozens of times. His ankle fractures were set immediately, but to improve skeletal alignment and speed up recovery times he was advised to adopt plates and pins. Like a bolt from the blue a terrible complication appeared: gangrene. He was urgently transferred to the infectious diseases unit. I looked after him attentively, but nothing could quench my anxiety. Late one evening, as I examined Elementi's infected leg, I realised that it had worsened to the point that his life was in danger. Without hesitation I had him loaded into an ambulance and took him to the hospital where I worked. The operating rooms were all closed. Rather than waiting for them to open I decided to operate on him there and then, turning the simple medication room into an impromptu operating room, in a race against time. I was determined to see that Geronimo missed his appointment with death – even if by only a few minutes. In that intent I succeeded, but only at the cost of having to amputate his injured leg.

Now, when he drops in for check ups or brings me his splendid children for specialist treatment, we embrace and cry like old soldiers. In his tears there flows that nostalgia for the world of racing which he never rejoined (although he did go back to riding a road bike), and in mine there is the regret of not having found any joy in the act of saving his life.

Earlier on I promised that I would only write about riders who had won world titles. In writing of Giuseppe Elementi I have had to go back on my word but, for once, I have honoured a higher justice that, while it does not take world championship points into account, solemnly respects those that have been scarred by misfortune. Like Giuseppe, Alberto Puig received a leg injury after falling at Le Mans. He was airlifted to exactly where he wanted to go, to his friend, Professor Villarubias in Spain. Alberto kept his leg, but it had sustained horrific multiple injuries, the pain of which was only mitigated when he finally stood on the podium in France. Even today, when he strolls around the pits where he works as commentator and team manager for young Spanish stars such as Elias and Pedrosa, his eyes convey an unmistakable sadness.

15. *The Caracas Lightning – J. A. Cecotto*

In September 1975 a budding young talent who had just become 350 cc World Champion was brought to me. His name was Johnny Alberto Ceccotto, and the fractured astragalus of his right foot was to bind us together in a story of great friendship (even if the medicines I prescribed him often ended up forgotten in a drawer on account of his preference for the consolation of beautiful women). To keep a closer eye on how the bone was healing we spent a long period living in the same house; the injury was a complex one, and there was a risk that the bone would die, thus compromising the shining career of a great motorcyclist. His convalescence was long and difficult. Six months later, in March 1976, Johnny Alberto Cecotto triumphed at Daytona, powering his n° 96 Yamaha to victory in front of some of the best

Daytona 1976: victory lane for Claudio Costa, Johnny Cecotto and Andrea Ippolito.

riders in the sport. That victory did him more good than all the doctors and therapy in the world.

That same year, Johnny took me to his hairdresser in Bologna – another dyed-in-the-wool motorcycling fan – and practically obliged him to look after my hair forever. This odd commitment had something of a superstitious ring to it and being superstitious myself, I accepted with pleasure. So, since then my hair has always been cut by Gianni "Sultan" Farioli, a keen burraco player with whom I was to establish a lasting friendship.

Back then I would often live at Johnny's house and he at mine. We also spent a lot of time together in his car, a lightning-fast Ferrari. The fear that bubbled up inside me whenever and wherever he drove soon dissipated, as I slowly realised I was in safe hands. Yet he soon made me anxious for another reason: his driving would attract the attention of the police, who stopped us on several occasions, their guns unholstered.

His love for cars eventually led him into automobile racing where he went on to drive in Formula 1 and all other sorts of competitions: motorcycling lost a splendid champion, and I a friend!

16. *The Clavicle – Paolo Pileri*

Pileri was so taciturn that when, in 1975, he fell at Brno in Czechoslovakia, no-one noticed that he had a displaced fracture of the collar bone for the simple reason that he didn't complain about it. The only person he mentioned it to was me, a young doctor gaining his first experiences as a motorcycling medic.

A fracture of the collar bone (or clavicle) will heal in three weeks of its own accord: all that is required is a comfortable figure-of-eight bandage, which need not even be worn constantly. Evidence of just how old this remedy is has been found in Egyptian hieroglyphics dated several centuries BC. The doctors of the time wrote that "a person with a fractured clavicle is laid at rest on a stone bed and a figure-of-eight linen bandage applied to his shoul-

Paolo Pileri in the crunch that snapped his collar bone.

der". The Egyptians also advised the injured person to eat honey served by fair maids. Over the centuries things have changed a little: the figure-of-eight bandage is no longer in linen and drugs are prescribed in place of honey. The latter are arid chemical formulas and – as the clinic has a shortage of fair maids – are given out by Paolo Fabbri.

The world of ancient Egypt is no longer with us and in arriving at modernity things have speeded up a bit: where riders are too impatient to wait the three weeks a surgeon can set the bone with plates and pins to accelerate recovery.

That day at Brno, Paolo Pileri didn't have time for plates or pins: his next race was just two hours away. Instead, he replaced steel plates with an iron will and pins with the raw desire to race. I tried to stammer a few words of dissent but in the end I was proud to bandage his shoulder as best I could before this rider, born in Terni, the birthplace of Liberati, left for the starting line. He rode like the wind, but on the last corner ran out of petrol as he was leading the race.

Envious of such greatness, the gods had transformed the last few drops of petrol in his tank into the silent tears that streamed down his face as he desperately pushed his bike towards a finishing line that had become unreachable.

17. *Sacrilegious – Marco Lucchinelli*

Already holder of the 500 cc World Championship title, Marco Lucchinelli fell at Vallelunga during practice, sustaining severe chest and lung injuries. A drain was urgently applied (this consists of a plastic tube inserted in the thoracic cavity which houses the collapsed lung, shrunken by injury:

Marco Lucchinelli: an enigma that feels no need to explain itself.

the tube runs into a machine that creates an artificial vacuum which helps the "bunched up" lung to expand and reattach itself to the wall of the rib cage). On entering his hospital room I immediately rebuked him: "Why are you smoking!?".

"Who, me? I'm not smoking?" he replied.

"So explain how that smoke got into the drain tube then!" I retorted. He pulled out a hidden packet of cigarettes and sneered that they couldn't possibly hurt him because the inhaled smoke, rather than stagnating in his lung, was in any case immediately sucked into the transparent plastic tube.

Sacred on the track and sacrilegious off it… this was Marco "Lucky" Lucchinelli. He continued motorcycle racing well beyond an age at which it might be advisable to call it a day and in this endless fight against time he battled with the weapons of recklessness and courage. During one such battle he fell at the Bologna Motor Show, which draws in the crowds by the thousands. This wintertime exhibition of cars and bikes, skilfully organised by Alfredo Cazzola and his entourage (Marco Cuppini, Giorgio Catalano and the "pensioner" Umberto Bassi deserve a special mention here), hosts what are true automobile and motorbike races. The rally events have seen Valentino Rossi shine like a diamond and motorcycling events have seen the participation of many a champion.

It was during one of these Motor Show races that Lucchinelli crashed violently onto the tarmac and stopped breathing: prompt action by the doctors of the Clinica Mobile saved his life and Marco made a full recovery. His story continues, a story that – when he's on the track – has not even a trace of the sacrilegious.

18. *A Breath of Life – Franco Uncini*

I pressed my lips against his pale, immobile and half-closed ones: I pushed my breath into his lungs and his chest rose timidly. I did this again and again and waited for that moment that every woman experiences when her newborn child takes its first breath. So it was with Franco Uncini. Silently. Because when a human being is born for the second time he cries no longer. The betrayal of that first birth has already been absorbed and the cry of dismay at being thrust into an unknown world has already been swallowed. Franco was reborn right here on the Fahrerlager corner at Salzburg: soon he would walk that courageous path which led to his 500 cc World Championship victory with Suzuki (1982).

Like Franco, I too got up from the muddy trackside where I had knelt to perform that almost religious ritual of artificial resuscitation. Unlike Franco, I took the path towards the Clinica Mobile which accompanies me all over the world – and helps breathe life into all those riders that need it.

Salzburg, 1st May 1977: Claudio Costa breathes life back into Franco Uncini.

19. *Sito – Alfonso Pons*

World Champion, his aristocratic features concealed a human energy that sometimes bubbled to the surface as anger. Anger at not being able to have it all.

Although I'd already met him, I got to know him better when he joined the outfit run by Roberto Gallina, an able team manager and excellent motorcycle rider. However, I always had the feeling that a complete understanding of Sito was some way off.

Only when he stopped racing to become a team manager himself did I get to know him properly: an able negotiator in obtaining the best for his team, an obstinate book-keeper whose need to square the team finances sometimes risked making him unbearable, a smooth mover within the

Sito Pons when he had no idea he'd one day become a team manager…

motorcycling politics and movingly human in his alliance with his injured riders as he helped them back onto the path of courage.

In this last act he would always bow to the immensity of aspiration and the rider's will to accomplish seemingly impossible feats. Very few people are capable of abdicating their power in favour of a superior humanity: one of those few is Sito Pons.

A man who, while having to balance the books, is never trapped by the cords of calculation. An essential part of him remains free, ready to aid riders who have pushed beyond the boundaries of common sense and prudence even when taking that path might destroy not only his earnings but his credibility: at heart, Sito remains a rider and I think he always will.

It was that free spirit that called me over to the pits to give Loris Capirossi's injured hand an injection of anaesthetic so that he could continue testing. Thus Sito Pons allied himself with the rider's desire to race at all costs and in doing so boosted the determination of the doctors at the Clinica Mobile.

...let alone President of IRTA.

20. *Aspar – Jorge Martinez*

I first met Jorge in 1981, on the eve of the 50 cc World Championship race at Imola, when he used to race with Ricardo Tormo, a heroic rider who came close to death after he crashed during a test ride on the roads near the factory, the mechanics acting as impromptu marshals. Today, the race circuit of

Jorge Martinez: kind and gentle off the track, a terror on it.

Valencia, constructed on the outskirts of the city just as Jorge Martinez wanted, carries the name of his companion: the Ricardo Tormo Race Track.

Aspar, as Martinez's friends called him, loved the Imola circuit and many a time confided that he had loved it a great deal more before the chicanes had adulterated all the fast, sweeping bends. Personally, I feel that where these bends have no safety run-off they should be replaced with chicanes. High-speed crashes into solid obstacles are not just dangerous: they are lethal.

Yet the chicanes that replace high-speed arcs already featuring extensive run-off areas are nothing less than foolish muddles invented by those too ignorant to know that falling onto sand or grass, even at high speed, is unlikely to cause serious damage. It is, in fact, in the chicanes that there occur the greatest number of falls with multiple fractures and it is on these sections of the track that some riders have paid the ultimate price for the thoughtlessness of inexpert legislators. Chicanes should only be placed where there is no safety run-off: otherwise they should be banned in favour of the wide, high speed arcs they are misleadingly intended to soften. Not only because the latter exalt the rider's skills but because the riders generally get up from their falls incredibly quickly to run back to bike or pit to continue living out that legend which is motorcycling.

21. *The Nomad – Carlos Lavado*

Unable to resist the call of motorcycling Carlos left his native Venezuela and headed for Europe. Here he wandered for years before settling in the Romagna, the place he would finally identify as a heartfelt home from home. Carlos "The Nomad" Lavado faced many obstacles during his career, some of which seemed insurmountable, and he fought constantly against the demons that lived inside him. In racing he found the exhilaration he craved, thus taming those fearful demons that were an innate part of his character and transforming them into fellow travellers. A solitary wayfarer, he had no fixed abode, yet in his roaming he never forgot his far-

Carlos Lavado, the man from Venezuela who settled in Romagna, Italy.

off homeland. He started off as a vagabond and became the master of all: world champion. After a terrible fall he once risked losing a leg because the arteries were inexorably compressed by broken bones: fortunately, the blood flow was restored by the prompt action of one of the "guardian angels" of the Clinica Mobile, and in that instant in which the life-giving oxygen resumed its journey, his life's travelling companions, the demons, finally became his friends.

He continued to wander with those friends and, at the end of his wanderings, returned to Venezuela. Yet sometimes, using the excuse of business interests, he returns to that town in the Romagna that he had chosen as his second home. Lugo always gives him a warm welcome, perhaps because the emblem of that town is the rearing horse, symbol of heroic aviator Francesco Baracca, evocative of the courage that lives in Carlos Lavado's heart.

22. *One Lucky Guy – Randy Mamola*

There is no better way to narrate Randy's wonderful story than to let him, the hero of his own private fairy tale, tell it in his own words:

"When I was just a kid the Beatles came to America and instilled a lasting passion for music in me. I dreamt of being Ringo Starr, so I asked my parents if I could have drumming lessons. I practised and played for four years, but then, at the age of 12, I got the motorbike bug and my parents asked me to choose the lessons or the bike: they couldn't afford both. I chose the bike. When I broke the news to my music teacher – Tom Jones' drummer – he burst into tears!

I started off with dirt track racing and immediately began competing – and winning. At the age of 14, I was already on race tracks as Kenny Roberts' understudy. I've raced on 50, 125, 250 and 750cc bikes. I've won a lot of races. In 1977, thanks to Gino Amisano, I was brought to Europe to compete in the Imola 200: despite the fact that I was only 17, he assured me that he would somehow get me into the race. He didn't, and I was barred from taking part. However, I did get permission to do 10 demonstration laps and the times I clocked up would have put me on the front row of the starting grid – and this was at a time when the line up included Kenny Roberts, Uncini and Walter Villa. Thanks to the resulting publicity, I got my first contract with Bimota to race in the 1979 World Championship.

So at the age of 20 I raced my first full season in 500 cc, when Kenny Roberts had already won two world titles. In 1980 he won his third title – with me coming in a close second: I lost that championship by just one race when a mechanical failure caused me to come fifth. Roberts came 4th and won the title. The following season I came second again, this time behind Lucchinelli, but got my revenge on Roberts who came 3rd in that particular championship: this time the title was lost when the engine seized during the warm-up at Monza. So I think it's sometimes a question of luck. I mean, I consider myself extremely lucky as I won many races, met a lot of people who were – and still are – extremely kind to me and never seriously hurt myself. However, at the crucial moment, my luck sometimes ran out.

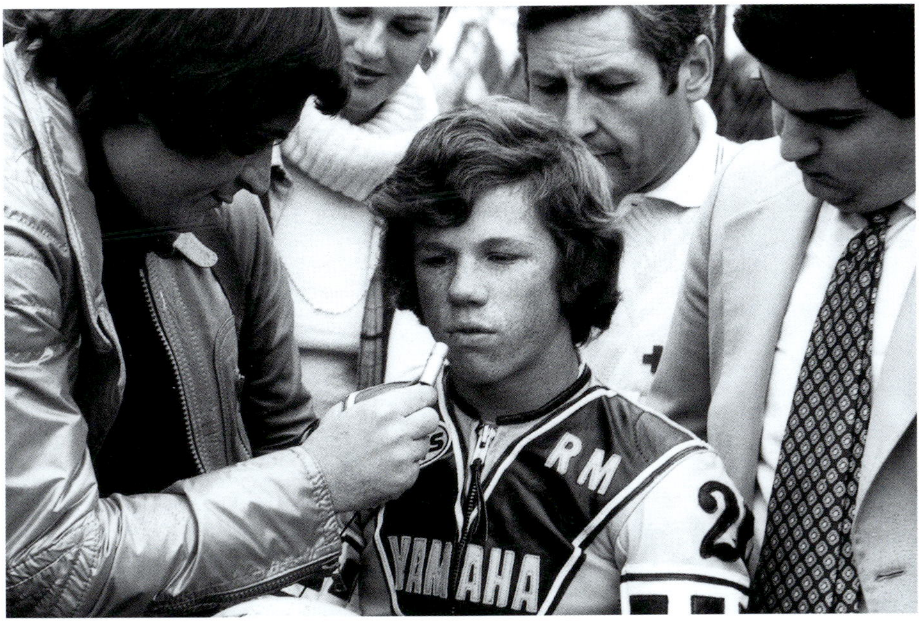

Carlo Costa interviews a boyish Randy Mamola.

Randy Mamola: from devil to angel.

Looking back, I had a satisfying career, I'm happy with what I've achieved and I think that's what counts: that, and the friendships I established with people over the years. I'm probably the only rider to have taken the podium in 500 cc in three separate decades ('70s, '80s and '90s) and that, I think, is the mark of a winner. For some, winning world championships is everything but not for me. A lot of exceptional talent has left motorcycling over the years… Schwantz, Lawson: I, instead, am still here, among people who still go out of their way to do me a favour. That really makes me feel like a champion.

I also feel immense gratitude at having had the opportunity to learn from greats such as Agostini and Phil Read: motorcycling's given me a lot, everything. Now it's my turn to do something for motorcycling. Nowadays I mainly work as a commentator for Eurosport. Thanks to my past and the fact that I raced for so many teams I have access to all the pits and everyone – riders and mechanics – treats me with respect. I'm the only TV commentator that can drop into the Honda team area and then calmly walk over to Suzuki. I also do promotional work for Marlboro Yamaha, taking pas-

Bernie Ecclestone and wife wisely make friends with Dr. Costa before their test ride.

sengers around race circuits on a Yamaha pillion Replica. It's quite a buzz: until we started doing this non-racers had had no idea what it was like to ride an official competition bike around a circuit. Now, instead, the fans can experience it first-hand. Giving them that experience is, for me, a question of pride. Sometimes I even get celebrities – I even got Bernie Ecclestone once! It's a job I'm lucky to have: in meeting so many people and having had such a long career I count myself as one lucky guy".

Of course, Randy Mamola has often asked me to take a ride with him. I've always been tempted, but have never taken him up on his offer. A lot of people ask me why not. Some smirk ironically, convinced that I'm too scared to. They're right, I am pretty afraid – but not of falling off or hurting myself. I'm afraid that if I get on that motorcycle I'll never want to get off it again.

23. *The Reverend – Walter Villa*

I have always been a friend to the riders. Their friendship and love is worth more to me than all the riches in the world. It should come as no surprise, then, that I formed a close friendship with that likeable rider from Modena who won numerous World Championship titles, Walter Villa. It was a bond tempered by the act of saving his life together with Dr. Caroli at Monza on that terrible Sunday on 20th May 1973.

This solid patient-doctor alliance wobbled just once, in 1976, the year in which Walter Villa competed in the 250 cc World Championship.

The "certainly reverend" Walter Villa.

That year I was doctor to a friendly youngster called Johnny Alberto Cecotto who had the habit of falling frequently. Fortunately, after each fall I managed to get him back on his bike and he was thus able to participate in all the races, including the one at Mugello which he won with a broken hand. The joy of seeing him win was quashed by the tragedy of the crash that killed Tordi and Buscherini: the skilled attempts of Attilio Fabozzi – one of our most skilled medics – to resuscitate them were in vain. A fine doctor, Fabozzi had the aristocratic traits of education and refinement and, despite suffering from a serious heart complaint, never deserted the hospital and often accompanied me with the Clinica Mobile to race events. The riders' injuries caused him enormous distress, as did the injustices inflicted on us by non-Clinic doctors. On that tragic Sunday I'm sure his weak heart suffered even further pain when he was unable to resuscitate those two heroes who will always be known to us as Paolo and Otello.

So, my friendship with Walter Villa became rather strained that year. This upset me somewhat so I asked him to elucidate. "Certainly, we're friends", Walter replied, "but every time Cecotto crashes you get him back on his feet – and his bike –and I risk losing the World Championship and…" What he then went on to say is, for the most part, unprintable.

Some gave Walter Villa the nickname "Certainly" (the word with which he began every sentence) while others preferred to call him "Reverend" on account of his kind, calm visage. On that occasion, though, "Certainly" was the more apt of the two as there was nothing priest-like about his words, which I have politely censored. Soon enough, the Reverend fell too: together we healed his broken bones – and our wounded friendship.

24. *Little Big Man – Eugenio Lazzarini*

Small in stature, yet several times world champion, the magic of motorcycling transformed him into a feared giant. His vigour and optimism may well have much to do with the fact that he was from Pesaro, a city brimming in history and the birthplace of men who would write some of the most glorious chapters in the history of motorcycling.

In the 1920's Pesaro became home to that renowned motorcycle manufacturer, Benelli: the creative genius of a whole family of manufacturing pioneers melded with the drive, courage and boldness of one of its members, Tonino Benelli, the Charles Lindbergh of motorcycling.

Going back even further into Pesaro's history, 22nd July 1909 saw the birth of Dorino Serafini, a vivacious, robust child who used to steal his father's motorbike and put it through every pace imaginable before obtaining his first racing bike from the Benelli brothers. With his iron constitution and lion's heart he won an incredible forty-five races; as he rode round the track he would often hear the speaker, especially when abroad, bellow "the Italian from Pesaro!", an acute reminder of just how far he was from the brine of the Adriatic.

The list goes on: there was also Giancarlo Morbidelli, employee of a Pesaro-based woodworking and furniture factory. Even as a child he used to play with rusty scraps of iron rather than toys and use them to build his "dream bike"; in the end his dream came true when he rode a real one to victory during his debut in the Shell Gold Cup, organised by my father in 1969.

Pesaro is also the city where my uncle Cirillo Costa, a skilled surgeon, lived; it was he who brought me closer to the world of medicine. It is also the town where many of my father's and Eugenio Lazzarini's friends have lived (Goffredo Tempesta, Egidio Piovaticci, Silvio Grassetti to cite just a few) and the abode of first-rate family friends such as Marcello and Roberto Berloni: their splendid villa has hosted not only numerous cultural events but a great many sporting ones too. There, at the end of 1993, we celebrated the "resurrection" of Corrado Catalano, the Rome-born rider who

Pesaro-born Eugenio Lazzarini sports the rainbow colours of the champion.

Biaggi and Capirossi: a spontaneous reconciliation defeats the hypocrisy of an enforced one.

had come close to death at Hockenheim a few months earlier. Attended by a gamut of motorcycling champions, the event was a moving one for everyone. As if by magic even Loris Capirossi and Max Biaggi, who had squabbled like schoolboys at Brno, seemed to get on peacefully, without anyone diplomatically or hypocritically having to tell them to.

The best kind of peace between two people is that which springs from forgiveness, a precious gift that rewards the giver much more than it does the receiver; when it touches the hearts of two opponents joy and happiness soon follow. The intransigence of resentment and rancour melts away at the sudden, unexpected appearance of the irrational desire to forgive. Forgiveness allows us to glimpse the most veiled, but perhaps most precious, parts of ourselves, transforming frozen obstinacy into something more fluid that moves towards humanity and meets it in a divine embrace. To forgive others is to forgive ourselves.

Eugenio Lazzarini, punished by the gods who had horrifically dismembered his brother in a terrible racing accident, forgave them. Like Abraham who accepted God's will that he should smite his best-loved son with the sword, Eugenio accepted his destiny and his brother's mutilated arms as an invaluable source of strength for his own small limbs. Thus, when he won the most coveted title in motorcycling he simultaneously crowned his brother and his native town of Pesaro.

25. *Smiler – Mario Lega*

A smile carries inexplicable fascination. Perhaps, in prehistoric times, showing one's teeth between half-open lips was a gesture of peace, a promise to the enemy that one's weapons (i.e. teeth) would not be used. This evolutionary view of things might go down well in academic circles but it falls

An evidently serene and happy Mario Lega.

well short of explaining that universe of sentiments embodied in a smile.

There is the smile that the newborn infant encounters on his mother's face, that irreplaceable visage that tenderly whispered words of comfort, serenity and trust in the dramatic aftermath of birth. In coming into the world we feel deeply betrayed because from paradise we are thrust violently into the absurdity of reality. The only thing that redeems us from this violent betrayal is our mother's smile. Mario Lega's smile recalls that of the most affectionate mother, and the smile that accompanied him onto the podium in 1977 when he won the 250 cc world championship title recalls the poem "Your smile" by Pablo Neruda:

> (...) Your smile rises skywards searching for me
> and opens all life's doors for me
> (...) Deny me bread, air, light, Spring,
> but your smile never.

26. *Claudio – Pier Paolo Bianchi*

Claudio is Pier Paolo's son. The name honours that doctor Costa who had helped his father many times: once I managed to save one of his legs from amputation. While everyone knows me as Claudio my full name is Claudio Marcello. This combination of names has always led me to believe that I would never be confused with anyone else. I assumed that this double Christian name (a relative rarity in Italy) might help me understand life's ambivalence; it gave me the hope that one day, in gazing into a mirror. I might find the answer to the enigma of my own identity. Am I my parent's dream, have I been so lucky that their dream in the end coincided with mine? I don't know – and maybe never will: Claudio Marcello remains the twin name of an ambiguity and a doubt. This enigma has been partially disentangled by the riders: like the arrow that knows its target they know who I am and what my origins are. Pierpaolo Bianchi, motorcycle rider, knew that my twin name had not yet revealed the truth: hence he named his son Claudio and nothing more.

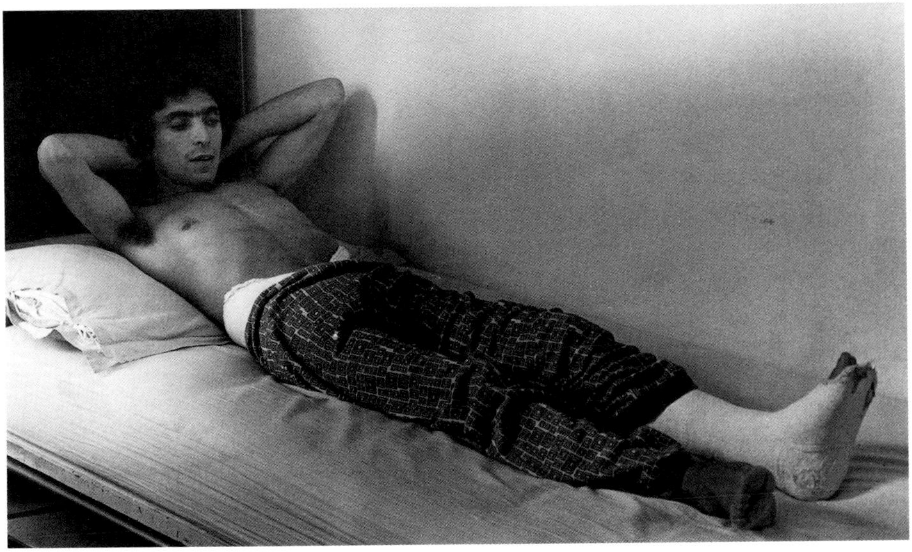

Adriatic brine fails to melt the plaster encasing Bianchi's leg.

27. *A Brain – Corrado Catalano*

In 1993, during the 500 cc race at Hockenheim, Corrado Catalano rode like the wind: as he roared through the chicane he fell and slammed against another bike that had slid off earlier; its rider had thoughtlessly parked it at the edge of the track. Despite the protection offered by his helmet Corra-

Corrado Catalano, the sphinx of life.

do received serious brain injuries and fell into a deep coma. He was transferred to Mannheim hospital for urgent surgery. To gain precious time I offered to help the skilled neurosurgeon I met that day, Dr. Adrian Wolf. The German anaesthesiologist was assisted by my colleague from the Clinica Mobile, Dr. Salvatore Marrone. To wait for the arrival of the second anaesthetist and second neurosurgeon who were on call would have cost precious minutes.

Spontaneously, I called Corrado's father and informed him of his son's critical – if not desperate – condition, yet solemnly promised him that he would pull through. The words "pull through" seemed to calm him: later, together with his mother and sister, he would keep a touchingly constant bedside vigil over his son. Corrado rose from that coma, his left hand clenching the pomegranate seeds that symbolise the riches acquired by those who descend into the realm of the dead... but only in his left hand, as he will have difficulty in clenching his right hand for the rest of his life.

28. *The Flying Imolese – Fausto Gresini*

Imolese (i.e. from Imola), twice world champion, the living expression of *romagnolo* genius and courageous in every circumstance. He began many of his races with broken hands or feet, exploits that rightly earned him numerous titles. Fausto is humble yet a connoisseur, straightforward yet imagi-

Fausto Gresini scans his palms perhaps in search of an endless story.

native and is as sharp now as he was in his heyday. With Fausto there remains just one doubt: at Imola, he often plays cards (traditional Romagna games such as *mattazza* and *beccaccino*) in a social club (The Tozzona) populated by likeable pensioners – and he's clearly the best. So why is it that he always loses against me?

The courage he displayed on the race track came to the fore again when he set up a winning team that he leads from the heart.

In 2001 luck paid him back with interest when it donated him a hero by the name of Daijiro Katoh. Fausto will continue to build on his intuition this coming year too by entrusting the world championship 250 cc

Daijiro Katoh: a child-like face masks true samurai grit.

Honda bike to one of Italy's most promising riders, Roberto Rolfo.

Katoh is a Japanese youngster with a smooth, almost baby-like face. His soft, almost beardless features confine him to an eternal childhood and his eyes are those of a youth blind to life's bitterness. His fragile body would have been the worry of any mother. Nobody would have foreseen a glorious future for him, only the humiliation that society all too often reserves for the weak or apparently defenceless. Yet Daijiro, when he sits astride his bike, is transformed into a samurai, righteous with himself and merciless with his opponents. From that slight body there bursts forth an unexpected energy that is living evidence of the mind's power to overcome any poverty, any weakness. Like David who downed the mighty Goliath, his resolve stems from that starlight the human mind scatters across the sky of life.

Rolfo's strength, instead, comes from his education and serenity, yet this state of grace is sometimes spoilt by the doubts that spring from unknown depths of his mind. I believe his alliance with Fausto will help him to chase the demons away and Roberto will then be able to aspire to being one of the greats and Daijiro Katoh's heir.

Roberto Rolfo engaged in a high-speed chase for his dreams.

29. *Club Foot – Alessandro Gramigni*

A club foot is one of the most common cases in infant orthopaedics. During my years at the Rizzoli Hospital in Bologna I treated many such feet, making countless little plaster casts with my tutor Laura and performing countless operations with my trusted assistant Giovanna. One such operation was on the right foot of a newborn child called Alessandro. Later, his mother would bring him in to see my mentor, Alessando Dal Monte, for regular check ups. When he was much older, Alessandro asked his parents for a motorcycle: on that motorcycle he hoped to hide the infirmity he displayed when walking and playing, and perhaps hoped that the motorbike would in some way recompense him for the punishment received at birth. Worried sick, his mother rushed to the Rizzoli hospital to try and get the duty doctor to dissuade Alessandro from his intentions: "But don't you think, doctor, that my son should stay away from motorbikes?".

"Oh, of course he can ride a motorbike" replied Dr. Lello Rubbini with a smile aimed more at Alessandro than his mother, "riding that bike will cure his foot much better than any doctor!". Even back then, Lello was one of those at the Clinica Mobile who had realised that a child's wish fulfilled is more powerful than any medicine.

On the track, Alessandro was a thoroughbred. At the start of 1992 he was leading the World Championship. But one day, biking out on the road, he was hit by a car. Unprotected, he sustained a displaced fracture of the right leg; his right foot, already deformed by destiny, was horribly mangled. His will to keep on racing was strained and the dream of becoming world champion was shattered by the reality of the hospital bed.

But unexpectedly, as usually only happens in fairy tales, something magical happened: during the night he was operated on by my cousin, Dr. Paolo Costa, Chief Orthopaedic Consultant at the Santa Maria Hospital of Reggio Emilia.

A few days later I stole Alessandro away from my cousin to take him to my home and get him started on a fast-track recovery program that would ensure he didn't miss even a single World Championship race. Perhaps the only person who took all this as par for the course was my cousin: ever since childhood he had known that I was a something of a reality-eluding dreamer.

One month later Alessandro Gramigni completed the Mugello GP and 42 days later, in Barcelona, came 4th. He still needed crutches to get to his bike, but when he reached it the injuries vanished: in the cup from which he had drunk so much pain the last few drops evaporated into the rainbow of the world title. His seemingly endless joy lasted but an instant, yet the book that tells us how Alessandro Gramigni became 125 cc World Champion in 1992 with Aprilia will last forever.

A confident Alex Gramigni caresses the asphalt.

30. *Digger – Wayne Gardner*

"Ciao Claudio, it's been 9 years since I've visited the Clinica Mobile to get fixed up by you and the team. As I've just turned 41 I can't tell you how grateful I am for all the great work you did on me. Even now as I get older I've had no ongoing problems with any of the injuries received. You are a

Wayne Gardner powers through the corner, buoyed by youthful spirit.

legend! Now that I'm involved in the sport again with the young Aussie rider, Broc Parkes in the World Superbikes – it's great to know that either you or your team will be there with your brilliant medical support for him and the other riders. My motorcycle career would never have been as good if it were not for you and your team. I owe you a great deal and am indebted forever. Not only did you heal my wounds you were always there as a great friend. I hope to catch up with you sometime soon...

Cheers, Wayne Gardner".

When I was asked to put the history of the Clinica Mobile on the Web (the address is www.clinicamobile.com), I felt a bit uneasy. I'm not a great fan of technology and see it as a form of "21st century slavery". Yet when an entry like the one above pops up in the Guest Book my hostility towards computers evaporates and I come close to something that looks ominously like forgiveness! Just as I feel life has so much to offer when I visit www.ducati.com and receive mail from and chat with so many unknown friends via Internet.

The words of Wayne Gardner are comforting: the years have gone by but he has not suffered any lasting effects from the multiple fractures he received during his epic racing career – despite the fact that I cured them by ignoring the traditional "dogmas" of trauma medicine and chose "action" as his cure and "desire" as his doctor. My fears that injured riders would, in old age, be transformed into cripples have been swept away by the above words of the 1987 world champion. That "faith" shown by convalescing riders is the most healing of medicines, not only in the short run but, perhaps, in the long run too. Nature offers us a doctor that we ignore only because we are blinded by technology and ensnared by the fascination of false sirens.

Luckily, human beings often open their eyes and, like Ulysses, steel themselves so as not to fall prey to the dangerously persuasive song of the siren. Released from the prison of false promises, motorcyclists are free to honour their destiny and enjoy riches dug from the mine of their own souls with a desire sharpened by faith.

Dear Wayne, so many times you descended into the terrible world of torment and pain and just as many times you returned with those pomegranate seeds that, in ancient Greece, symbolised the riches conquered during that disturbing journey. So many times we suffered together on the eve of a race and then celebrated afterwards when you conquered the podium. At the inauguration of the 3rd Clinica Mobile at Imola, on 21st

Wayne Gardner.

May 1988, you were the first to enter it not only as one of its "godfathers" together with Giacomo Agostini, Kenny Roberts and Franco Uncini, but also, because of the fractures in your right foot, one of its patients. The day after, when you came in second behind Wayne Rainey, I was happy. When you limped over to me, hugged me in tears and donated the money you had just won to the clinic I was moved. Our tears, mixed with joy, showed the world that pain and delight are inextricably entwined and that men should not be afraid to drink from the cup of suffering because in it, perhaps, they may well find happiness.

31. *Steady Eddie – Eddie Lawson*

I write willingly of Eddie – even if he was cantankerous, introverted and a man of few words. My father liked him a lot though. In 1983, "King Kenny" Roberts was about to abdicate to Freddie Spencer and saw in his young team-mate Eddie Lawson a potential ally: Eddie would help him knock

Eddie Lawson: when he had something to say he let his bike do the talking.

the Honda rider into third place in the last World Championship race of the season in Imola, thus allowing Kenny to conquer his 4th world title. For Kenny, victory at Imola would not on its own suffice: for him to win the title it was vital that Spencer do no better than third place. That day, the first Sunday in September 1983, Eddie Lawson did the exact opposite of what was expected of him and spent the whole race drifting in the anonymity of the bunch; his attitude drew anger, criticism and rebuke from many, the things that hurt worst. Yet to despise others and laugh at their weaknesses only masks the fragility and fear of those who harbour a creeping uneasiness: in the words of Camus, "Of course, I was aware of my weaknesses, and I regretted them. Yet I forget about them with a deliberateness that was almost praiseworthy. Instead, my own criticism of others continued unabated". My father had no such uneasiness: with his almost Franciscan looks and a spirit to match, had taught me that other people's failings are also ours and that lies irredeemably condemn those that speak them to the category of the mediocre, the weak and insecure. With a smile of veiled superiority he said, "Eddie Lawson is the best in the world; all he has to do is get used to being

Jim Redman, Freddie Spencer, Claudio Costa, Luigi Taveri.

away from home and then he'll win more titles than Spencer". This incredible prediction transformed me into one of Lawson's biggest fans: subsequently, my arguments with Freddie Spencer's fans became legendary. My biggest clashes were with the photographer-artist Franco Villani, and Dr. Lello Rubbini of the Clinica Mobile (a keen favourite with Luca Cadalora for saving the wrist he had fractured badly in Sweden).

Those arguments ceased only after Eddie won his fourth world championship title against Spencer's three. My greatest satisfaction, though, was that my father had predicted it all: he had read the rider's future. He'd already done this with Lomas, McIntyre, Agostini and Roberts, speaking of them as heroes before anyone else had even heard of them. His most poignantly remembered forecast, though, regarded Keith Campbell. Keith arrived at Imola in the 50's after being invited to take part in the Shell Gold Cup. Poor and unknown, my father hosted him at our house, the "Feudino", because he knew that Campbell had no money for food and accommodation. My father was utterly convinced of his riding skills – all he needed was a little help. That day I learnt that hospitality makes the host happy. In the evening (as we sat and ate the delicious food that only my grandmother Maria could cook) I saw this Australian rider give my mother a bouquet of flowers and learnt that in poverty there often resides great nobility. When I was told he had scraped together the cash for the flowers by asking people to lend it to him I was moved: just as I was when he became World Champion with Guzzi in '57.

My father rarely left Imola: his whole world was the "Feudino", his birthplace. From here his imagination would reach out to visit far-off countries and take a close look at their riders. Then, one by one, he would bring them, nameless, into his theatre – the Imola race track – and send them on their way with a name and the unexpected title of hero.

For all this and more, I loved Eddie Lawson – and loved him even more when he won with Cagiva.

Claudio Castiglioni, builder of the Cagiva legend, has not only led it to victory. He has, in this new millennium, gone the extra mile and fired the nostalgic dreams of motorcycling fans by resuscitating the name of MV Augusta.

32. *The Man from Monterey – Wayne Rainey*

On 5th September 1993 Wayne Rainey fell at Misano at corner no. 1. A fall from which riders usually recover quickly, running off to grab their bikes as if afraid of missing communion. But the three times World Champion wasn't getting up. His agitated arm-waving and the bustling of the marshals indicated that something serious had happened.

Wayne Rainey lay on the sand paralysed from the waist down; immediately transferred to the Bufalini hospital in Cesena the doctors there managed to halt the massive haemorrhage invading his chest, thus saving his life (the doctors of that hospital later received many letters of praise). He was then transferred to a hospital in Los Angeles, California and on Christmas Eve he returned home to the beautiful city of Monterey and the love of his family.

That day Wayne Rainey fell into the abyss of his own drama and in the desert of his condition began to listen to the voice of his soul. In the darkness of this terrible suffering there appeared a timid sunlight, the "black sun" described by the French poet Bousquet.

Wayne Rainey miraculously began reliving his life and regained control over it, a control which he exerts to this day.

It has been written that a near-death experience makes life much more vivid and authentic. The injuries that opened terrible lacerations in Wayne Rainey's body have forced him to spend his life in a wheelchair. Yet this terrible experience has also allowed him to reach a new world – full of an unexpected energy and light that cannot in any way be confused with the everyday light you and I see. The rent in his body has yielded that strength which is the forerunner of poetry.

Those like Wayne Rainey, who live their lives in wheelchairs and have crossed the abyss of their tragedy at the terrible price of torment, discover a precious core of courage that the bulk of humanity will never perceive. Only these "lucky few" will be permitted to see the world from a new, original viewpoint.

Their tears reveal a place illuminated by a different light – a place where they will walk and run thanks to the guiding hand of their own imaginations.

In this fantastic, sublime place all the world's Wayne Raineys run to embrace each other while society's everyday inhabitants remain imprisoned in their shells, bound by the cords of omnipotence and power, crushed by technology, overwhelmed by convention, robbed of brilliance, creativity and imagination, mesmerised by fashion and a consumerism that fails to respect even time itself.

A person forced to live in a wheelchair faces a multitude of new challenges: he also learns to put up with things that the average person is probably unaware of, such as the humiliation inflicted on him by society's false solidarity and hypocritical kindnesses.

It is a society often made up of people who fail to recognise neither the people who live in the same street as them nor their next door neighbours. Yet the person actually in the wheelchair learns to acknowledge diversity and understand others, miraculously transforming his problems into rare gifts.

Wayne Rainey: joy and pain are drunk from the same cup.

33. *Lorito – Loris Reggiani*

His difficult childhood made him authentic, and the terrible injuries received by his frail body tempered his spirit and mind even more. I well remember the day in which we found him near death: together with Dr. Giancarlo Caroli, who shared emergency duties with me at the Imola race track during motorcycle events, I raced against the clock to return him to the joy of living and the thrill of racing. In those dramatic moments we took advantage of everything science had to offer.

During the night we transferred him first to the Resuscitation Unit at the Rizzoli Hospital (where I worked) and then to the Sant'Orsola Hospital for delicate surgery. Most of the bones in his skeleton had been smashed by the truck he had slid under as he rode out of the driveway of his house to test a new motorbike, the brakes of which had suddenly failed: to transport his shattered body we "packed" him in a vacuum mattress which immobilised him perfectly. Yet the mattress was so bulky the doors of the ambulance wouldn't shut.

The minutes that separate life from death were ticking away fast, so one of the Clinica Mobile staff lay on the floor of the ambulance and held the doors half-closed with his hands, while Dr. Caroli and I continued to treat Loris as best we could.

The journey was made and the first battle won. Later ones were fought by Dr. Antonio Di Gennaro who I recall here with great affection. It was he who, one night in February 1977, skilfully operated on my father (after he had been involved in an accident with his friend and gifted interpreter, Giancarlo Galavotti).

In piecing together Loris Reggiani's crushed pelvis Dr. Di Gennaro was helped by Dr. Giancarlo Caroli and Dr. Aristide Guerra. The former is now Director of the Villa Laura nursing home in Bologna and the latter Head of Traumatology at the Hospital of Ravenna.

Loris Reggiani made a full recovery. That he also returned to racing owes much to the fact that Ivano Beggio, the founding father of Aprilia, put his absolute trust in Loris and gave him a bike to race with. In my first meeting with "the man from Aprilia" I told him that Loris would, in the end, be saved not by medicine but by a demonstration of unconditional trust. There was, quite simply, no other way to save him. To help things along I told a worried Ivano that this was the viewpoint of many a philosopher and that these words of trust were the same that Christ had uttered to Judas.

I didn't really know Ivano Beggio back then, but his reply convinced me he was a man, not the ruler of an empire. He said "I shall worry myself sick that Loris won't be up to it, but my Aprilia is all his". The miracle had happened: his irrational trust had opened the doors to the indescribable greatness of this rider who first won his own private battle and then started winning races.

The recompense for all this is to be found in his gaze which, when he looks at me, offers me a warmth and tenderness that is touching. It is a recompense that becomes even more human when accompanied by the delicious *tagliatelle* that only his putative mother, aunt Marisa, knows how to make.

Loris Reggiani: his bike was his family, his everything.

34. *A Different kind of Rider – Luca Cadalora*

Luca has never liked the reality of this life, not at all. This may explain the ease with which he descended into the vaults of his own soul to obtain the precious nutrition that would slowly but surely bring out the best in him. The ancient Greeks would have said that Luca was able to descend to the netherworld and from there return with the pomegranate seeds that symbolised renewed spirit. Mick Doohan held him in the highest esteem, defining him as his most feared opponent.

Francesco Chionne, one of the Clinica Mobile physiotherapists, wrote: "It is difficult to interpret a man when he conceals his inner qualities behind an apparently bashful and introverted personality, yet it is equally pleasing not to seek a rational answer to that mystery and enjoy, instead, the enigmatic fascination that a man like Cadalora inevitably arouses".

Luca was a "different" kind of champion. His motorcycling was based on an authentic passion that fed on the most primitive and thus most emotional of rationales: to race against oneself, to win the challenge that springs from one's core, that self that always seeks out a reason for its own being.

The key to understanding how Luca managed to stay at the top for so many years is this: not only did he, of course, try to win as much as possible, he also sought out, with every new race, new stimuli and new reasons to help him do what he loved so much even better. This made him unique. A connoisseur of motorcycle mechanics, he adopted a riding style that reflected his philosophy for living: it was not the rider who should adapt to the bike, but the bike that should bend to the will of its rider; it is not man who should adapt to circumstance, but events themselves which should follow a fervent, determined will.

Luca, more than any other rider, celebrated not only his victories but his defeats too: because everything that Luca did, successfully or otherwise, he had chosen to do, driven by a will that extended far beyond the needs of those that worked with him and even beyond the expectations of those who wanted him to win – but were never able to fathom his sentiments. Cadalora surpassed himself on a thousand occasions. When, for example, he demanded – for his official bike – a hand-made frame or even a standard tyre produced by a rival company! When, still able to race with the best, he accepted the role of test rider. When, in all those races in which he realised he wasn't riding the bike he'd demanded he would quickly – and controversially – return to the pits; rather than take unnecessary risks he would ensure he got the bike he knew he deserved in the next race. Thanks to this willpower, Luca, as his career matured, walked a path of courage that was lit more and more by the light of reason than the light of "folly"; reason became the custodian of passionate consistency. To take unnecessary risks would have meant depriving himself of the happiness of living life according to his own designs. With Luca, this is perhaps the crux of things: in his long career, which saw him triumph in both individual races and championships, Luca was not once seriously injured.

His unwillingness to compromise came to the fore again and again. In 1996 he chose a standard production Honda instead of the official Yamaha, which failed to arouse the enthusiasm that had brought him so far. Just about everyone thought it was a bad move – a practically guaranteed race lo-

Barcelona, June 2001: Honda celebrates 500 victories, many of which belong to Cadalora.

ser! Perhaps Luca had already figured that out himself... but from the height of his own convictions it was a choice he had to make; he had to know, cost what it may, that he would not have to wonder for the rest of his life what would have happened if he had not followed his instincts.

For those that knew how to appreciate all this, Luca, while failing to grasp that hoped-for 500 cc crown, quenched a thirst for a different kind of victory that has nothing to do with standing on the highest step of the podium but has everything to do with self-esteem and unconditional observance of your beliefs. In this Luca was not just a rider, he was a guiding philosopher. In this respect he deservingly became champion of his own dreams and since then his standard white, sponsorless 500 cc Honda has come to symbolise one of the most glorious chapters in the history of motorcycling.

35. The Texan – Kevin Schwantz

The history of the third Clinica Mobile is a rich one. One particularly memorable chapter regards Kevin Schwantz who became a "regular" at the Clinica Mobile after breaking his collar bone at Assen in 1988. It is a story with a series of incredible episodes. In 1989 he came third at the Paul Ricard ra-

Kevin Schwantz: a smile lights up eyes brimming with the desire to race.

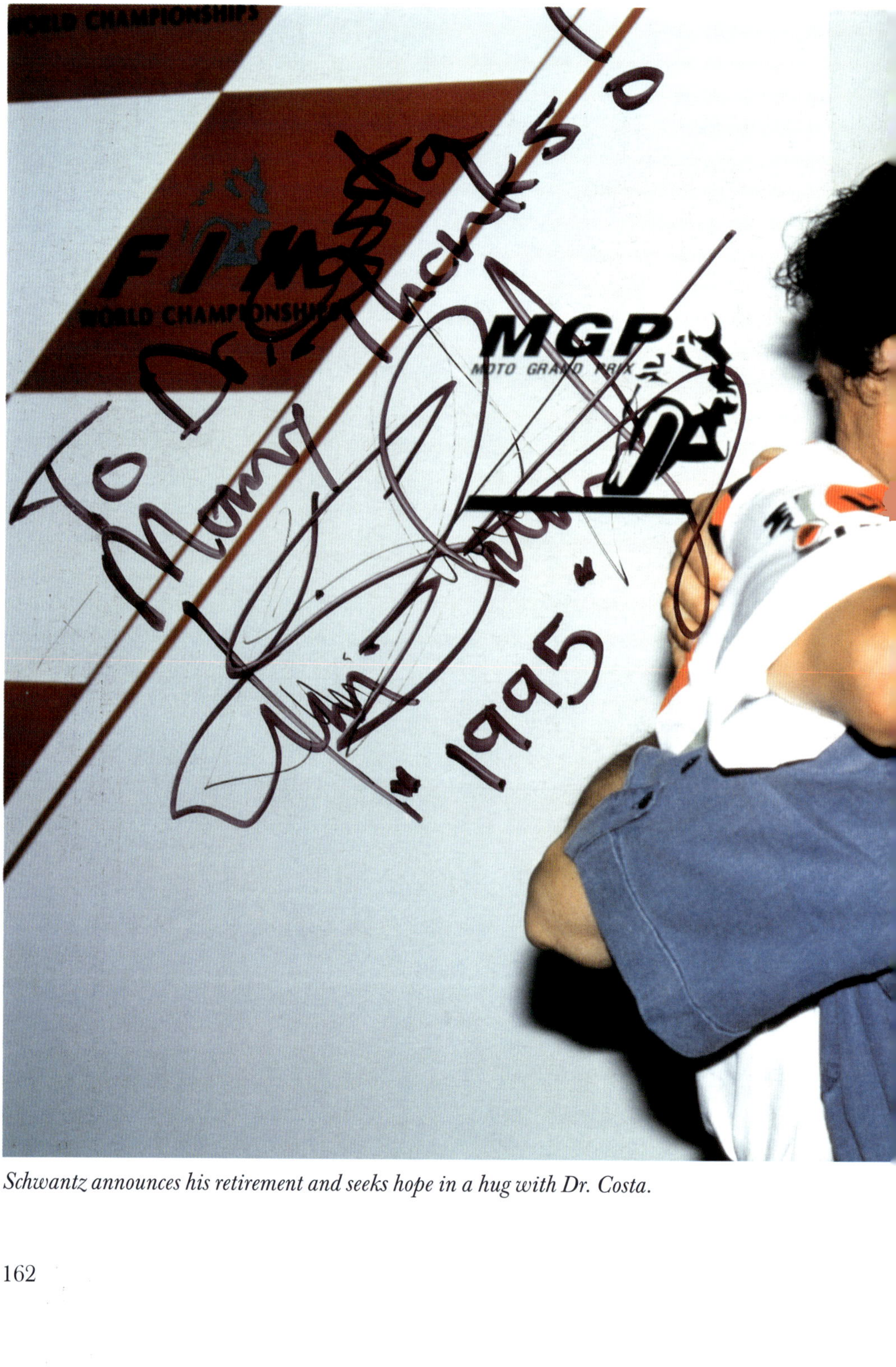

Schwantz announces his retirement and seeks hope in a hug with Dr. Costa.

ce track after crushing his right knee cap two weeks earlier at Spa in Belgium; in 1992 he came in fourth at the Hungaroring after breaking his left wrist and fracturing his right pelvis just two weeks earlier at Assen. In 1994 he hurt his left wrist for the umpteenth time during the warm-up at the Assen GP, this time suffering the worst wrist injury in the book; yet he still wanted to take part in the race and continue his quest for the world title. With his fractures and dislocated wrist set in Scotchcast he returned to the pits with Paolo "master of plaster" Fabbri and Clinica Mobile doctor Michele Macchiagodena to see whether, in this condition, riding the bike was feasible. Amazingly, not only could he ride it, he dominated the field for almost the entire race. A fortnight later he came third at Mugello and a month later, still encased in the resin bandages invented by 3M, competed in the Donington GP and won.

During a charity auction for children in need Kevin was presented to the crowd by ex-Beatle George Harrison as a legendary hero; the Scotchcast that had harnessed his wrist during his marvellous journey to championship victory was sold for a fine sum (a curious coincidence would later see Geoff Britton, the drummer who worked with another ex-Beatle, Paul McCartney, treated at the Clinica Mobile for exactly the same kind of fracture). After the thrilling, moving victory of Donington in 1994, Kevin never won again; suddenly feeling the physical and mental strain of years of competition and injury, he announced his retirement. The staff at the Clinica Mobile wrote the following letter:

"When Kevin Schwantz told an unbelieving crowd that he was going to retire from racing, his listeners were suddenly overcome by a void too great for their tears to fill. The greatest rider of the last ten years was stepping off the stage as a mere mortal, a stage he had dominated like a god: only the poetry of nostalgia and the love of his admirers will ever bring him back to Olympus. But Kevin Schwantz's retirement from racing, announced in June at Mugello, had already been decided during the Japanese Grand Prix at Suzuka, when the Texan, with his aching shoulder, wrist and hand, realised that the age of heroism was coming to a close and that the age of humanity was about to begin. Nobody understood or could understand this tense drama... but in the falling rain of Suzuka, on a stormy, dark day, something marvellous happened. Loris Capirossi, rapidly drawing up behind Kevin Schwantz, although unaware of the stirrings inside the American rider's heart, had a sudden inkling of what was going on. Kevin Schwantz, the fans' most beloved knight, invincible on the Japanese tracks and in the rain, was about to give up motorcycling. Loris understood: in a split second, he grasped the sad truth. And when, on his roaring Honda, he swept past his rival among myriad splashes of rainwater, he was unable to prevent his heart from ordering his body to make one of the most splendid gestures of his career as a champion. Almost bowing on the unreliable and slippery asphalt, his left hand still aching from a heavy fall in Malaysia three weeks before, Loris lifted that injured hand, not so much to beg Kevin's pardon for overtaking him, as to offer Kevin the gift of true solidarity, the solidarity of the new up-and-coming champion with the still greater one on his way out. An ancient gesture, which recalled to memory the chivalry of Medieval tournaments when, perhaps, human dignity met with greater respect than it does today, crushed underfoot as it is at every moment. Capirossi's steed, without his hand's guiding control, went wild and cast its rider onto the wet asphalt and the mud at the side of the racetrack.

Everybody, their minds the prisoners of prejudice, shouted that he had made a mistake, criticised his error, accused him of inexperience. But, amidst the water sprayed into the air as the motorcycle skidded crazily among the puddles, a sudden rainbow appeared, enchanting against the backdrop of that dark day. In legend a rainbow is a light woven from many colours that rises out of a pot of gold and spreads out to touch another, equally precious, one… That day, a rainbow arose from Kevin Schwantz's suffering to illuminate Loris's chivalry and honour a gesture which only the blind could not or would not admire and ponder. But fortunately, motorcycling fans love these gestures, they understand them, they know that – beyond the mathematics of classification – there exist exciting enterprises which can create rainbows in the dark and make us love a champion even when he falls… or retires!"

36. *The Legend – Mick Doohan*

The story of Mick Doohan is, quite simply, a fairy tale. Children hear many such tales before drifting off into sleep. Such tales often speak of the youngest of three brothers whose parents would sometimes disappear or be ever-present.

Once upon a time, then, there was the youngest of three children, Mick, thrust into the world behind two brothers who already occupied so much of that limitless space that children so desire. Yet he found that his mother's strength and determination made up for this. He loved her so much that he decided to make these qualities his own. Helped by these virtues, he cultivated a healthy sibling rivalry that would, without him realising it, drive him towards destiny.

Despite his gifted imagination, he had no idea that he would become a motorcycle racer, as he honestly thought that "you'd have to be crazy to want to ride around a track at that speed!". Yet destiny is unpredictable and his brothers, always pushing him towards confrontation, urging him on in his struggles, were amazed at his talent. Sibling rivalry evaporated to reveal a dream shared by all three: the world championship. Thus the fairy-tale began and Mick knocked on the door of motorcycling's castle, realising that he had not arrived but was just starting out. To conquer its throne he would have to fight with other hardened knights who harboured the same dream. Throughout his life, whenever he had come to the fork that divided an easy path from a difficult one he had always taken the latter, a habit that would ease the coming climb up the mountain of adversity.

Using his innate talent to sharpen his weapons, he fought his first duels and, soon afterwards, started winning them. He went on to dominate, becoming the undisputed leader. And here the story may well have ended with an "and they all lived happily ever after". Yet to conquer the kingdom of motorcycling more was needed: hence Mick entered a dark forest inhabited by ghosts and ghouls and steeled himself to face further danger despite serious injuries. At the crucial moment, just when his destiny seemed to be tormenting him, someone came to his aid, promising him that the kingdom , despite adversity, would be his, as would, perhaps, the love of a beautiful young woman who would give him a marvellous daughter.

And it is here that the most human part of the story begins, that part which narrates dangers to be faced and obstacles to be surmounted, telling the story of man's romantic attempt to escape from the prison of reason and embrace the world of sentiment.

On 26th June 1992 Michael Doohan, undisputed leader in the world motorcycling championship, fell at Assen (Holland), sustaining a 4th distal spyroid displaced fracture of the right leg. At the Clinica Mobile the doctors

Mick Doohan: his eyes promise us that paradise has not been lost.

suggested that the fracture be treated without actually operating so that he could compete in the last race of the season: all he would have to do to win the world championship would be to come 5th. But Doohan turned down the idea because he wanted to *win* the race, not calculate a strategy for extra points. He wanted to be operated on as soon as possible so that he could throw himself back into the fray quickly; finding the agreement of a team of Dutch doctors, surgery was performed on his leg. Yet terrible complications arose and Mick Doohan risked losing not only his leg but his life. His desperation, like that of a caged animal, was infinite. Together with the doctors of the Clinica Mobile I flew with a specially equipped aircraft to steal him away from that Dutch hospital. Kevin Schwantz, admitted to the same hospital for a broken wrist and dislocated pelvis, also flew with us. Once in Italy Mick Doohan underwent intensive therapy (medicines, hyperbaric treatment) and, to cure his now almost lifeless mangled leg, a daring operation was attempted: the healthy left leg would be joined to the right to nourish and save it. The operation was a success and both legs recovered. And with healing returned desire. Forty days went by and Mick expressed his wish to get back to racing: a Dionysian folly so great as to find the equally "mad" support of his doctor. He raced in Brazil (where he came 11th) and in South Africa (6th) and the 1992 World Championship was lost by just two points. His legs bleeding under pads specially prepared by Paolo Fabbri, Mick cried out his disappointment as did the few friends surrounding him. I had followed him step by step through this minefield of folly and was almost unable to resign myself to the injustice of it all. Yet, as a doctor – and thus mere mortal – I had no idea that the future would later grant justice by seeing Mick win at Mugello in 1993 and become World Champion at Brno in 1994.

On 7th September 1994 I wrote this letter to my friend Mick Doohan:

"Dear Michael, as you lay one night on a hospital bed after a terrible operation, we cried together, and I thought there must be a reward for so great a suffering. I instinctively felt that on leaving that bed of pain, you would manage to win the world championship of 2 years ago, and when this failed to happen I suffered as I had done during those nights in hospital.

I felt that you had been betrayed, that the world had deserted you. But the greatness of your spirit, free from the imperfections the human being bears in his body, let you write yourself a new destiny. A beautiful story in which you became the key protagonist of the whole motorcycling scene.

Assen, June 1992: Mick Doohan races towards his destiny.

Cornering the Doohan way: one technique for right-hand turns, another for left-hand turns.

Phillip Island, Australia, 1998: the exhilaration of victory and the pride of the flag.

With this enterprise, you have not only proved your own greatness, you have also shown every motorcycle rider how to give meaning to pain, and you have given the world a breath of hope.

In knowing you, I can finally say that life is worth living, and what I do is worth doing.

Your doctor forever, Claudio Costa."

After Mick won his 4th Championship title, I wrote him this second letter:

"As you lay on a bed of thorns, wounded by fate and man's arrogance and as your tears glinted in the faint light of the hospital room, we thought those tears would never fill the abyss of your distress or soothe the suffering of your injury... and indeed they soon ceased to stream down your pain-struck cheeks and in an instant those feelings of hope and desire which sustain a human being as he shoulders life's burdens returned to the fore: the hope of going back to racing and the desire of going back to winning.

And when you did go back to racing, your wounds still bleeding, we saw

Claudio Costa and Mick Doohan on the podium in Australia: a joyous moment.

your spirit bloom, invading your being as if emerging from some half-sealed casket. But time, unrelenting, continued to yield only pain, suffering and disillusionment, and desire was unable even to find shelter in the sweetest of harbours...

Then, suddenly, that casket of treasures which every human being carries inside himself opened completely and you, Michael, saw your entire self, from the depths of your soul to the heights of reason. You had become world champion for the 4th time. And in the joy of that instant, you felt that the theatre of pain had vanished, that it had ceased to exist, and you learned that time, which had so cruelly defined your suffering, no longer was. You realised how in happiness the human being becomes, in that precise instant, eternal, and you breathed immortality in the embrace of victory.

You felt yourself to be fortunate. Yet fortune is the ally of those who know their own soul: man can write his own fate. With you, Michael, we witnessed something wonderful – how pain can be transformed into happiness through that fortune which is no prisoner of destiny, but the most treasured quality of every human being. That, dear Michael, is why you kept on winning, and with your every victory, you redeemed your pain and that of all those who suffer. Some sports reporters, steeped in prejudice and stock comparisons, have hesitated in placing you on the right page of the history books. And perhaps they are right! They are unable to write you into the pages of history simply because you, Michael Doohan, are history, and perhaps, some day, will be our own history."

The legend of a man who, with his boundless pain and valour, made the gods turn pale just as dusk dims the day.

In 1998, Michael Doohan won his fifth world championship in the last-but-one race of the season on Phillip Island, and insisted that I, his doctor and friend, join him on the podium. In the winter of the same year, I was honoured to be able to present Mick with the Motosprint Caschi d'Oro award. The kingdom was conquered but Mick Doohan's ideals did not consist so much of conquest as self-improvement: he had set himself the unattainable goal of discovering his own limits.

In the lucid words of the great psychologist Gustav Jung "an unattainable goal does not lose its value because ideals are guides, not goals". Thus Mick attempted the not to be hoped for sixth title and met with his terrible accident in Jerez on 7th May '98. His injuries were so severe that he was forced to

The cage imprisoning his leg would soon fling open the door to a wondrous victory.

leave the castle of motorcycling forever: a world that he had, perhaps, already subconsciously left to pursue the infinity of his own heart.

That limitlessness of heart is seen in his work as adviser to a Honda team which had once been his and, today, nurtures his marvellous heir, Valentino Rossi.

Whenever we meet a nostalgia for the past appears in our eyes, eyes that will never forget and promise our friendship will last forever.

This promise of friendship fascinates us and is renewed whenever Mick comes to chat with me at the Clinica Mobile during motorcycle Grand Prix events or for a physiotherapy session with Bernard Achou, just like the good old days. Sometimes he visits me at my home in Imola (which is as much his as it is mine) and when we are far apart we write. And at this point I recall my response to his letter that was published on the Clinica Mobile web site:

"When I "scroll" the Guest Book at the Official Clinica Mobile Web Site (www.clinicamobile.com) I am thrilled and sometimes moved by the complements, encouragement and words of praise that come from so many and so far.

The words and ways of communicating are many, but in all the messages one thing shines through: love for the Clinica Mobile. This "creature", my family's offspring, destined to serve the heroes of motorcycling, has become a symbol that reunites the joys and pains of many.

Among the many names that pass before my eyes one in particular, a flash of nostalgia, stands out: Mick Doohan, wishing me a quiet week at Assen 2001. Assen, the circuit where, on 26th June 1992, after his terrible accident, his story, the story of motorcycling and perhaps part of my own story became entwined.

Knowing that he is my friend relieves my mind of existential doubt, recreates a sense of future and gives me the courage to face it. Mick's friendship is the very best payment that I could ever receive for the work I do. His visits to my Imola home and my residence (La Riva, meaning The Brink) in the beautiful valley of Fontanelice are frequent (the name of the house comes from Dante, Inferno, canto 12 verses 55-57 "...the while they raced along the brink, as when their game they hunted in the world of men"). When I greet him, his charming companion Seline and splendid daughter Allexis, it is a little like reliving the most intense moments of our story. I'm happy, just as I am when he enjoys the local food, the *piadina romagnola*, lovingly prepared by Luciano. In Allexis I see the natural strength and light of a budding child: the same light and strength seen in Mick when he was

Two friends.

condemned to the dark prison of his accident in June '92. Now that I have met and played with Allexis I realise that I have always known her. I have no doubt that it was she, with her child's strength, who led Mick by the hand from that Dutch hospital to an aircraft that would carry him towards his destiny. The courageous path taken by her father had been illuminated by her child's light.

I understood that Allexis had lived even before her birth, in Mick. As Wordsworth said, "I believe that nature, when she wishes to form a favourite from the very first dawn of infancy, she often creates a gap in the clouds that seems as if it has been split apart by lightning". Mick opened this gap and showed us Allexis.

Allexis Doohan.

The Feudino.

The Riva.

PART THREE
The Temples of Speed

38. *Imola*

Unluckily, I am neither a writer nor a poet. So, in writing of the Imola race track, I have taken the liberty of drawing inspiration from the book "Un viaggio in Romagna" by my father's close friend Dario Zanasi, a journalist with the Bologna-based daily *il Resto del Carlino*.

Dario Zanasi and Checco Costa belonged to that unselfish, idealistic, slightly mystical generation of men who loved to give and had cancelled the verb "to take" from their vocabulary. Just as ancient kings and princes used to do everything in their power to make sure that, on Sunday, every subject had a chicken in his pot, so my father, Francesco Costa, a mild-mannered, almost Franciscan graduate in Agriculture, did his utmost to ensure that all Italians had not only a chicken (and, with luck, a tasty side of beef) in their Sunday pots, but also thrilling motorcycle races like the Shell Gold Cup and the Imola 200.

And on those dream-like days, on the other side of the turbid waters of the River Santerno, the suggestive world of motorcycling would gather its vehicles, tents, picket fencing and the caravans which housed the gods of the motorcycling World Championship, those heroes who in coming so close to death had discovered what it meant to be truly alive. A beautiful, dare-devil world, chaotic yet picturesque, characterised by peaceful pauses and long-lasting thrills. During these events Imola put on a multi-coloured show without equal.

Just below the track itself the River Santerno slides past lazily. Horse chestnuts, acacias, fir trees, cypresses, pines, elms and vineyards grant the surrounding hills a harmony interrupted only by the graceful ribbon of the race track. Believe me, without this race track that natural harmony would have been destroyed by man. When Leonardo da Vinci drew his famous map of Imola he let the river run free but later generations, in too much of a hurry to mix cement, would adulterate Leonardo's plan. Yet the race track – about which there is nothing blind – has respected the map drawn by this genius and defended it. Without the race track no-one would have understood these sublime places, just as no silence can be appreciated without some intermittent background noise to define it. The silence of the night is more mysterious, fascinating and wistful when it is interrupted by the patter of rain, the jets of a fountain, the whistle of a departing train, the trill of crickets.

I believe the race track should be the town's symbol, an emblem for *Imolesi* to carry on their travels around a world that recognises the town on account of that track. The circuit should symbolise the thoughts and feelings of its inhabitants.

It is my hope that this temple will once more embrace the religion that consecrated it, that it will, once more, be inhabited by the cult of the motorcycle and repopulated by the heroes of the World Championship and the Superbike as they do battle around these "hills of passion", packed with fans celebrating the return of the centaurs.

I will be happier for them than anyone, but envious at not being able to live the race from the heart like the fans, these authentic connoisseurs of courage free to cheer on their heroes – and mine. And on the pit lane wall, next to the tower by the starting grid, there will shine a ceramic plaque

1996: the Town Council of Imola dedicates the Acque Minerali corner to Checco Costa.

in memory of Checco Costa dedicating the Acque Minerali corner to him forever. When I unveiled that plaque my voice cracked tearfully as I pronounced the following words: “so that the ashes of memory may not be swept away by the wind”.

Because in those ashes there lies the enchantment of a father whose memory has become my own and who has entwined his life with mine. In that moment my eyes were filled with countless images, memories that rose up as if by magic to remind me that the present only exists to contemplate a past that sometimes seems to mean and explain all. And through the blur of my tears I clearly saw that the achievements and inventions of one’s life are the sole explanation of its enigma – and the only passport to immortality. Before my eyes I saw endless riders and the melancholy drove me to seek out the seemingly inexistent words with which I could describe them…

A Dicer with Death – Ray Amm

His full name was William Raymond, born and bred in Rhodesia. I met him for the first time at the Imola Moto Club in 1954 where I used to spend the bulk of my free time and where, on the eve of the races organised by my father, I used to help his secretary (first Bruno Bizzi then Armando Bertozzi) stamp the tickets.

Ray Amm was a risk-lover: using the irrational willpower of a man attempting to break free from the chains of physics he was even capable of keeping his balance by touching the tarmac with one foot as he swept round corners. His special blend of physical and mental skills was honed to perfection.

During the race he kept up a sort of running dialogue with Death: with his gentle smile, Ray admitted that “if, even for just a moment, I felt the cold fear of death I would stop racing that instant as I would be unworthy of the coming corner or race”. Death kept him in credit for a long time, allowing him to win a great many races, but tragically decided to call in his debt at the “Rivazza” corner as he raced his 22nd lap at Imola on 11th April 1955.

Amm left the world behind, but his opponents carried the challenge forward, just as they do today and will forever… and when, one day, another motorcyclist encounters that mysterious figure dressed in black, he will simply ask “What makes you think you’ve won?”

Imola, 11th April 1955: Ray Amm rounds the Tosa. He has just two miles to live.

The Iron Duke – Geoff Duke

Geoff used to pore over his bike as if it had a soul; he would practically court it, touching it with pure chamois leather gloves. He was a man who had strayed from everyday reality to attain a perfection unmarred by human flaw. That humanity, which he had kept at bay so long and so successfully, would be returned to him in '57 at Imola during the legendary Shell Gold Cup as he lay in the dust of the Acque Minerali corner.

Checco Costa, Carlo Costa and the champion, Geoff Duke, astride his Gilera.

The Chinaman from Bergamo – Carlo Ubbiali

Even today, Carlo (whose nickname stems from his quasi-oriental features) continues to tell me that he dedicated the best and happiest years of his life to motorcycling and swears it is a world he'll never leave. He has just one regret: the suffering he caused his worrying mother who, whenever Carlo went racing, hid herself away at home to sob away her fears. Over the years I've met quite a few of these worried mothers! Even my father would

Monza: Carlo Ubbiali just before passing in front of the stands and giving his Mum a smile.

have slunk away to cry if I'd raced motorcycles. To spare himself that pain he forbade me to ride… and I obeyed him. That submissive obedience has persecuted me for decades now and becomes painful, even piercing, when I read the following verses by Kahlil Gibran.

"Your children are not your children
They are the sons and daughters of Life's longing for itself
They come through you but not from you
And though they are with you yet they belong not to you
You may give them your love but not your thoughts
For they have their own thoughts
You may house their bodies but not their souls
For their souls dwell in the house of tomorrow, which you cannot visit,
not even in your dreams."

It is not that I do not understand a parents' anguish when their sons engage in competitive motor racing (or simply ride their mopeds home from school); the fact is that I have also come to understand that in fulfilling their desires in this regard they are not running risks but making the decision to live. Hence, when Carletto Ubbiali took his mother to Monza and accompanied her to her seat in the stands and promised to give her a smile every time he went past she stopped crying. If only all mothers would stop crying when their sons start smiling! Even John Surtees was often accompanied by his mother: she used to remove his trademark black-striped white helmet from its worn out case, remind her son that it was time for him to get changed, then help his frail, bony, curved body into the black leathers and rouse him to greatness with words of encouragement for the coming race. In that magic moment, as he listened to his mother's words, John would become a tornado, flying into a rage if someone tried to get in front of him. Like a lightning bolt he flung himself out of the little London suburb of Catford where he was born to conquer eight world titles – seven on his motorcycle and one in Formula 1 with Ferrari. During the course of his career he uttered two phrases that remain engraved on my memory to this day: "If you fall get up quickly, because if you don't you'll be in the dust forever" and "If you fall without finding any explanation as to why, then it's time to stop racing". But not everyone saw it the John Surtees way. Bob McIntyre "the Flying Scotsman", in fact, fell dozens of times without ever bothering to ask himself why… for the simple reason that he seemed to have no understanding of the laws that govern balance or physics in general. In 1957 he won at Monza on

John Surtees at the chicane inserted by Count Agusta to slow the riders at the Tamburello.

a Gilera, in an epic battle against Guzzi. At the end of the race he began feeling ill and was taken to a clinic in Milan where X-rays showed one of his vertebrae to be broken: despite this dangerous crack in one of the skeleton's most delicate bones The Flying Scotsman had cruised to a fantastic victory. Destiny had dealt Bob McIntyre an uncommon dose of bravery, yet that same courage has been seen in plenty of riders over the years. Fate seemed to have smiled particularly favourably on Gary Hocking, who, in just four years won eighteen GP's and two World Championship titles. The boy who had pushed his plough in the fields of Bulawayo, Rhodesia and been galvanised by the feats of Ray Amm, conquered the world motorcycling scene in just a few years. For this lad, with his sad smile and a heart unable to hold onto happiness if not for a few fleeting seconds, nothing was impossible. So he decided to go in for the Tourist Trophy and achieve something that motorcycling would remember forever: then he would retire. So to Douglas on the legendary Isle of Man, populated with its odd-looking Manx cats, Gary Hocking went. In a fearful accident during preliminary tests he escaped disaster by the skin of his teeth. He discharged himself from hospital and,

Bob McIntyre, the Flying Scotsman.

battered but not beaten, set himself an impossible goal: to win the race and beat the fateful average of 105 mph. It was a dream... yet he made it come true. True to his word he pocketed his eighteenth world title and abandoned motorcycling... but only to head for Mallory Park and take the wheel of his first racing car, a Lotus. In his very first race he led the field, but was forced to pull out when a wheel came loose; most people assumed this unlucky incident to be the source of Gary's post-race mope, but in truth Gary Hocking was always gloomy because he wanted everything to happen in a hurry. He didn't care whether he lived or died as long as eventually found out just what it was which tormented him and wiped away his smile in moments of joy. During the GP in South Africa, the country where he had met Ray Amm, the Dicer with Death, he perished at Devil's Corner in a mass of coiled steel. Just as Dr. Faust had consulted Mephistopheles, perhaps Gary had asked the Devil himself to provide some of the answers to the torments and absurdities of life; the difference, though, was that Dr. Faust was saved by the gods while those same gods, perhaps envious of his skill and bravado, left Gary Hocking to his fate.

Gary Hocking: the sad smile of a rider unable to find joy even in victory.

The Wild Genius – Umberto Masetti

Motorbikes and women fascinated him, causing him to dream like a knight of olde, envisaging his escape on horseback with his sweetheart. He even tried his luck – several times – with a glittery circus star of the time and was thus forever the focus of gossip. Masetti was an easy target in this sense, but a much harder one when it came to singing his praises, or explaining the greatness with which he enchanted the world with two world titles on a 4-stroke Gilera. Today he moves through motorcycling circles with suave nonchalance, telling of his epic duels against Geoff Duke's Norton. He also speaks willingly of Bill Lomas, although he has yet to forgive him for the joke the latter played on him at Monza a few years ago. That day, as the veterans sped round the track on vintage motorcycles, Umberto Masetti fell and was bruised all over. As Masetti was being treated at the Clinica Mobile, Bill Lomas, who had won the event, was telling the press that Umberto had fallen because he had been distracted by a circus girl who had appeared at the edge of the track. He ended these words with a burst of raucous laughter – that froze in his throat when he met the icy stare of Masetti's current companion.

Masetti, like Valentino Rossi years later, rides the n° 46 to world championship glory.

The Kangaroo – Jack Findlay

Accompanied by the kangaroo painted on his helmet, Jack achieved World Championship victory in the 750 cc class. He often came to Imola and would engage in incredible race fee negotiations with my father vis-à-vis the Imola 200, a race he sorely wanted to compete in. He probably wouldn't have asked for any money at all and would have stayed in the paddocks to watch the 1978 race from the stands if he'd known that he would fly off during his descent of the Acque Minerali corner and instantly stop breathing. Fortunately his breath was pushed back into him by the doctor stationed at that corner, Claudio Macchiagodena, thus saving his life. Now, in the paddocks, Findlay is Technical Director and Macchiagodena is Medical Director, his task being to ensure that the medical services provided at all world championship circuits are up to scratch. Twenty years on from that accident, their respiration is still synchronised. During breaks in testing and qualification Dr. Macchiagodena always goes off with him to the Clinica Mobile's hospitality room for a bite to eat. During this frugal meal they spend most of their time joking together, often reprimanding me for the lack of air conditioning in "this restaurant".

Jack Findlay. Proud to be Australian? Just take a look at the helmet!

The Thunderclap – Tarquinio Provini

With immense self-satisfaction he used to enjoy saying how, when he was sure he had an Imola race in the bag, he would allow himself a curious extravagance. Instead of exiting the Rivazza in fourth he'd engage third gear: while this inevitably slowed down his incredibly angled bike, it also made it back-fire in a roar that thrilled the crowds clustered on the "Hill of Passion", a growl that rebounded back towards him as thunderous applause.

What's changed since those times? A lot, perhaps too much. Today we walk around the track with phonometers to take noise level readings. Today, motorcycles stand in a dock built by those that want, at any cost, a world dif-

Tarquinio Provini at Imola, where he won more and earned more that anywhere else.

ferent from that which actually exists. Our sophisticated instrumentation and that installed by the "guardians of silence" acquit even the motorcycles with which riders race GP or Superbike events. Believe it or not, noise levels are well within the strict limits imposed by law. Even the bikes which ride into the everyday wind of the public highway in search of boundless freedom are innocent of the crime of noise pollution as they are subject to severe government standards. Yet it's hard to believe that this "paradise" is in any way marred when some "romantic" centaur "cheats" a little and hikes the rumble of his exhaust above the permitted noise limit.

Soon, though, without having to commit any such sacrilege (not even the unleashing of an unbearable roar) motorcycles will be able to return to their sacred temple: the Imola race track. There they will be able to race without disturbing the residents on the other side of the River Santerno (who, in truth, are endangered only by the silence of their own souls and the unease of civilisation). In following the bikes I shall comply with and observe those noise level laws. It's only fair, after all: but that obedience will never explain why I used to find the smell of burnt engine oil so inebriating. Or why I used to feed on the rumble of the Gilera 4-cylinder, the Guzzi 8-cylinder and that unmistakeable growl of the MV Agusta. I have no idea. All I know is that they were sounds in which I intuited the unheard sounds of my soul. Now that I no longer hear them, there is only a silence that I have never been – and never will be – able to interpret.

Golden Boy – Dickie Dale

Dickie Dale really was the Golden Boy of motorcycling: he won more Shell Gold Cups – the most important race on the World Championship calendar – than anyone else. His first win came in 1956 after overtaking Kenny Kavanagh ,who was, that day, riding the mythical 8-cylinder Guzzi in its debut race.

On that stormy day the public, heedless of the bad weather, filled the stands and the trackside to bursting point. Dickie Dale gave them their money's worth with a victory that was unimaginable: on his one-cylinder wonder (another Guzzi) he beat the bike that would go on to become legendary.

Fate has, many a time, failed to reward the good sense and measured risk-taking demonstrated by some riders. Thus it was with the "measured" Dickie Dale, swept away in a corridor darkened by the tall trees of the

Twice winner of the Gold Cup, Dickie Dale shows the Midas touch.

Libero Liberati, the impenetrable Gilera champion, with a youthful Claudio Costa.

Germanic forests of Eifel. His life was simply snipped from beneath him by the unbending Atropos, the green-eyed fate of Greek and Roman mythology who cuts the thread of life woven by her stern and gloomy sisters, Clotho and Lachesis.

The Bold Knight – Libero Liberati

A bold knight, silent with a careful, measured riding style – that was Libero Liberati. Perhaps only Libero himself had any proper idea of his own greatness – but at Monza, in September 1957, when he beat Geoff Duke and rode his Gilera to World Championship glory, everyone knew he had become legendary. Even though I was a Guzzi fan, I was fascinated by Libero and was proud to stand at his side during the 1955 Shell Gold Cup. Two years later, just after his fantastic victory at Monza, I got him to autograph the publicity photo below.

Yet I was unable to enjoy his victory to the full because that same year Gilera, Guzzi and Mondial indignantly pulled out of racing in protest at the scant industrial support then offered by the Italian government.

Despite this disappointment, he continued to race on an unofficial motorcycle, the fuel tank of which continued to carry the logo of his beloved Gilera.

While testing that bike on the outskirts of his home town of Terni, in Umbria, he met with a fatal accident and carried away the secret of his greatness forever.

On the day the riders left the theatre of my own imagination and left the Imola race track, a happy custodian was left on the paddock tower to keep watch over the track and the riders' feats. It was the unforgettable figure of Francesco Costa, austere, silent and seated in a pose of expectation. There he remains, a silent witness, clutching his chequered flag like a signalman waiting for the arrival of a ghost train. Yet when the motorcycles once more return to Imola Checco Costa's voice will be heard again through that of his best-loved son, Carlo, who will breathe life back into a timeless nostalgia. And when the unmistakeable voice of the commentator, Checco's son, announces the event of the year we shall be there to listen to it, and when he shouts "Thirty seconds. They're away! Fabulous!" the figure of Checco will once more stand smiling on the paddock tower and unfurl his chequered flag.

39. *Monza*

In the '50's, when I was a child, my father took me to Monza. I was nearly beside myself with excitement. It was a time of innocence, an age in which time seemed eternal and illusions reality. On entering the Royal Park, which could then be crossed at will, I was a bundle of energized antici-

Monza, September 1957: the camera captures Libero Liberati's victory perfectly.

pation. The natural beauty of the setting, while it in no way distracted me from the race I had come to see, was deeply fascinating. Perhaps inevitably, the promise this beauty held on that fantastic day has never been maintained: even the air and light seemed different then, wrapping you in an atmosphere that seemed everlasting.

Spectators and riders invaded the park peacefully, steadily occupying the most sought-after positions of Lesmo and the Parabolica. The passion of the wait was palpable.

Then came the start, the first lap and the riders reappeared out of the blue on the corner where you had ensconced yourself, leaving you breathless. Such was the eagerness to see your heroes – everyone's heroes – that they seemed to take forever to ride round the track and come back into view.

My youth's mind began to form the first preferences, likings and loves for this or that rider. I learnt devotion for Bill Lomas, a rebel from head to toe – forelock included – and adoration for Fergus Anderson (the Michelangelo of the motorcycle). On 12th September 1954 I froze when the competitors rode the first lap of the 125 slowly and sombrely to pay homage to a small Austrian named Rupert Hollaus, a former world champion who had died the day before during qualification when he crashed on the second and extremely demanding corner at Lesmo. By incredible coincidence Jochen Rindt, another Austrian racer, would also meet his end at Monza.

Now, when I return to Monza, the innocence of my youth has been replaced by a heavy guilt at not having known how to live closer to nature and the fear that life is not really so very long after all. The standing I enjoy now is not enough to cancel this weight and fear, and melancholy sweeps through me, turning to quiet tears when I see the old medical centre (now used for other purposes), where, on 20th May 1973 I knew pain and desperation as I beheld the lifeless bodies of Jarno Saarinen and Renzo Pasolini.

Occasionally, that sad darkness lifts, especially when the places where I had dreamed as a child flash back into my thoughts. Because dreams cure melancholy by transforming them into the most beautiful of human sentiments – nostalgia. And when I return to Monza, I sometimes find that, deep down in my heart, it's still there and think, maybe, that I can still dare to dream.

40. *Nürburgring*

The reporters of the time, perhaps more poets than journalists, called Imola "the little Nurburgring". It was a name that my father, a lover of the German Romanticism of Wagner, Goethe and Beethoven, was proud of. It is thus easy to intuit, then, how "Checco" (the endearing nickname, pronounced "keh-ko", with which everyone referred to my father) became a close friend of Ludemann, then Director of the German race track.

Ludemann was solemn and ceremonious. On our arrival he would welcome us into his office under the old wooden stands and propose a toast to his Italian friends. Then he would offer us tickets that allowed us entry to the pits and paddocks. The most exciting thing was that you could actually drive round those 23 kilometres of racing history. My father drove fast and nonchalantly through the circuit's 170 sweeping bends, forcing us to pull in our elbows which protruded from the windows into the hot German summer.

The elbows, by the way, belonged to Roberto, Bruno, Giacomo, Zino, Gianfranco and Annibale: in short, my most trusted friends, whom I used to take with me one at a time on this "motoring holiday" so as to have, during the following winter of scholastic suffering, someone with whom to share its unforgettable memory. Even now, our schooldays long since over, those experiences continue to help us by reminding us of the value of true friendship and the light-heartedness of adolescence. Hardly anyone is able to live his life in solitude or bear the fear of the unknown alone. Luckily, this human weakness is offset by love and friendship.

My own life-long fear of the unknown has inflicted deep wounds that my friends have always succeeded in soothing. Only my friends have ever been able to understand – and abide – my many defects. Friendship is a generous gift and I have always taken what my friends have offered me gladly. Perhaps I've even been lucky in love too, as I've received so much of it from racers and everyday motorcycle riders alike. Yet a terrible doubt remains: has the love which I've returned to my riders freed my sentiments from the ice in which I often feel they are imprisoned?

41. *Le Mans*

La légende s'écrit dans vos yeux: the legend is written in your eyes. These words are written on the gateway to Le Mans. And they're true. It was 1967, the year in which I graduated, that I joined that party with which the entire city of Le Mans celebrated – and still celebrates – the famous 24 hour race. The crowds lining the 12 km route prepared themselves for the night, not only for the event in itself but to have a good time around their fires, eat good food and forget everyday mediocrity. The blinking fires were little altars of humanity that gave off much more warmth than the burning firewood: it was a warmth released by hundreds of hearts waiting expectantly for the start of a race, a fire fed by imagination and hope, a flash that illuminated different people in a symbolic alliance that would help them experience the event as one. Everyday problems, existential rage, intolerance of life's injustices seemed to vanish spontaneously and everyone was filled with a seemingly endless festivity. Even today, my memory of those electrifying nights has not dimmed and the twinge of nostalgia is strong. When the crazed cars of Lance McKline and Pierre Levegh smashed into the packed stands, killing dozens of spectators and casting even more into an abyss of pain and suffering, the Le Mans 24 hour race, rather than dying with those unknown martyrs, continued, in the agony and mourning that rose from those stands, to live on and exist. A fatality is hard to accept because it flings the crude truth of reality in our faces. When something horrible happens, we instinctively look for the guilty party, kidding ourselves that, without somebody to blame, nasty things just can't happen. We live out reality as if it were a wrongdoing, so as to deny its cruel meaninglessness. Vice versa, the ancients had made Fate one of the most respected deities and in doing so they had redeemed reality from wrongdoing and life from its absurdity. In accepting even the most tragic happenings one conquers the enigma of existence and the disturbing truth about life. Forgiveness must not be implored but given freely. Forgiveness does more good to its giver than its receiver. It does not depend on reason but reason's crisis, which abdicates in favour of a more sublime kingdom where there is no longer blame but true solidarity and responsibility shared by all. Le Mans was forgiven...

42. *Tourist Trophy*

My copy of *Tourist Trophy: dicing with death* by Mario Donnini carries the following author's dedication: "Thanks for giving me the best chapter of the book". Proud of that compliment, there follows an excerpt from Marios' chapter nine: "The exorcist's opinion".

"There's no way round it. If you want to find out about the devil you have to go and interview the exorcist. To gain a true understanding of the Tourist Trophy there's no way you can ignore the thoughts of a man who fought against TT racing for a long time, seeking to have it banned. That man is Claudio Marcello Costa, a specialist in orthopaedics and traumatology. More importantly, he is also the founding father of the Clinica Mobile, the travelling hospital which gets injured World Championship riders back on their bikes with a speed that, in more traditional medical circles, would be astounding: for the riders it is the lighthouse that saves the castaways of the race track. Claudio is son of the late Checco, the founding father of the Imola race track and, for many years, the doyen of Italian motorcycling.

Dr. Costa, what makes TT riders different from the rest?

For a long time everyone raced in the Tourist Trophy. There was no real distinction between those that raced here and those that raced on other circuits, many of which were just as frightening. Then, after losing its status as a World Championship venue, only a few remained faithful to the ritual of the Isle of Man. Deep down, everyone finds risk irresistible. Dicing with death has always had its fascination and modern day competitors in the Tourist Trophy are those that feel the pull of that risk more intensely than the rest.

With death? Sounds like a citation from Ingmar Bergman's masterpiece, The Seventh Seal, in which the mysterious Knight battles it out on the chess board with Death.

Exactly. The concepts of destiny and death are interchangeable.

Why do you think the Tourist Trophy has withstood the test of time?

Because it embodies and symbolises the history of motorcycling. It's a race that can reward its participant with the joy of victory, that most Dionysian part of life, and at the same time inflict tragedy and grief. Like life itself, the Tourist Trophy is ambivalent, mysterious, unknown – practically a metaphor for life itself. You see, man differs from every other creature in that his brain has elaborated a marvellous concept: desire. Who knows, perhaps in prehistoric times everything began with an ape that looked on the dominant male and decided that he wanted to be like him without actually wanting to eliminate him. Within our minds – especially the minds of those who race – one of life's most sublime desires takes the form of risk. Imagine Michelangelo's Sistine Chapel, with Adam's finger outstretched towards God's, tantalisingly close but never touching: that's risk.

As a man who, for decades now, has fought hard to improve track safety, you're sure to hate the following question. Dr. Costa, do you like the Tourist Trophy?

Like the Tourist Trophy itself, my answer to that is an ambivalent one. Back in 1976, at the International Motorcycling Federation congress in Bruges, Belgium, I fought hard to get it removed from the World Championship. I did my utmost to ensure that World Championship riders would no longer have to return to the Isle of Man. But that was a long time ago and things have moved on. If I answer your question as a Federation man then I'd have to say I'm dead against it. But if I respond on a more personal level, I'd have to say that TT racing has the fascination of the legendary. To ban it now would be to render its sacrifices worthless. While you might be able to stop the Tourist Trophy, you can't cancel the race from memory because, in the history of motorcycling, TT racing has been the supreme test and – for many, unfortunately, the sacrificial altar. Those who have lost their lives deserve respect, just as today's competitors do, because they have accepted one heck of a challenge. Generally speaking, I find that people who don't have the courage to face death can be pretty scary: in refusing that test they reroute their qualities elsewhere. Sometimes they take other roads, perhaps getting involved in violence or even war, or ending up in the news for all sorts of wrongdoings; yet I have nothing to fear from a man willing to race round the Isle of Man: his character is above suspicion. You want the short answer? If you'd asked me back in'76 I'd have said that TT racing was dreadful. Now I find it utterly human.

If you had a magic wand what would you do for the Tourist Trophy?

Talk about it in this book.

If a mountaineer, parachutist or yachtsman dies everyone feels a deep sense of respect for the victim, yet if something happens to a ri-

der or driver there's an inquest, a circuit is closed, the guilty party is sought out. Why do you think this is?

In the first three cases the challenge takes place in a natural setting. With the racer things take place in a more social setting and so-called common sense is called into play. Somebody's died doing something dangerous? Some think it might be the case to investigate, to change something. Yet in doing so they forget that life's often a search for knowledge and this often involves a certain degree of risk. A life worth living can't be lived without risk, and that's why I believe it's a mistake to place common sense above all else. Look at today's world. How many authentic, passionate people do you know? Few. Most of us are frozen stiff by our own common sense and will probably only be thawed out by the flames of hell. Sorry, but I've no taste for frozen meat: I like men who dig beneath the surface of their own souls, even if they have to run risks.

And those that enter the Tourist Trophy?

They dig even deeper, digging into the depths of their own minds as they race. The ancient Greeks believed that these "diggers" would be rewarded by Persephone, a divinity of the Lower World, with the pomegranate seeds that symbolise unheard-of riches.

Why is TT racing so popular with the older riders?

Youngsters still think that life can be different from how it is. The older man has no such illusions. For him, things aren't quite so clear cut. He understands that he only has so much life and accepts seemingly absurd compromises, enjoying every last yard of a race like the Tourist Trophy. A young TT racer, instead, sublimates the desire for invulnerability. The older rider simply accepts that some of the challenges faced as a youth can still be faced.

Race aficionados have noted that the Anglo-Saxon approach to risk and death is colder than its continental counterpart. Some see it as the cultural humus in which TT racing has its roots. Do you see it that way?

Great Britain is an island. TT racing takes place on a smaller island within it. It is a country that was born, grew up with and lived shoulder to shoulder with a supreme risk: the sea. Everyone is a captain who measures himself against the storm and accepts risk and the possibility of defeat – death – in full. I totally agree with you. Anglo-Saxon culture takes risk more in its stride. Land-locked Europeans, instead, tend to hide themselves behind other symbols. France has its Revolution, Germany its army, Spain bullfighting,

Holland its dams, Switzerland its mountains. Italy is, unfortunately, something of an orphan in this regard. Its symbols change continuously; that's why a win by Ferrari at Imola generates a sudden surge of collective identity. The Anglo-Saxon, on the other hand, knows that the storm is there to be weathered. Grief has been evolved to a higher level and is accepted more readily. Thus they share their lives with the terrifying circuits of the Ulster GP or Isle of Man.

Resolve the paradox: if you were asked to take the Clinica Mobile to the Tourist Trophy, would you go?

If my son were to start gambling, I'd try and dissuade him from it. If I weren't able to dissuade him I'd teach him to be a hell of a card player. If, for some reason, the Tourist Trophy re-enters the World Championship circuit, there's no way I'd allow my riders to face it without me.

Do falls in TT racing involve a specific type of injury?

They certainly do. Unfortunately, the damage is tragically similar to that seen on the everyday race track of roads and motorways. You get just the same kinds of accidents in the Tourist Trophy, but worse.

Have you ever treated a rider injured in the Tourist Trophy? If so, how did you feel about it?

Yes! More than anything I felt an overwhelming admiration for him. An example? The emotion of seeing Tarquinio Provini injured just made him seem even greater in my eyes.

What sort of psycho-physical preparation would you recommend for someone entering the Tourist Trophy?

Before answering that I'd better point out that I don't want to push anyone into TT racing. Absolutely not. Yet your question deserves an answer. From a physical viewpoint I'd recommend a preparation similar to any such sporting enterprise. From a psychological standpoint I'd advise a rider about to tackle the Isle of Man to think seriously about how that island's made, how it's swept by fog, rain and sun. And I'd beseech him to watch out for surprises, because TT racing's full of them: just when you think you know everything you realise you've learnt nothing.

How would you improve rider safety?

His only proper defence is his freedom. If you have to enter a cave inhabited by a dragon – which is what the Tourist Trophy is – there's no point in going in armed to the teeth. Go in naked. The best weapons are those God-given ones found only at the bottom of your heart.

43. *A World of Symbols*

Ideally, I'd like to explain all the emotions that the riders have given me over the years (but doing so would almost certainly stop me from ever finishing this book!): emotions that have, in part, cracked the ice which has always frozen the sentimental side of my life. That iciness, perhaps, explains why I just adore the snow, the way it blankets nature's myriad colours in a crystalline white. The trees and bushes bow under its weight yet retain a proud natural strength, which allows them to survive and bud again in Spring. That same promise of Spring is felt when I sink my feet into the fresh snow covering the pathway to my house in Fontanelice. Even that indefinable crunching of my footfalls tells me that there's hope in everything. There is absolutely nothing to be feared in this spectral landscape: its ghosts have simply melted into the whiteness reflected by a hesitant starlight. Yet their whisper of hope is clearly audible. It is the same message of hope whispered to me by the dreams of my riders, whispers that have helped me to live and sustain my conviction that "life is worth living". For this simple reason I can't stand hearing how the riders "owe me a lot", because it is from them that I have learned to weather life's tempests, to navigate the dark storm into which existence has thrown me.

...And now I know that we must lift the sail
And catch the winds of destiny
Wherever they drive the boat.
To put meaning in one's life may end in madness,
But life without meaning is the torture
Of restlessness and vague desire
It is a boat longing for the sea and yet afraid.
(Edgar Lee Masters, *The Spoon River Anthology*)

There is nothing I would love more than to return to the childhood pleasure of seeing the sun rise from the Castellaccio hill of the Imola race circuit, to eat home-made bread baked in a wood-fired oven, to tuck into a succulent roast chicken prepared during the night by the mother of my friend, Carlo Grandi, to converse in the company of the other spectators, pretending to know something about the riders and their stories of heroism. Sat on the grass of that hill, as a child full of illusions but equally full of the hopes that accompany life's Saturday, there is nothing I would like better than to cheer them on in a flurry of admiration.

Like my father, I was mad about Guzzi, while my brother was a true Gilera buff. Yet when my father was welcomed by Count Agusta and *Commendatore* Gilera during winter to agree on the participation of these glorious teams in the Gold Cup, I forgot my allegiance to the legendary Guzzi and sank into an unconditioned state of admiration for all motorcycles. Since then I've felt that the motorcycle is much more than mere technology, cold metal or merciless electronics, but, rather, a natural, instinctive, almost luminescent symbol which, together with its rider, recreates the centaur of Greek myth-ology. Even now, I don't see Ivano Beggio, Federico Minoli or Claudio Castiglioni as industrialists but sovereigns of a kingdom where motorcycles are forged by imagination and genius.

Their bikes symbolise that part of mankind which wishes to escape from the mediocre façade of the daily. And there's no shortage of symbols in motorcycling: these sacred signs, hidden in men's hearts speak the language of dreams and are the forerunners of future action, accompanying the world's motorcyclists towards their common goal of blending cold reason with the warmth of natural folly. Symbols link past actions with future ones to form the concrete coherence of action. A symbol is not mere significance but an act of salvation: that's why they are so common in the world of motorcycling and so scarce in Italian society. Society, orphaned of symbols, becomes restless and sinks into the violence of madness. This is terrible. Analogously, the rearing horse of Ferrari is an unequivocal "good", bringing together people from all walks of life in the dream and hope that a "red" win will free them from the confines of the workaday world and give them a measure of happiness.

The same happiness that I experienced as a child, when my father took me to Enzo Ferrari's birthday party on 20th February (the great Drake was actually born on the 18th, but a heavy snowfall postponed the registration). On such evenings my child's joy made me feel as much the centre of attention as the legendary Ferrari himself. I remember being sat on the knee of the great Fangio: of all the stories he softly whispered to me, one stands out in particular. He said "if, one day, you decide to race motor cars and you find that you can take a corner at top speed (full throttle in fifth: what brilliant words) and the others can't, well then, never actually do it in fifth unless you must in order to win the race or championship. If, vice versa, you fall victim to a sense of omnipotence and always take that corner in fifth, you'll die". This story had a solemn ring to it, not just because it was told by Fangio but because of the spirit that pervaded it: in life you need a sense of risk but should only dare as much as you have to. That is the marvel that can change us all from ugly ducklings into splendid swans.

Juan Manuel Fangio's words would come back to haunt me years later when I read the news reports of Luigi Musso's fatal accident at Reims in 1958: "Fangio responded that the Calvaire could be taken at full throttle. Caressing the kerb, almost courting it as if it were a beautiful woman, sticking to it all the way round, the Calvaire could be taken at full throttle. But everything had to be kept under tight control. You had to hold your breath and remain as sharp as a pin. Nothing could be left to chance. You had to feel how the car vibrated at the end of the straight. You even had to watch the leaves on the trees: if there was wind the attempt would have to be put off, but if the leaves were still you could go for it. You had to enter into the corner with your foot on the floor and not raise it for any reason whatsoever" (from *Gli indisciplinati* by Luca Delli Carri).

These experiences nurtured me as much as the "classics" I studied at the Benvenuto Rambaldi Grammar school of Imola. I remember that school with nostalgia because I spent the best years of my life there. It is where I formed lasting friendships, learnt how to face up to others and constructed ideals and close alliances which promised to be invincible. Paolo, Bruno, Carlo, Gastone, Gianfranco, Giorgio, Giacomo, Oriano, Vittorio, Zino, Celso, Gabriele and Roberto (the last two have sadly passed away) formed a round table where there was no King Arthur, just loyalty among friends. We were happy because in friendship every thought, desire and attraction was born and experienced with secret joy.

That school was the altar at which we worshipped the symbol of friendship. Symbols have always fascinated me. So I seek them out where they're most at home: in motorcycling. I even hope to be able to translate them into words for the readers of this book. An impossible feat? When are words ever impossible?

44. *A Motorcycle*

The motorbike is a symbol of energy. It is not, as most might think, technological, but natural. It is that animal part of the ancient centaur that safeguards our instincts and frees them to ride out and seek the answers to questions which torment us.

Not even the fury of the wind can stop this quest for freedom, this attempt to seek answers different from those society palms us off with daily. It is certainly no chance occurrence that Aprilia, on presenting its team for 2001, decided to bring a lion into the proceedings. This superb beast, stalking up and down its cage around the motorcycles, seemed to become one with them, brushing up against them as they were his impalpable and impossible soul. At that presentation, the lion took on an almost divine strength that shed a different kind of light on the bikes themselves, making them appear alive.

In the Superbike, in fact, the praises of the bike are sung even more highly than those of the rider. Here the bike symbolises the light that illuminates all of motorcycling. The engines roar, albeit with a voice perhaps more feeble than in the past, on tracks surrounded by enthusiastic spectators who have come to the event on their own bikes – not dissimilar from the ones being cheered on the track. I see this fabulous interaction as a glorious dance, a heroic return to the epoch of the Frontier, when man danced with wolves.

All of motorcycling dances to this music, transported by a harmony that is diffused throughout the world by two brothers, Maurizio and Paolo Flammini. They are the humble priests of SBK, a temple where the motorcycle has re-conquered its soul. Many flock to this altar and many fall silent in reverence. Many work there too; there is the organisational talent of Roberto and Renata Nosetto who write the sacred books of this religion. In the Clinica Mobile, Dr. Massimo Corbascio and Dr. Ruggero Mattioli heal the pain of the injured centaurs, their own private recompense for paradise lost.

I too listened, huddled around this altar on 23rd April 1972, when Paul

Smart's Ducati number 16 and Bruno Spiaggiari's number 9 cut across the finishing line of the first Imola 200 organised by my father. That day I was born to motorcycling as a doctor and consigned myself to its magnificent history.

On the eve of the last race of the World Superbike Championship, held at Imola on 30th September 2001, the Ducati which stood in front of the pits re-evoked that event perfectly. That day I was officially invited to participate in a moving commemoration and, as if by magic, I found myself standing next to that fabulous bike which had – thirty years previously – won the first Imola 200 mile race.

Paolo and Maurizio Flammini.

I hugged a new-found Paul Smart, sheathed in a beautiful Dainese replica of his leathers of yesteryear.

A few moments after the short ceremony began, my voice quaking with emotion, I pronounced the following words: "My father Checco is unable to be here today and so I shall have to, although I don't really deserve the honour, represent him".

I stretched my hand out to touch a marvellous past and a fantastic future, symbolised by Paul Smart's Ducati number 16 and its present day counterpart number 21 ridden by the 2001 World Champion, Troy Bayliss. My father's dream lives on.

Renata and Roberto Nosetto.

The postcard for the 1972 Imola 200.

September 30th, 2001: thirty years on, Troy Bayliss and Paul Smart commemorate that race.

45. *St. Francis' Strange Sister*

On Sunday, August 23, 1998, I was coming out of Mike Doohan's pit in Brno, as sad as he was that fate had now laid out a difficult, almost impossible path for the Australian rider towards the greatness which had, only minutes before the race, seemed so firmly within his grasp. In that moment Carlos Checa came to mind.

The race was nearly over. As I approached the Spanish rider's pit area I had an odd feeling, as if I were about to enter an unusual, almost holy place. Its occupants were there as usual, all heads turned towards the TV set, yet... something impossible to define, something peculiar was hovering in the air. Carlos finished his race, everybody was satisfied, and – for some inexplicable reason – those present lined up like devout friars along the sides of an altar which could not yet be seen.

A few seconds later his Honda number 8 thundered into this area, coming to a halt like a tired but still powerful animal. The voices had many things to say to the Spanish rider, yet the tone and the joy seemed to be contained, almost reserved. The rider bent his head over his motorcycle, as if to kiss it, then slid off in a faint and lay down on the ground. His hands covered his forehead as if to protect his eyes, those eyes which at Donington had stopped seeing the light of day on account of a cruel illness.

With an almost inaudible whisper Carlos said, "I am tired...". Yet his eyes were alive and filled with light. Expert hands checked the wound which ran across part of his body. His pulse was strong and although he was breathing somewhat laboriously, it was no cause for worry. The light in the eyes of the rider became even more intense, deep, almost mysterious. Carlos outstretched his hands towards some unknown person; something or someone invisible drew him up... he rested one hand on the shoulder of Sito Pons, more a friend than a team manager, and the other on his number 8 motorcycle. His eyes were seeing with a light which was not of the sun, but an inner light which illuminated the universe of his soul.

I left him with his friends, and went towards the "victory lane", the area set aside for victory celebrations and the podium ceremony. I spoke to Alex

Carlos Checa.

Barros, his eyes swollen and burnt by the wind. I shook hands with Alex Criville, who had managed to race thanks to the medicines he had taken for a troublesome sickness which had been afflicting him since practice began. Biaggi, who had won, was surrounded by a great many people, a distinct crowd of celebrities, especially the sweet and beautiful Anna Falchi to whom Max was saying "thank you".

I felt this ceremony was missing something. It was missing Mick Doohan, and as I thought of him, I was overcome by nostalgia; in a flash I saw his entire life, I saw the light in Carlos Checa's eyes, and then, taken aback, I realised who had helped Carlos pick himself up and sustained him back in the Pons Team pit. It was the same "Old Lady" who had befriended and saved him in Sherwood Forest near the hospital of Nottingham and Donington, and had become his friend. The Lady no one remembers or wishes to remember. The "Lady" Saint Francis affectionately referred to as Sister Death!

46. *A Cat with a Collar*

As Alex Criville fell during the Dutch GP in 1997 his left hand got caught up in the handlebars of his bike. The fault lay squarely with the useless invention of a new type of glove. Its makers, in their hurry to create a "trend" had forgotten that protruberances and jutting parts are, quite simply, dangerous.

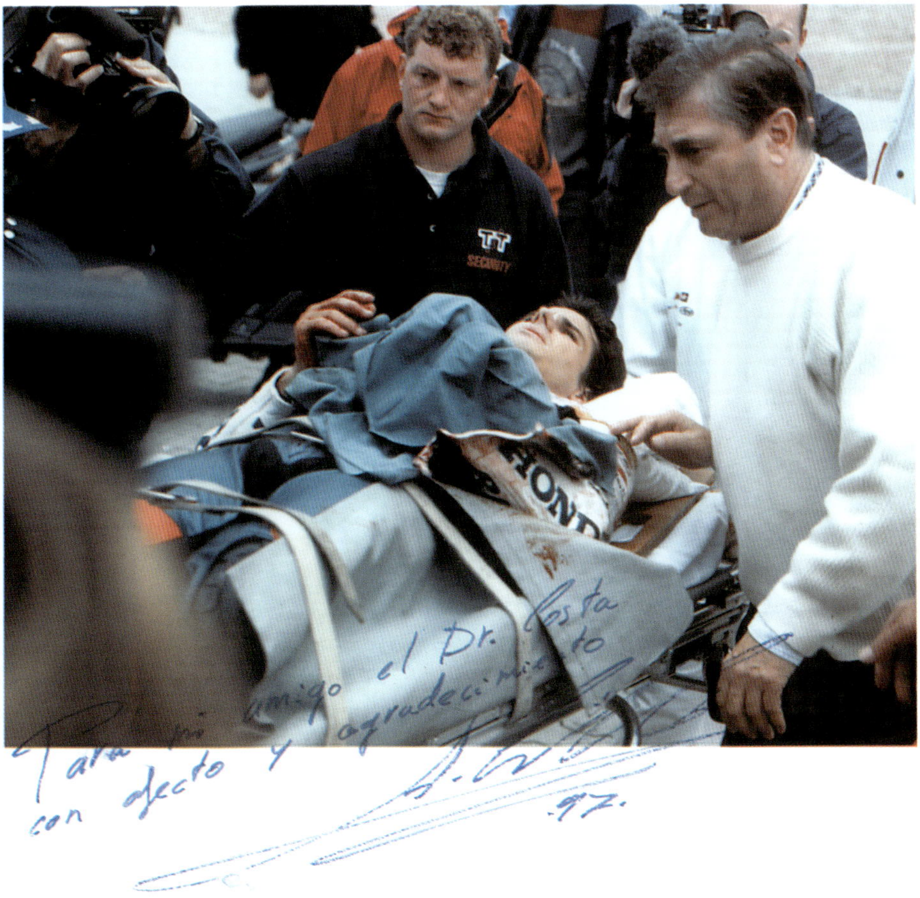

Assen, June 1997: a sheet hides Alex Criville's dreadful hand injury.

Those who insist that their cats wear collars to make them look good run the risk of one day finding them strangled on the branch of a tree. Fashion is worse than death, it is a plague that has spread across the globe, killing off customs, rituals and history.

Alex Criville got "hung on a branch" and massacred his left hand. When he arrived at the University of Groningen Hospital the situation was a delicate one: there were a lot of emergency cases that had priority over his and he would either be forced to go through an excruciating wait or, equally excruciatingly, end up "jumping the queue" to the detriment of other people perhaps less deserving of a similar injustice. A difficult decision had to be made and I was lucky enough to come up with an effective solution to this regrettable dilemma. With the help of Franco, an interpreter that the Dutch TT organisation has placed at my disposal for some years now, I suggested that the hospital managers call all the off-duty specialists needed to cure Criville's hand and their personnel on call so that we could get one of the spare operating rooms up and running. I promised that the expense would be honoured by the Spanish rider's insurance policy. I also promised the hospital director that no expense would be spared and that once the case which I was, of course, most interested in had been resolved he could keep the operating room – which would otherwise have lain idle – open for business. This initiative has since become law: in motorcycling GP events injured racers now find a fast-track channel that is activated on their arrival and, more importantly, this service does not deprive anyone else of his or her inalienable rights. Statistical surveys over the last ten years have shown that number of hospital admissions or examinations per race season is, on average, no more than 5. This highlights just how effective the trackside Clinica Mobile and Medical Centres are. Alex Criville cried a lot after the surgery that rebuilt his hand: some say because of the pain, others say out of the fright he'd had and many because of his fear of never being able to race again. I stayed with him in his room, the darkness chased away by that diffused, cold, violet light so typical of hospitals. As I tried to encourage him, whispering that everything was proceeding all right, I realised that the tears streaming down his face shone with the light of desire, and realised that Alex needed his tears to fill the gap that separated him from his return to racing. Unlike the others, I saw his tears as a message of hope. A few weeks later he made his comeback at Brno and missed the podium by seconds. I was happy for him. Men's tears are not just "surrender and resignation" but sometimes the sublime exaltation of desire.

47. *An Enchanted Hand*

A story … a hand … a legend. On a morning in June 2000, during the usual pre-race tests that precede the Dutch GP, Capirossi fell badly and broke his left hand. His eyes were full of tears and not only because of the pain: there was already an encroaching nostalgia for a race he now feared would

Loris Capirossi: an idol.

be denied him. Unexpectedly, a light went on in the depths of his brain and a spark arrived in his eyes. It was the spark of desire, and the rider suddenly had only one thing to say: "I want to race". The Dutch doctors immediately forbade it: no, the Italian racer would not be allowed to take part in the Grand Prix. Yet Capirossi's tears had succeeded in winning him a final medical examination at 1 p.m., just 60 minutes before the start of the 500 cc race. At the appointed hour in came the Dutch doctors to examine Capirossi. The examination was a "cruel" one, his hand being bent back and forth in a way that would have caused pain to an uninjured hand. Loris met his "torturers" with a smile that the doctors found disarming and, almost

Assen 2000: Roberto Brusi soothes Capirossi's badly fractured left hand with ice.

miraculously, his hand regained its functionality. Loris Capirossi was given the green light. He had chosen the most difficult of two paths, the one paved in jolting pain as opposed to the smooth surface of prudence. The treatment, bandages and medicines undeniably helped him, but the pain remained. Loris demonstrated greatness: first he tried to ignore the pain, then got to know it and finally, made it his friend. As he bravely battled it out on the track first place seemed within his grasp: then the race was rained off. In the ensuing interval there was more treatment, more medicine, new and painful infiltrations, then back to the track. In the end he would attain a stunning 3rd place. Crying with pain and joy he was helped up onto the po-

Tears of pain and joy.

dium by the one who had believed in him, the one who believed that human beings are carriers of hidden worlds rich in resources, unimaginable strengths and marvels.

This is just one of many stories that makes us proud to work at the Clinica Mobile. Once again love – and a smile – won out against the rigid laws of society. The love I offered Capirossi at the Clinica Mobile that day came back to me when it was I who was laid up in hospital: after a "terrible" operation I opened my eyes and saw Loris holding my hand. His eyes held the promise of my own healing and smiled as they had done that day at Assen.

The friendships shows: Claudio Costa and Loris Capirossi smile happily.

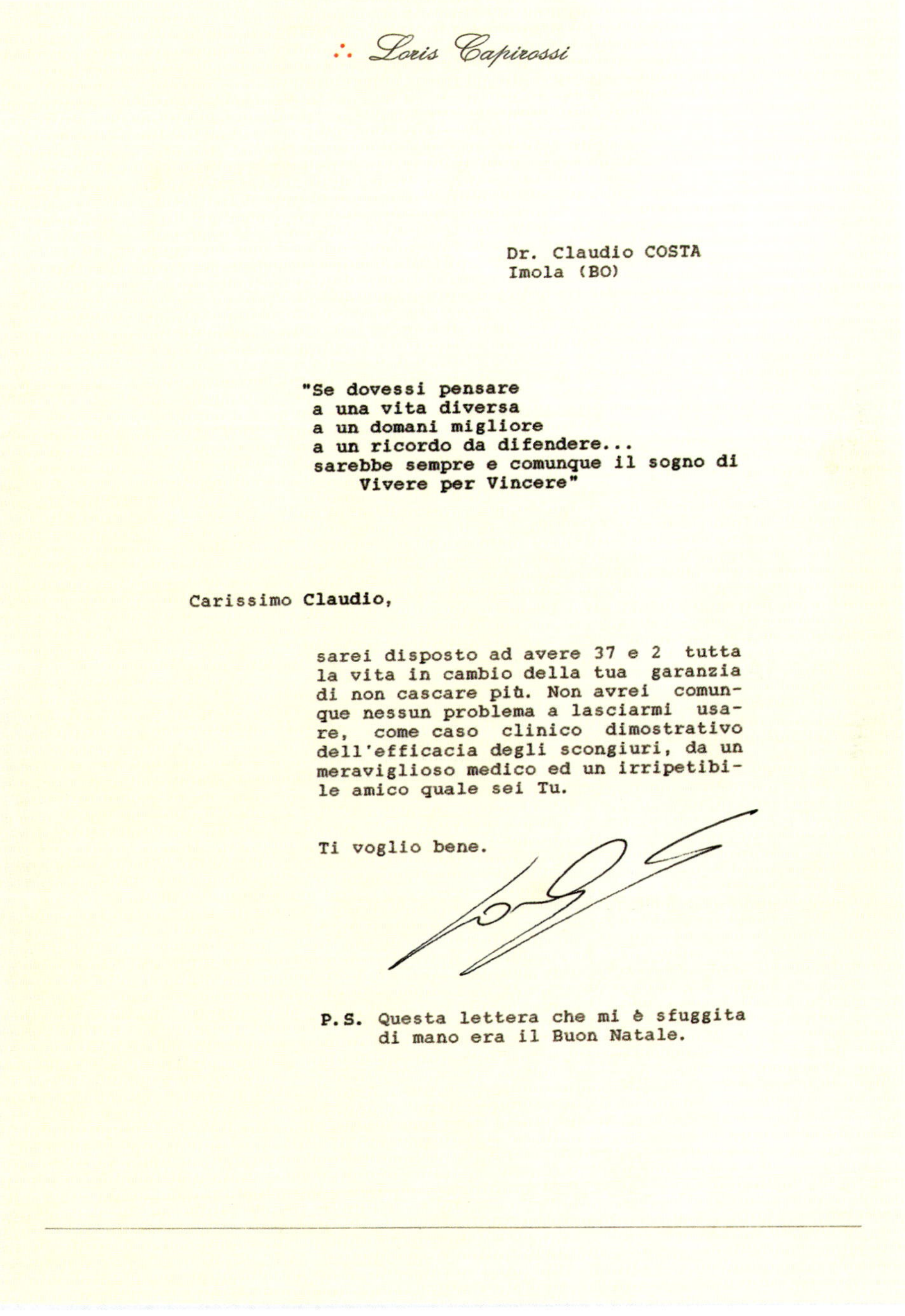

∴ Loris Capirossi

Dr. Claudio COSTA
Imola (BO)

"Se dovessi pensare
a una vita diversa
a un domani migliore
a un ricordo da difendere...
sarebbe sempre e comunque il sogno di
Vivere per Vincere"

Carissimo **Claudio**,

sarei disposto ad avere 37 e 2 tutta la vita in cambio della tua garanzia di non cascare più. Non avrei comunque nessun problema a lasciarmi usare, come caso clinico dimostrativo dell'efficacia degli scongiuri, da un meraviglioso medico ed un irripetibile amico quale sei Tu.

Ti voglio bene.

P.S. Questa lettera che mi è sfuggita di mano era il Buon Natale.

A treasured letter: Loris Capirossi thanks his friend and doctor.

48. *A Magic Glove*

Things are more important than we think they are.

We strain our imaginations to find appropriate names for them and invest considerable amounts of energy in those efforts. If they didn't exist our world of meaning wouldn't be here. Things magical abound everywhere, especially in fairy tales (boots, gloves, swords, slippers etc). The fairy tales of motorcycling are no exception: one of them regards the story of Noboru Ueda who fell at the Paul Ricard track in 1998. He received devastating injuries to his right arm, sustaining a displaced fracture of the humerus and snapping one of the three nerves that control the arm and hand (the radial nerve to be exact). The resulting paralysis was total and he couldn't feel his hand at all: dramatically, he was convinced the limb had been amputated. Sobbing, he insistently asked for his glasses, the French doctors clueless as to why. They gave them to him and as soon as he got them on he looked at his hand – still attached to his arm – and let out a relieved "I'm so happy to have that hand, thank you Claudio".

The fractured humerus, if operated on properly, would heal in three months. The radial nerve was another matter: there was no way of telling when or whether it would heal. Tearfully, Noboru (or Nobby as his friends call him) asked me "When can I start racing?". The gravity of his paralysis made a rational answer difficult. I hesitated, then instinctively said "in one hundred days". We took him to the hospital where his humerus was operated on by a skilled French orthopaedic surgeon and his nerve by an equally skilled neuro-surgeon from Marseilles. Three days later he arrived at my home in Imola and, euphoric, told Lucio Cecchinello, who had accompanied him there, that he would begin racing again "in 100 days", at Barcelona in September. I didn't dare disappoint him and promised him that, yes, it was possible. If, after one hundred days, his hand were still paralysed he would use a "magic glove".

As he settled into his room – already known to him as he'd stayed with me plenty of times before – I told him about when I used to work on the Paediatric Ward of the Rizzoli Orthopaedic Hospital in Bologna. I told him

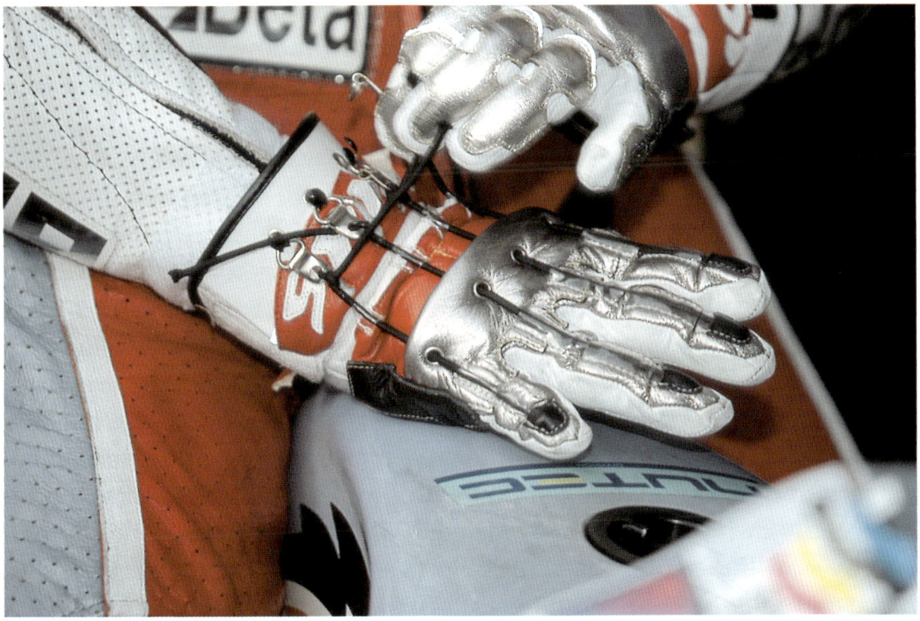

Barcelona, September 1998: the magic glove crafted by Spidi.

The glove does its stuff: Ueda celebrates a good race result.

Temperature, humidity, acceleration and heart rate sensors have been fitted inside the suit intelligently, without making it bulky or stiff. Data recorders, housed inside the "hump" that protects the rider's back, can transmit telemetric info back to the pits. Moreover, at the core of the hump and inside the helmet a small radio transmitter allows the rider to keep in touch with the rest of his team.

At the Clinica Mobile this invention is known as Marsyas, the satyr of Greek mythology who, because he had had the nerve to challenge the gods, was flayed and tied to a tree by Apollo. Marsyas lost his skin because he had dared to invent the flute and music itself: in this modern-day invention, that skin has been rediscovered. Man's creativity stretches out to challenge the gods once more, but this time they will be unsure as to which skin – the human one or the suit – needs to be torn from the centaur as punishment.

At the Sachsenring Valentino Rossi played the "role" of Marsyas, just as Max Biaggi had done at Jerez, by putting this new Dainese-made suit – complete with its comprehensive set of hump-housed data registration devices – through its paces.

In tradition, the hunchback is a bringer of luck. Popular belief often assigns a magical value to imperfections, thus lightening the defect for the person who has to sustain it. This wonderful way of thinking is also seen in love, where the defects of loved ones are totally ignored and even remembered with poignant nostalgia.

Unfortunately, outside of love and popular wisdom, people suffer their defects enormously or simply hide them. Moreover, hidden behind the rigid mask of society, they hit out at others' imperfections with squalid lies, showing a petty hostility to anything different. In the words of Perls, "If you can hate anything outside of yourself, that thing is yourself, no matter how hard that is to believe".

The "hump" in the suit looks like an imperfection, yet supports the riders head and, without in any way limiting his freedom of movement, contains a casket of precious help: comfort, flexibility plus acceleration and heart rate monitors (good for training purposes, especially in motocross). Acceptance of a defect sometimes opens the way to unhoped for resources and energies. As wise old men used to say, the hump brings luck: it's just a shame they never got to meet great champions like Valentino Rossi and Max Biaggi.

Valentino Rossi and Claudio Costa pack sensors into the hump of the special Dainese suit…

…and Max Biaggi tests it out for the world's motorcyclists.

50. *An Enchantress*

Armando, father of the lovely and delicate Manuela, the companion of Roberto Locatelli, 125 cc World Champion in the year 2000, is the Director of the workshop where we have the Clinica Mobile trucks repaired. The tractors that pull them are the magnificent creations of Renault and the VAI plant in Brivio, Lecco – one of the best in Europe because the work is done with dedication – that special dedication which is attention fuelled by love. The work is also done with the tools of sentiment, a must in the construction of any human feat.

As chance would have it his workshop was once graced with the presence of a beautiful "enchantress" and her knight. The name of the enchantress was Brigitte (or Brigitte Nielsen as she's known in the movie world) while her

Brigitte Nielsen works her magic on Falappa, leaving him open-mouthed.

knight, able to tame the wildest "horses" in the realm, was called Raul. Even enchantresses, though, sometimes need help and Armando decided that Brigitte's troubles would best be cured by the Clinica Mobile. Believe me, the fame and beauty of that fair lady paled in comparison with her alluring mysteriousness. If the authors of a present-day fairy tale wanted to invent an enchantress only she would be able to play her. Armando was luckier to know this enchantress than King Arthur was to know Merlin.

Armando thought of his daughter's companion, Roberto Locatelli, as one of his knights and trembled every time he went into battle. When Roberto was injured Armando wanted him healed instantly as if by magic. Unable to heal him instantaneously, we did at least help him believe he was getting better, even though his wounds were still open. So Roberto returned to the tournaments with the other knights and did so many times, almost forgetting about his broken bones, his lost spleen and snapped ligaments. Roberto Locatelli and Armando Gilardi have learnt that people's injuries sometimes help them understand more about the world and understand it better, their wounds sometimes opening a gap that provides an insight into the truth.

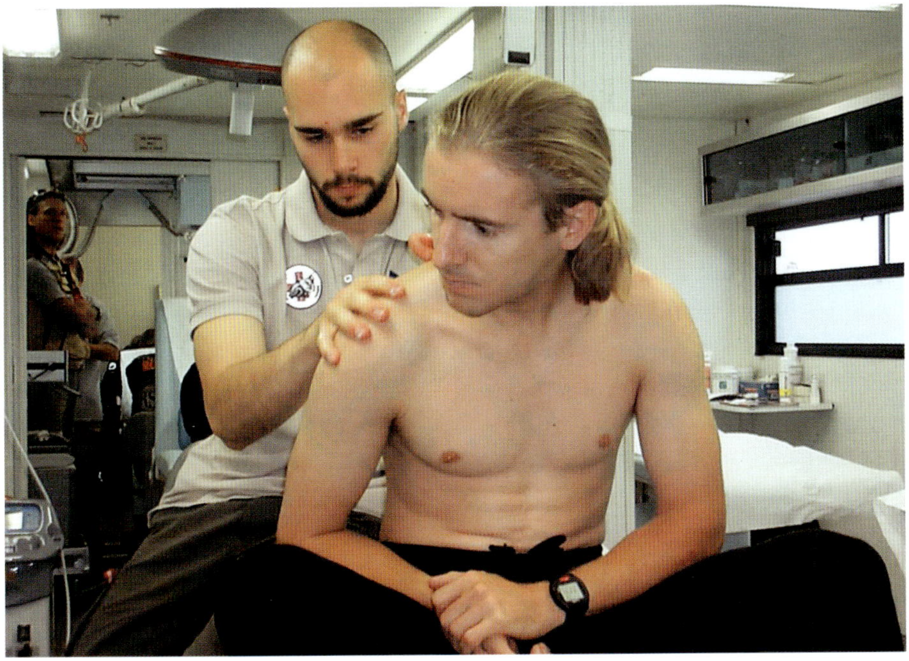

Francesco Chionne gets injured knight, Roberto Locatelli, ready for a new joust.

51. *Youth*

Leon, seventeen-year-old son of the legendary Ron Haslam, and De Angelis, the San Marino Kid, recovered easily from their complex fractures to the left wrist. Leon injured his hand at Le Mans on 18th May 2001 and De Angelis received a similar injury at Donington on 8th July 2001. Youths heal quickly, helped along by Mother Nature, to whom only they have remained faithful.

That special knack children have of finding the guiding light offered by nature also seems to be the prerogative of motorcyclists. Just as instinct, spontaneity, curiosity and a sense of marvel accompany children at play, so they accompany motorcyclists. As he darts along on his bike, the rider is illuminated by his inner child; in the theatre of that light imagination, creativity, brilliance and the pure exhilaration of the race play leading roles. Riders are children capable of astounding feats and, youth being what it is, they sometimes squabble in the backyard, just as Valentino and Max did at Barcelona in June 2001 and Manuel Poggiali did with Elias at Donington one month later in that backyard of their home from home which is motorcycling.

When children argue, they are either faced with "imperfect" parents who understand and acquit them or parents who have been made "perfect" by the rules and regulations of society.

The latter are parents who only know how to criticise, judge and condemn: they fail to recognise the child's inherent mix of wildness and brilliance or see the light that flows from their joy because their own light has, in the words of Wordsworth, been extinguished by the light of an ordinary day.

Those who failed to understand the argument at Barcelona between Valentino Rossi and Max Biaggi and the scuffle at Donington between Manuel Poggiali and Toni Elias have totally forgotten their own inner child. The result of that forgetfulness is daily denial of their own emotions and self-im-

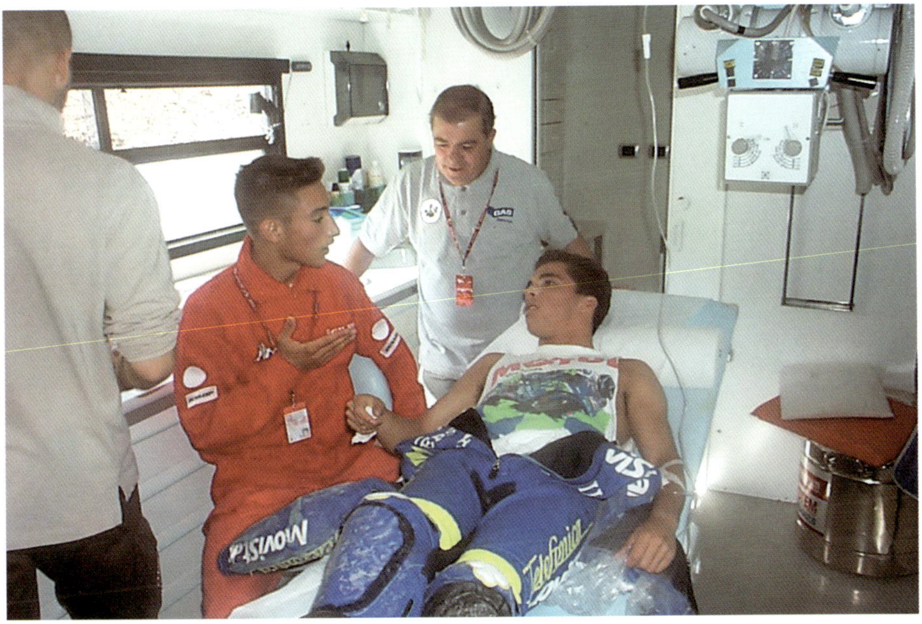

Manuel Poggiali and Toni Elias continue their on-track argument in the Clinica…

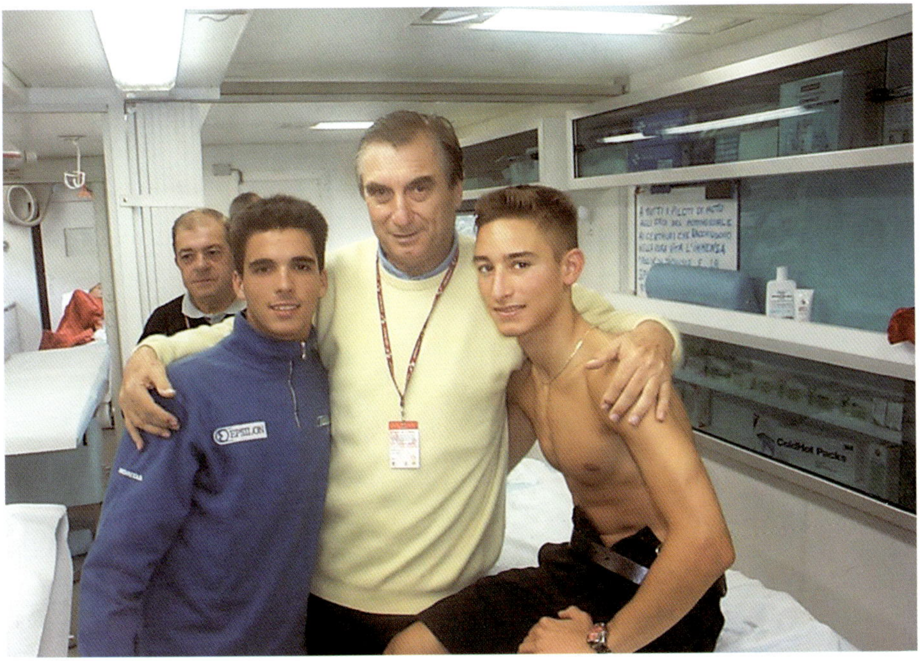

…and then put the magic of forgiveness to work.

prisonment of their minds in misery. Such people are simply terrified by any show of vitality and thus shout and holler to bring things back under their own rational and moral control. This enforced peace is born of minds that have screened themselves off from life because they fear its spontaneity.

Hypocrisy is worse than argument because while the latter is human, the former is based on a falseness that is the forerunner of betrayal. I do not – and never will – betray Valentino Rossi, Max Biaggi , Manuel Poggiali and Toni, especially when they argue, because their child-like brilliance has given me some of life's best moments. They have made me forget just how much hate and violence resides in the rigid morality of "perfect" parents. Parents who, in order to be perfect, have abandoned truth to embrace misguided convictions and frozen institutions; parents who have been chased out of childhood's paradise and confined to a world studded with acts of cruelty which I can only hope that they too, deep down, hate.

That's why youthful friction deserves understanding and why, when they make up afterwards, their peace offering has a sincerity that is moving.

52. *Heart*

Every new life is driven into being by a newly beating heart. As soon as we are born its warmth and strength dissipate every fear. Its throb evokes the soothing voice of the mother, that comforting reassurance that the heart may not understand yet is able, like a magic wand, to conjure up with a cry or a tear as if it were a magic wand.

Yet when that wand no longer works the heart is gripped in fear and terror, its vital resources are stretched to breaking point. This is a devastating experience for the newborn heart, and children that have suffered it and been thrown into the chasm it has opened beneath them are countless.

Why are we so dependent on others? What if they abandon our heart and extinguish our smile? It would be the end. In truth, very few people are capable of resisting such anguish: yet those that do miraculously strengthen a weakened heartbeat and fearlessly recommence their race along life's path.

Max Biaggi's heart has already run this uplifting path and, thanks to his enormous talent, it is a course he continues to follow. His heart, which has been studied carefully as part of Dainese's Pro-Com project (known to us at the Clinic as Marsyas) has surprised us enormously: nothing, it seems, can weaken it. Its vertiginous, vivacious response bears witness to Max's rare zest for life and the enormous thrill he gets from racing. Only in the heat of the challenge is this heart, so calm before the race, stretched towards unbelievable heights, the peaks of which point to an infinity that makes the fog of the valley from which he has climbed but a distant memory.

Max's heart, in rising above that fog, has glimpsed the light at its very source and captured its intact energy. Yet someone like Max Biaggi can never get enough light or energy, hence his insatiable thirst for victory. This constant tension crafts incredible feats of skill which, as soon as they are completed, are forgotten in the quest for new ones.

A youth's heart is seduced by curiosity; it is not interested in things known but in things difficult and intricate. An insatiable longing for knowledge blends with curiosity to open up the dimension of play, one of man's

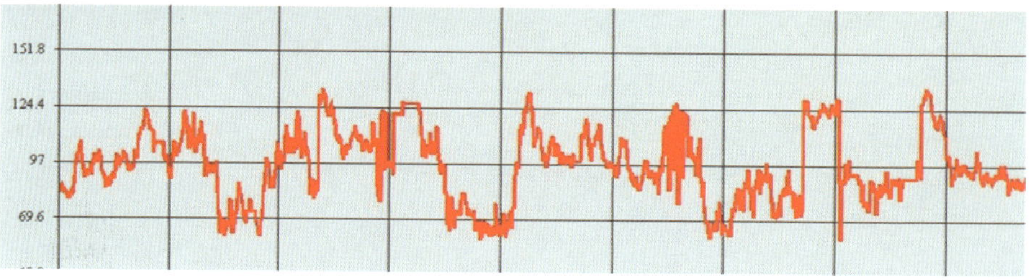

Valentino: the ECG of a kid caught up in play.

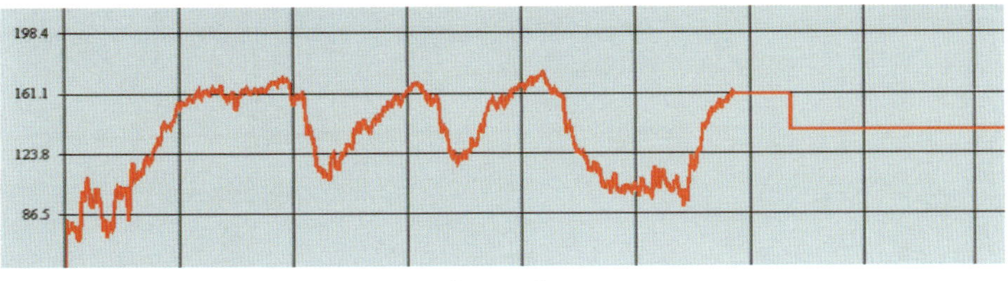

Max: an ECG that beats out a rhythm of pure talent.

Max "D'Artagnan" Biaggi.

Valentino "Peter Pan" Rossi.

most marvellous tools in his quest to create, know himself and know others. And it is perhaps in their sense of marvel that youths begin to admire the world around them and find the spur with which to construct their own reality through spontaneous creativity.

Valentino Rossi's heart is that of a child, who plays to have all that surrounds him – and perhaps all the world's riches – at his complete disposal. As he leans body and bike this way and that in the heat of the race, his excitement is complete. His own marvel at that which he is capable of spurs him on to even greater heights to win control over the kingdom of his own desires. For Valentino, the race is the half-way house between dream and reality, a gateway to a vital dimension of individual creativity. Like all great artists, he will still be playing when he's 30, 40, 50... To live a hopeful life is to play with imagination while you wait for your dreams to materialise. To play is to joke, and a joke is often that much-needed trick which gives a clear-cut sensation of reality. The ease with which Valentino enters and exits that reality is achieved through a jokiness that is one of the purest forms of play.

Valentino abandons himself to creativity of the mind so that he can play the game of life according to the carefree rules of the child. He is so sure that he can generate his own world that, in the theatre of the race, his heart has neither the time nor the inclination to worry itself.

Valentino is light years ahead of that flat unconsciousness which defines a dull existence. Instead, his awareness extends infinitely into a world where nothing is unknown. His response to the uncertainties of that world is the almost acrobatic, theatrical harmony displayed on his bike. Valentino, rather than being self-aware, is awareness itself. During the race, his crystal-clear fluidity raises him to a state of grace, exonerating him from crises and disruptions in a way that ensures his next move is as smooth as the last. The pre-race rituals constitute a valuable store of tried and tested actions that have proven their worth: his lunch at the Clinica Mobile and his massage under the skilled hands of the physiotherapist Marco Montanari bolster his strength just before it is needed most. The 3M breatheright plaster is meticolously put in place to aid his respiration. These simple gestures of good omen are the lead-up to a new session of play, a new race. And with every race fate deals the card that hides the secret of success or the disappointment of defeat: for Valentino, though, that card holds no secrets.

53. *A Wise Old Man*

The day on which Ivano Beggio, President of Aprilia, presented Marcellino Lucchi as their official GP rider for the 250 cc class, I told Marcellino about the Clinica Mobile web site.

That same day, Marcellino sent me the following message: "Claudio, although I didn't have any doubts about it before, your splendid web site has made me realise just how lucky I've been throughout my riding career to have had the physical and moral support of you and your team. Thanks to that support I can still allow myself – even at my age – to pursue that splendid sport which is motorcycling. Ciao, Marcellino Lucchi".

I replied: "Dear Marcellino, the letter you wrote after visiting our web site has made me very happy indeed. Similarly, I hope that the following

Lucchi submits to the revenge of his younger rivals.

words, written to you some time ago, are still capable of giving you an equal amount of happiness.

"You, Marcellino, are a rider who has succeeded in stopping time. The youth in you continues to live on even at the dawn of adult senescence. Your continuing battle with the youngest riders is a message of hope for the entire world of sport. And not only. The energy spent so lavishly to stop time has created happiness. We bear witness to this extraordinary achievement and, as your friends, promise you that the Clinica Mobile will always be at your side. In the words of Richard Wagner, "joy and gladness are not to be found in things, but in ourselves". When he walks the path of courage man is ageless and you, Marcellino, in walking that path have shown that time should not be measured as it is boundless and incommensurable.

Yours fondly, Claudio Costa".

54. *Grace*

The South African Grand Prix, 2001. The 500 cc race is over and its winner, Valentino Rossi, salutes the crowd in inimitable style before embracing his splendid, unbending rival Loris Capirossi, their hands united in a moment of mutual joy.

We begin our return journey. Over the high plains the contorted clouds seem low enough to touch; the smoke from the chimneys of the nearby mines blends with the outstretched darkness of the sky hovering over a mesmerising mix of savannah and farmland. The rain, as forecast, is on its way, creating a fairy tale landscape that sparks the imagination and demands contemplation.

Suddenly, we spotted the flowing mane of a lion, that regal animal that Ivano Beggio had borrowed from nature to present the Aprilia 250 cc last March. Despite a clearly injured right paw, there was no mistaking the beast's elegant, feline gait. That same elegance would soon be seen on the track at Welkom, the lion's mane transformed into the short, tawny head of hair of Marco Melandri, who, in rising from injuries he had received two weeks earlier in Suzuka, Japan, had entered into a state of Grace. Grace is that dimension which cancels out geometries, mathematical results and reason. It is the condition that, even in defeat, allows you contentment; it wins you everyone's love, even that of your opponents. Grace is the divine fluidity with which Marco completed the clash with his rivals.

Fausto Gresini, Team Manager of the GP's tiny yet tough Japanese winner, Katoh, while happy, was amazed to see someone happier. I would later tell him that while victory sows the seeds of joy, the capacity to give meaning to torment and pain, as demonstrated by Marco in racing with a dislocated shoulder, sows the seeds of Grace. Suddenly Katoh himself remembered the previous championship in which he had finished 5th at Le Mans; when he crossed the finishing line his injured hand had bent him to tears. Yet he had been happier then as a "loser" than he was, now, as a "winner" because, like Marco, he had discovered Grace.

Marco Melandri skims over the South African asphalt of Welkom…

…and, enraptured by the grace that has made him forget his shoulder, wheelies in joy.

55. *An Angel of Light*

The shining light of the divine was donated by Lucifer, the most beautiful of angels. So dazzled was he by that light that he rebelled against God: defeated, he was banished to Hell. To shield earth and man, also banished from Paradise, God stationed two guards, Gabriel and Uriel. These faithful angels not only had the task of watching over a desperate humankind; they also had to prevent Lucifer, now the Devil, returning to take possession of Earth. Lucifer was not to be denied and succeeded in gaining access to mortal Earth, raising sin as his banner of revenge.

In today's world we brush shoulders with angels and demons alike, but Tetsuya Harada does not know this. He mistakenly believes that there are only angels and that the Devil exists only as a far-off, forgotten symbol of evil. It is perhaps no coincidence that his helmet depicts a devil, Lucifer himself banished and cast into hellfire. I met this Japanese rider for the first time when Alessandro Valesi introduced me to him in Pavia as the team-mate of Francesco Chili, one of the best riders in the bunch. I looked him in the eye and caught that unmistakeable twinkle of light that had been abandoned by Lucifer as he fled from God to embrace darkness. Such was the strength of his gaze that I could not, no matter how absurd it might seem, stop myself from blurting out "Light !". Now, whenever I meet him that is my greeting: this gentle lad from Japan always responds with a smile that softens his gaze with tenderness. That light is the source of an incredible strength that mends his injuries, fractures and illnesses with astounding haste. A strength that allowed him to bounce back from his crash at Donington, where many fell but only Harada was hit hard. Just as fast was his recovery from the terrible fall at the Piratella corner at Imola when he lost control of his 250 cc Aprilia. The next day he raced – together with his broken ankle. He fought a close-run battle for victory with Valentino Rossi and fell. Unbowed, he ran to his bike: despite his displaced fracture, his stride was an even one and he managed to rejoin the race.

Only a few dullards failed to realise that the light of the mind and the gods of the heart can cancel bodily hurt. Unfortunately the light of day is

Imola: Tetsuya Harada leads the field with a fractured ankle.

Brands Hatch: after the race Kevin Chili gives his Dad flowers picked from the trackside.

less illuminating: Tetsuya Harada failed to see the Devil's shadow gaining on him in the midst of the Argentine pampa as he neared the end of his marvellous ride, seated on an Aprilia 250 cc that seemed destined to take him to World Championship victory. The Devil on his helmet took the human form of Loris Capirossi and both of them rolled off into the crunch of the gravel trap.

When they got up, it was Capirossi who triumphed in the earthly battle, yet the light left in the defeated Harada's eyes traced a rainbow that was far different from the one claimed by his rival. Loris Capirossi conquered the earthly reign of humanity and Tetsuya Harada re-conquered Paradise lost. Since then I have called him Angel of Light.

56. *Rain*

The races organised by my father were a source of endless excitement for both heart and mind. The entire family would participate in the event with almost religious fervour. But on the eve of the race everything that had seemed so wonderful became the source of a growing unease. Fear flattened our hearts and the demons that inhabited our minds began to whirl faster and faster. And just what was this spectre that we tried to ward off with amulets, superstition and anything else we could get hold of? It was rain.

The eve of the race was a sleepless one, spent gazing skyward, sometimes hoping for an encouraging glimpse of starlight among the clouds. As dawn drew closer our drowsy minds would anxiously settle on one of the stone tiles on the bedroom floor and wait for the sun's rays to filter through the win-

Alex Barros: a lightning bolt in the eye of the storm.

dow and illuminate it. As that sunbeam struck the floor it rebounded into our eyes and filled us with unutterable delight. Yet far too many times that old stone remained as dark as the others around it and the anguish became as great as the joy we would have felt had it been sunlit. To paraphrase Kahlil Gibran, it was as if the well from which our light and laughter had flowed was now filled with darkness and tears.

The Clinica Mobile that now travels all over the world has no stone tiles: but the memory of that anticipation remains, nostalgically reminding me that joy and pain are inseparable. Like the organisers, many of the riders, on the morning of race day, seek solace in the sun's first rays – but it is equally true that there are others who seek it in the rain. To them Gibran whispers "your joy is pain without its mask" and so, as the rain spatters onto the asphalt of a track watched over by raincoated marshals, the riders enter the arena: some full of anguish, others joy. Through the falling drops I can make out just about all of them, but the happy at heart are few: Alex Barros, Kenny Roberts Jr, Jeremy McWilliams, Pier Francesco Chili. But the real rainman is the inimitable Alex Barros.

57. *The Titan*

Although he thought he'd lost everything the day his father died, Manuel Poggiali soon realised that the saddest thing in life is not death itself but the waste of talent that would have occurred had he let himself fall into the arms of desperation. That acute realisation – plus a vigorous "tomorrow's another day" attitude – pushed him back onto his bike immediately. One of those tomorrows would see this youngster from San Marino scale the mountain of motorcycling to win the World Championship.

In Greek mythology Prometheus took pity on man's helplessness; with his fellow Titans he assaulted the mountain of the gods to steal the divine secret of fire and give it to mortals. San Marino is perched on a steep craggy mountain, Mt. Titan, named in honour of Prometheus. Like Prometheus, Manuel scaled a mountain, this time to steal the fire of his own glory: he reached the summit on 3rd November 2001 on the race track at Rio de Janeiro.

One day I was invited to Palazzo Sersanti in Imola (this houses a social club, where, as a youth, I used to meet up with my friends to escape the oppression of everyday ordinariness). I had been invited to the prize-giving ceremony of the annually held Youth Games. I asked Manuel, then just 15 years old, to come with me. He turned up punctually with his father and spoke to the crowds of kids; he told them that the best thing in life was to try and win the World Championship. The kids knew what he meant, but some of the grown ups wore a confused frown, somewhat disturbed that a near-child should "recklessly" risk his life to seize a mere laurel; the fact that their own kids had not had to risk their lives to gain their glory was a source of pride to them and their comments showed they actually felt sorry for poor Manuel.

Yet they were missing the point: he who has risked nothing has never really lived. Luckily, Manuel's father knew that there is a time for courage and a time for caution and that the ability to distinguish them is the prerogative of the great. The father smiled at his son and whispered that now was the time for risk. In whispering those courageous words he also

Rio, November 2001: Manuel Poggiali is World Champion.

Manuel Poggiali releases a prayer of thanks in remembrance of his father's smile.

cast a sideways smile at death, which even then was slowly stalking him with a fatal illness.

That was a long time ago. I thought I'd forgotten that smile. But when it re-appeared on Manuel's lips as he kissed the World Championship winner's cup, his father's beaming face came back to me with an almost disturbing clarity. The same smile was also seen on the faces of Claudio Verna and Gianpiero Sacchi, the Team Managers of Gilera, the motorcycle on which the kid from San Marino had just won the world. In the 50's, Gilera, together with Guzzi, symbolised motorcycling. Back then their riders were the indomitable Duke, McIntyre and Liberati. The best loved and most talked about rider of those years was Umberto Masetti, who in 1954 won the first Gold Cup, the legendary April race organised by my father that kicked off every motorcycling season.

Sadly, Gilera pulled out of racing after winning the World Championship with Libero Liberati in 1957 (the season ended in an epic duel at Monza with Geoff Duke). Guzzi and Mondial soon followed in this sad abandon. Italian motorcycle manufacturers pulled out of racing because the government of the day, as always, had forgotten the marvels of motorcycling. Unfair tax laws had hit motorcycle manufacturers hard, just as they do today.

Sadly, politicians have yet to learn the meaning of motorcycling. Like the horse before it, it is a symbol of freedom. It is a means with which to slim down the chaotic traffic created by impotent legislation. It is a means to regain that sensitivity that has, over the last hundred years, been mislaid. It is an inner sentiment that, far from bowing to technology and power, can actually help man grasp his dreams, win him the tranquillity of his own true identity and wake his mind to reality. If the planet's politicians realise, before it's too late, that the sentiment at the heart of every human being is the only symbol capable of changing the world, there will be a new dawning and everyone will be able to walk towards that faint light that motorcyclists have been racing towards for years. In truth motorcyclists have always led the way along this magical road, the road that triggers that which is truly human. Here, man's deepest feelings will free him from the chains of false needs and the obsession of the instant, liberating a society that has traded in happiness for false promises of reassurance. Manuel Poggiali and his fellow motorcyclists have redeemed that happiness by ignoring those promises.

Manuel shows the world that Gilera has hit the high it last attained at Monza in 1957.

58. *A Writer-Journalist*

Eternally elegant, an athlete, writer and, of course, journalist, Ezio Pirazzini was the understudy of Severo Boschi and Dario Zanasi, men who had transformed journalism into poetry. Ezio was press office manager at the races organised by my father in Imola. His favourite saying was that it was "better to write than work". I met him when I was still a child. Blessed with eloquence, he was a source of fascination not only to women but all those who listened to him. He was nearly always congenial and agreeable. Although he never really understood why my father risked everything for his races and his riders (to the point that his house was laid bare by the bailiffs) he admired him passionately and in his books and articles he sang his praises loudly, nicknaming him the King Of Risk.

When, as was only fair, Ezio had to write about other race organisers, my father would see red: he would underline all the sentences that praised the other organisers and then stride into Ezio's office and stick the offending article to his chair. My father disapproved of Ezio's liberal lifestyle. This pained him greatly, not only because he was consequently kept away from the exquisite foods my father admirably cooked up at his home and birthplace, the Feudino, but because he lost his consensus. Citing and paraphrasing Oscar Wilde, Ezio later told me that if my father had exonerated him for having had so much fun with women of "ill repute" and generally enjoying life to the utmost, these "contemptible" acts would have been the most beautiful and sacred of his life. Those same words are found in Oscar Wilde's *De Profundis*, written in the dankness of a prison into which he had been slung by men whose rigid morals were far worse than any of the vices attributed to this great English poet.

To Ezio, betrayal was a word both sacred and sacrilegious. For him true paradise was right here on Earth, the lost one inexistent. In the Imola Moto Club he nourished himself on my father's feats and adventures, inspiring him to write his books on motorcycling; but betrayal brought Ezio face to face with himself and he thus made it his friend. When he wrote his book on the Imola Race Track it's title was *The Ferrari Race-Track.* I was, to

Here comes trouble: from left, Agostini, Pirazzini and Hailwood.

Mike Hailwood and Ezio Pirazzini.

Ezio Pirazzini gets it on the record vis-à-vis Saarinen and Lansivouri's fee.

say the least, indignant at that particular betrayal, yet ended up forgiving him, just as my father did. I realised that Ezio's charm resided in his outrageousness, a way of being which gave him completeness, calibre and an intricate personality.

Perhaps my father figured this out very early on. I, somewhat more slowly, have come to see the same thing: an elegant man in jacket and bow tie sporting an enigmatic, mischievous grin, leaning on a walking stick that supports the hope that a world with a pinch of betrayal is better than paradise. Yes, despite everything, his world was a paradise, "a paradise illuminated by the glow of the inferno, but a paradise nevertheless" (Vladimir Nabokov, *Lolita*): maybe this is why I love Ezio. Over the years my esteem of newspaper and TV journalists rose steadily because they had begun participating more closely in the human drama of the riders and started narrating their stories with sincere sentiment. I am always amazed that the riders' "mad" decisions generally win the virtually unconditional support of motorcycling journalists, these difficult decisions being praised far more than they're condemned. Unconditional praise for a rider who has made his choice and chosen the hardest path instead of the easiest. Exaltation instead of arid criticism and controversy. So, in the journalist, the injured rider often finds a friend. A journalist will often be seen rushing to the Clinica Mobile to interview him but it is just as likely that he's rushing to see if he's all right. I've seen journalists moved, grieved, critical and cheered: I have seen men who, in praising happiness and pain, have put poetry into their prose.

"Like troubadours
Let us dance among saints and prostitutes,
Between God and world, the dance!"
(Friedrich Nietzsche, *The Gay Science*)

59. *A Photographer*

The camera captures the image, the brilliance of the photographer paints colour into it and the emotions and feelings of the onlooker bring it to life. Like an old, worn out, unreliable camera, my mind has fixed some unforgettable images of the people and things I've loved: my father, my friends, my riders and the artist-photographer who immortalised their feats, Franco Villani.

When I first met Franco in the theatre of the Imola race track I was fascinated by him. More than just a photographer, he prowled around the circuit with the severity of a priest patrolling his temple. By comparison the other photographers were mere altar boys. He photographed the first Clinica Mobile; he immortalised our first successes and taught us that images are a godsend. With his keen interest in biology he would have liked to have been a doctor while I, a doctor, would have liked to have been a photographer.

He was an artist of both photography and enjoyment. Franco, in fact, was a symbol of undergraduate revelry, an essential part of studies at the University of Bologna. It was a world to which, unluckily, I had only marginal access. While Franco was undoubtedly a born reveller, his altruism was enormous and he went to Hungary to help refugees during the upheavals of the 50's without hesitation. He entered into the Clinica Mobile as one of us and learnt to love the spirit of this travelling hospital perhaps even more than us. We shared countless hotel rooms and airport delays, successes and disappointments, approval and hostility. He told me stories about the bawdy student parties in which costumed participants would temporarily throw off the yoke of banality and organise get-togethers in ancient castles, their bodies and minds guided by ceremonies written in codes of love and honour. One such uproarious ritual, known as the "fox hunt", would see all the female party-goers escape into the woods outside the castle. Their male counterparts would then attempt to track them down: the prize for a "catch" is easily imagined.

There's no need for me to officially remember Franco, or speak of him,

Franco Villani: poetry in pictures.

his wife Mirella and son Luca as we still meet at work daily. When the Clinica Mobile does something to be proud of he's there to photograph us, not with his camera but his gentle, attentive gaze.

He adored his delightful companion Mirella and his son Luca with a love that seemed inexhaustible. With that same love he taught me that images are worth more than words: he was the very first to extol the virtues of the Clinica Mobile in pictures. It is a habit he has passed on to all motorcycling photographers. Today, they continue to capture our work on film and – in this digital age – on disk. Sincere friends, they continue to honour their communion with the Clinica Mobile. Like Franco, they give us splendid photographs – and if you look closely enough you will see that heartfelt commitment which is in the background of every single one.

60. *Power*

Life is full of attractive, dangerous baubles: one of them is fashion, another is power. Slave to money and earnings, power yields an arid existence that devastates the emotional side of man's life and casts him into a cold lake inhabited only by violent, inexhaustible anger. From power comes lack of respect for others. Power knows no empathy, that feeling which allows us to see our fellow humans' sufferings as our own. Power is a thorny plant from which roses never bud. Power tramples truth and is blind to reality, hating everything it cannot have. It envies the beautiful and deserts imagination, seeking to abuse anyone authentically trying to lead a more artistic life. Power is the begetter of slavery, the promoter of the death penalty. We at the Clinica Mobile have run into power plenty of times; it has imposed on us and tried to kill us with the potent weapons of humiliation and abuse.

When Daryl Beattie lost the toes of his right foot as it came into contact with the wheels of his bike during pre-race testing at the French GP, he was immediately taken to Le Mans hospital. The toes, which had been gathered into a small, sad bag of sterile liquid, could not, unfortunately, be reattached. All we could do was sew up the wounds and acknowledge the reality of amputation. Even those of us at the Clinica Mobile had to bow to this cruel truth and we advised the rider to accept it. Yet in this tense, delicate moment we were "ordered" to load the rider onto a helicopter bound for Paris where a renowned professor was waiting to operate on the foot and invert the reality of amputation. I gave the go-ahead, hoping that this time the immense power of a multinational would provide what we couldn't.

When I arrived in Paris with Daryl and his bag of lifeless toes there was no professor, only a few relatively inexperienced duty doctors in the casualty department: the doctors back at Le Mans were, by comparison, Nobel scientists. Meanwhile, all this wasted time was threatening Beattie's entire foot. Recovering quickly from the disappointment and, now driven by a sense of urgency, I asked the duty doctors to send me as fast as possible to the microsurgery centre run by Dr. Vidal, known to me on account of his extremely interesting publications. Soon afterwards I was in the operating theatre with skilled colleagues, finally able to do something for the Australian rider's foot: although his toes could not be saved, the rest of his foot could. When I left the Paris hospital room where Beattie was recovering from the delicate operation, I found myself alone. Not even one of power's representatives was anywhere to be seen; perhaps convinced they had managed to save Beattie's toes, they had returned to their affairs, unaware that their superficiality had nearly caused the rider to lose his entire foot, not to mention his career.

The anaesthetist I'd worked with in the operating room gave me a lift to the station on his motorcycle. From there a fast, comfortable train took me back to Le Mans. I arrived late in the evening. No representatives of power met me at the station, just Roberto Nosetto and his wife Renata, worried about the rider's condition. My team had waited for me at the Clinica Mobile as had been decided earlier, and we had supper together. The next day, I informed press and TV reporters that the operation had been a success: Beattie's race team managers boastfully claimed the merit for saving the rider's foot.

Even today they are totally unaware of the truth: the "expert" they had chosen to save the day failed to show up at the hospital in Paris and their hysterical anxiety and incompetence had placed Beattie's entire foot at risk. Humility is a rare quality in the powerful – and intuition inexistent: all they had to do was trust those who really care about the riders, those with a good understanding of motorcycling medicine. Those who try to save the species all too often end up sacrificing the individual.

61. *IRTA*

The International Road Racing Team Association stands at the heart of the city of Motorcycling. This association has given the inhabitants of the Grand Prix world dignity. Its first heads were the never-to-be-forgotten Michel Metraux, Mike Trimby, Paul Butler, Garry Taylor, Carlo Pernat, Tony Merendino, Dieter Stappert and Jeremy Ferguson. Those that would follow them – Sito Pons, Herve Poncharal, Luis Dantin – wanted the Clinica Mobile there with the teams and managed to give it a standing that FIM policies have never been able provide.

IRTA has always had a fondness for the Clinica Mobile: they have used their sovereignty to defend it and have ensured it continues helping riders recover from injury and illness. If our capacity to perform this uplifting task has been improved over the years, much of the merit is theirs.

IRTA also instituted the "unfit riders" list. Riders injured during testing or qualification are examined by doctors from the event's host country and then judged as fit or unfit to ride. Riders who fall during the race are listed on an official sheet which is passed on to the doctors of the next GP so that they know who to examine before competition recommences.

Since 1994 a Medical Director has been appointed to every Grand Prix race in the World Championship.

The Medical Director is a doctor with expertise in organising race track rescue services. Prior to every race he actuates any necessary tests, modifications and improvements to rescue and medical services and checks the professional qualifications of medical team members. In Race Control he coordinates first aid operations, ensures they are performed correctly and does his utmost to ensure their successful outcome. During racing and testing the MD has to make important decisions. The most difficult of these is deciding whether to allow a rider to carry on after a fall or stop him for a check-up at the Medical Centre. These tricky decisions have considerable responsibility attached to them; it is easy to intuit just how hard such decisions can be. That the Medical Directors have been chosen among the doctors of the Clinica Mobile is a source of great pride. The two doctors who perform these tasks impeccably are Dr. Claudio Macchiagodena and Dr. Ruggero Mattioli. IRTA also ensures that everyone in the paddock has the night-time phone numbers of the Clinica Mobile doctors so that they can easily be consulted or called in case of need. Advice issued by the Clinica Mobile regarding climate, clothing, use of drugs and country-specific health precautions is diligently filed away in the

Mike Trimby, irreplaceable "soul" of the team.

IRTA archives and sent out to all the people in the paddock as and when necessary.

We are guided not only by IRTA's organisation but also its members. A brotherly hug always welcomes us into their stupendous mobile office and the warm smiles of Irene and Linda can momentarily wipe away the worries of just about any problem (even pass problems). Mike, Paul, Sito

Paul Butler, "Captain" of the race control tower.

Pons, Franco Uncini, Jack Findlay, Geoff, Daniel, Mark and Tony come to our aid not because they have to but because they're proud to see their hospital being run as it should be. The annual dinners are a friendly affair; gifts are exchanged in a carefree atmosphere that is evidence of the love that recompenses us for the time and effort willingly spent helping the world of motorcycling.

62. *Dorna*

When, in the 90's, Bernie Ecclestone won control of motorcycling I went to meet him in London to decide both my fate and that of the Clinica Mobile. The "godfather" of Formula 1 had finally entered motorcycling: yet motorcycling is a different world altogether and Ecclestone was forced to accept

Carmelo Ezpeleta.

its values, one of which is the Clinica Mobile. With Bernie I had no contract, no fee: I entered into his organisation on the basis of a handshake. No waster of words, this magnetic personality of motor sports had just one thing to say to me: "Doctor, look after those riders!".

A few years later Bernie Ecclestone left motorcycling in the hands of another organisation, Dorna. In committing as much passion and heart as it does professionalism and technology Dorna has kept the fire of motorcycling burning brightly. Similarly, the Clinica Mobile's mission is, in the midst of cold technology and protocols, warmed by genuine Spanish passion. Carmelo Ezpeleta is a first-rate Spaniard: his enthusiasm fans the flame of motorcycling. Amiable and polite, he guides the "chariot" of motorcycling with a firm hand – a chariot pulled by two horses, one black, vivacious and crazed that soars skywards and another, white and wise with its hooves firmly on the ground. All I can hope is that the boss of motorcycling never forgets that motorcycling needs both those horses.

For the Spaniards, bullfighting symbolises the exorcism of man's darkest, most ferocious inner brutality, extinguishing it with the sacrifice of the bull – and sometimes the bullfighter. The chariot of motorcycling will only be able to accomplish that same exorcism if the charioteer guides its two horses with devotion to race them swiftly towards life's finishing line. Carmelo, we wish you every luck in that race.

63. *Two Martyrs*

The appalling images transmitted from Imola on 1st May 1994 during the Formula 1 Grand Prix are among the most tragic in the history of motor sports. Those images raised a cry: “Enough is enough, stop these races!”.

As the son of the man who created that race track I too wanted to cry out in anger. Yet my mind, wrapped in the torment of the tragedy was only capable of responding with a silent refusal to blame everything and everyone.

Thoughts flashed through my mind. Why do racers choose to live so dangerously? Just why do they risk their lives to steal a few centimetres from the track, a few tenths of a second from the clock? Just where does this fatal attraction come from? Perhaps because the clear and present danger of losing your life makes it that much more intense?

Imola, 1st May 1994: Ayrton Senna’s eyes seem to anticipate his final destiny.

This romantic reflection is not enough. So… perhaps my studies of the classics can help: the racer's supreme challenge against death might be thought of as allowing him to explore beyond nature's limits, beyond the boundaries of being. To help him satisfy a need to know not only more but know differently: to satisfy a need for answers.

To challenge death is to open the casket of human riches, to understand oneself, to free the spirit from the prison of the unknown and explain its hidden horizons, to offer it up on the altar of the most beautiful religion there is – self-understanding. In this race against death the racer commits no monstrosity but, rather, commits himself to his destiny. In seeking death he seizes life.

I believe (and perhaps, subliminally, always have done) that racers are "truly" alive, that their lives run on a parallel track wedged between reality and dreams, a life we cannot share with them. And so the pre-packaged "wisdom" of those that want racing banned rings false.

To me, the "common sense" that criticises speed is too restrictive and the apparent absence of any "common sense" in the racers themselves is only

Roland Ratzenberger's bows his head in his confrontation with death.

to be expected: it is alien to their philosophy for the simple reason that they live wholly different lives that have little or nothing to do with that day-by-day ordinariness which looks so much like true death. That dead men should ask racers to betray real life is, quite frankly, incredible...

In my heart of hearts I know that the fog of tragedy that has fallen over Imola and its race track needs to be swept away. That theatre of speed needs to be revitalised so that racers can continue living a life that we can intuit but never experience. Only when this "rebirth" has been brought about by the mutual love needed to make it happen will Ayrton Senna and Roland Ratzenberger return to race in our hearts.

64. *A Hero*

Michele Alboreto, a hero of motor racing, had a sneaking admiration for motorcycling. Shortly before the 1986 Monza GP, Michele, then driving for Ferrari, slipped up in his bathroom (or was it off a motorcycle?) and dislocated his right collar bone. He was rushed to the hospital casualty department. The diagnosis was clear: there was no way he could race at Monza. The doctors suggested that he be admitted to hospital for minor surgery and, well, with any luck, he would be fighting fit in two months.

Shortly afterwards I got the phone call I'd been waiting for since I was a child. I was asked if I would treat Michele Alboreto's injured shoulder. I hesitated, and asked if I could think about it for a few minutes: in those few minutes nostalgia flooded through me and I was a child again, fantasising

Claudio Costa fastens a pained Michele Alboreto into his cockpit, the throne of his glory.

about being the sole saviour of Ferrari's hero. A helicopter landed in the Imola football ground (I can still remember the amazed look on the groundsmen's faces) and whisked me away to a countryside villa not far from the Monza race track where I met Michele Alboreto. He was lying in bed, obviously in pain, naked from the waist up; his right arm lay limp at his side, and his left was raised in welcome. His gentle, fawn-like eyes twinkled with a light that masked the pain of his injury. He uttered his words with a disarming softness. "Doctorcosta" (all in one go, as pronounced by so many others) he said, "I'm in your hands: I want to race!".

I looked into his eyes once more, and found the answer to his question before he could utter it: yes, he would certainly race that GP. My hands glided over his injury: the broken collar bone hurt him enormously and he couldn't move the shoulder, but I already knew that Sunday would see him on the starting grid. It was a conviction based not on reason or the belief that my treatment would have the desired effect, but the simple sensation that, inside Michele himself, the miracle had already happened: like the Three Wise Men, I had the impression of being the only witness to this surprising event.

After "torturing" him with a series of injections I applied a functional taping and prepared the medicines to be administered later. Lunch was announced, giving me an opportunity to explain that the diet they had put him on was a pack of lies that stemmed from the ignorance of someone who has yet to realise that eating is a ritual celebrated through the overly-neglected senses of taste and smell. Simply by calculating the quantity of food and the time his body would take to assimilate it, he could have anything he wanted.

The rapport of complicity that Michele and I so quickly established did not, however, allow me to feel totally at ease during that lunch. Not even the enjoyable company of Michele's close friend, Riccardo Patrese, was able to wash away the discomfort I felt at being sat at a table of rich guests, served by white-gloved waiters feigning indifference. I was so ill at ease that when the waiter offered the roast rabbit I felt too embarrassed to confess that I couldn't eat it on account of my superstitions, and hastily declared "no thank you, I don't eat meat". Secretly, I hoped there would be another dish, and soon enough there was. The waiters returned with a tray of delicious Wiener schnitzel, a meat dish in perfect agreement with my superstitions – and my mounting hunger. Just as the gloved hand was carrying the tasty cutlet towards my plate it was stopped by the sharp voice of our host "Ambrose! The Doctor doesn't eat meat". All I could do was sit in silent dismay, condemned to hunger by superstition and shyness.

That day, the Friday, we decided that it would be best if Michele just rested to speed up his recovery. On Saturday, Michele's helicopter touched down at the Monza race track and he was almost swallowed up by cheering Ferrari fans. Out of all the shouts and cries, there came one unforgettable comment: "He's with Doctor Costa' from motorcycling... he's going to race!". I entered the Ferrari paddock in trepidation, but was soon put at ease by the friendliness of the mechanics

We gently eased Michele into the cockpit and tightened his safety belts: he was about to give us all a lesson of courage. It was a rare courage that Enzo Ferrari had seen before: although initially adverse to Michele's participation, the driver did so well in the Sunday morning tests that Enzo Ferrari gave him the go-ahead, realising that he could do it even though he had clearly not yet recovered. Michele's car leapt forward from the starting grid and sped along the shores of a sea of red flags. The gods, envious of so much glory, brought his Ferrari to a halt when he was leading. Perhaps the same gods, challenged again at Dresden, stole him away not out of envy, but to keep one so valorous in their company forever.

65. *Memory*

"I want that which I love to continue living
and I loved you and praised you above all else…
…I want you to live while I, asleep, await you
I want your ears to carry on hearing the wind
And for you to continue trampling the arena that we trampled together."

It is with these words, written by Pablo Neruda, that I solemnly remember all those who live on in our nostalgia.

To Ray, Gary, Tommaso, Pat, Randy, Sauro, Paolo, Otello, Guido, Lorenzo, Michel, Patrick, Nobuyuki and the many others who once strode through the arena we still stride through today.

67. *Thought*

Luckily, the gods gifted us with thought: if they hadn't, life's absurdity would have turned us into madmen.

When, on 11th September 2001, those suicide planes ploughed into the towers of the NY World Trade Centre I wanted to scream. I wanted to

The eyes say it all: Claudio Costa meditates life's enigma.

run off and hide in the small Umbrian village of Gubbio in the mad hope that I might meet St Francis and join him to speak only of nature and never again man.

I wanted to take part in one of the many ensuing peace rallies, I wanted the omnipotence that would allow me to change reality. These days, the road to St. Francis is now immeasurably longer than the one that actually links my house to the woods of Gubbio. To speak with that saint you need to whisper with the voice of your heart: learning that divine language can take a lifetime and in my case, would take much longer.

To march for peace, to fool ourselves that everything might magically fall back into place as it was the day before the tragedy was a terrible mistake. Because the absence of sentiment on the day before – and throughout a long period preceding that tragedy – had, in part, favoured it.

The omnipotence I craved was not given to me for the simple reason that I don't live in heaven but in an earthly Inferno. Yet just as my feelings were at their lowest ebb and the only hope left was that from chaos there might come order, I received a letter from an American doctor of New York, asking me to take him on as a member of staff at the Clinica Mobile. In many ways an application like any other, yet unique in its significance. It was as if this American doctor was asking us for a new home because the world's folly had destroyed his own.

On 30th September 2001, on the finishing line of the Imola race track, just before the start of the World Championship Superbike race, the entire staff of the Clinica Mobile, the doctors from the hospital of Imola, the Flammini brothers and the Mayor of Imola, Massimo Marchignoli, gathered together to welcome Dr. Donald Dishman. They promised him that he would indeed work with both the Clinica Mobile and the race track Medical Centre and that he would always find a home there – that no-one would destroy.

Those who recapture and live the emotional side of their lives create a world in which a hug is a hug for all humanity. That hug is the only thing that will save us from annihilation. The alternative is an abyss without sense or sentiment. And in that abyss, in which our arrogance has erected false gods, our punishment will be severe. The one true God will strike at us with a vehemence that will recall the anger with which he drowned all in the flood. But back then there was an ark, and an ark is no longer seen today because it no longer exists.

68. *Alex*

Alessandro Zanardi's terrifying accident at the Lausitzring circuit near Berlin during a Formula CART race sent a shiver into the world of sport and beyond. The voices raised in protest against the dangers of motor racing became deafening. Why continue racing? Isn't there already enough misery in the world? Hadn't the calamity of New York violently warned us of the horrible reality of death? Would it not be better to bow in reverence, hang our heads and halt the pain? Stop the racing, stop the crying!

In the wake of Alessandro's accident and the disaster of New York many wanted it all stopped: just as many wanted to see it continue. In the midst of all this confusion the truth is difficult to see as it wears many faces, all equally credible. In the words of Saint-Exupéry "The essential is invisible".

After the New York tragedy team managers urged their drivers on without pause out of a respect for their profession, their sport. Niki Lauda openly affirmed that one had to carry on because that is the very nature of motor racing. Some drivers matter-of-factly stated that they're paid to race and that the spectators deserve their money's worth. Others, though, given the enormity of the attack on New York, thought it might be better to stop racing even if only for a moment because painting an American flag on a racing car or bordering it in black as a sign of bereavement was, quite simply, not enough to honour America's victims. No, for a people hit so hard a stronger gesture of solidarity was needed.

So, when the world of sport did come to a halt and opposing teams and competitors held hands the vision of that unity was incredibly moving, testimony to a new-found humanity. In that still, hand-holding alliance the future suddenly seemed less bleak. It was right that the world should stop for a moment to honour the victims of a crime perpetrated not only against America but humanity itself. I too bowed my head. A lot of sports events were cancelled and this new-found unity gave us hope. In this moving meditation there appeared long-neglected feelings, and perhaps a pause in motor racing seemed only proper too. Yes, the sport that unites the world in rivalry, the sublime symbol of challenge should stop in solemn reflection.

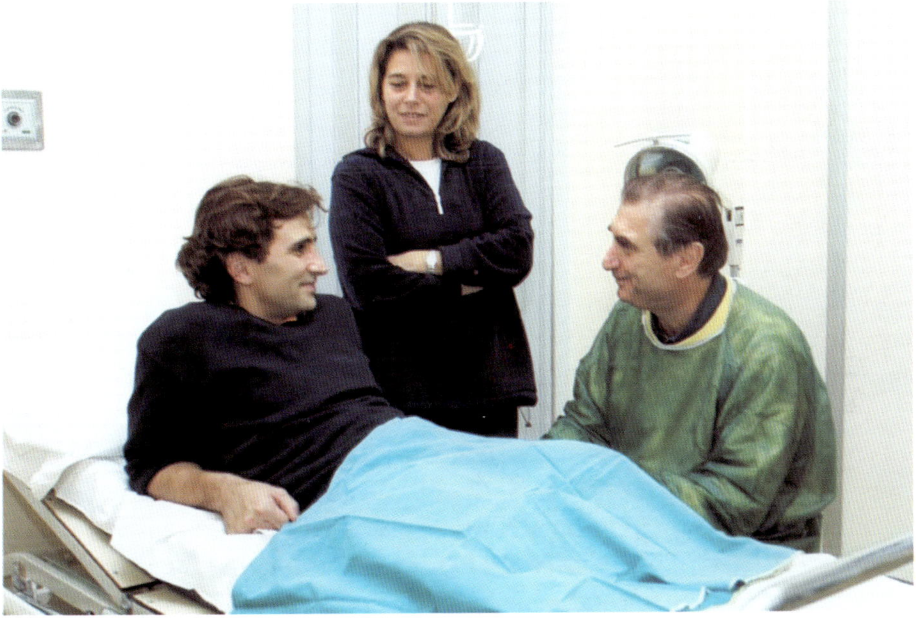

Imola Hospital: Dr. Costa chats with Alex Zanardi and his wife Daniela.

Zanardi's son recognises the violence and accepts it with a kiss.

Yet when I imagined those horrendous images of the suicide jets slamming into the Twin Towers, where so many people had been engaged in their own daily race for life, committed to everyday battles that might allow them to conquer their dreams or a future for family and children, I felt a wholly different kind of certainty. Yes, the world of sport should, out of respect, stop for a moment. But not the racers. Not for a single moment, especially after the tragedy of New York. Because racers of cars and motorcycles have a duty to sit straight back down in front of life's chess board and continue playing with risk, danger and death.

They *had* to throw themselves onto the oval track at Berlin, they *had* to race through the rain in Valencia, they had to face the dangerous chicanes of Monza and stand shoulder to shoulder, brothers in arms, to fight for victory. In doing so they were, effectively, defending that place at the chess board occupied by the mysterious knight in Ingmar Bergman's The Seventh Seal. In exhibiting such overwhelming courage and energy, I am convinced that man was able to shift the gloating figure of Death from the ruins of New York and oblige him to take his place at the chess board where men of bravery were challenging him. From underneath those crushed towers it was as if the cry "Death! You have not won!" could be heard.

As these races were being run, Alessandro Zanardi opened his eyes in the intensive care unit at the Umfallkrankenhaus of Berlin and witnessed his terrible wounds: both legs had been amputated. To his life's companion, the strong yet tender Daniela, he whispered "Death, I have won". And the sadness that I had always seen in the depths of Alessandro's eyes, that sadness which means that happiness lasts but an instant, disappeared to be replaced by hope. Death's secret hides at the very heart of life, and Alessandro's heartbeat will continue to tap out its message.

69. *Faith*

Luca Delli Carri is a sports journalist and author of the fascinating book *Gli indisciplinati*, a collection of five stories about racers as undisciplined as they are human (published in 2001 by Fucina). In the following interview I provide answers to Luca's intriguing questions on the meaning of motorcycling.

How did this enormous passion for motorcycling come about?

My entire family has always loved the sport. My father designed and created the Imola race track back in the 50's and as a child, instead of toys (we were pretty poor and I wouldn't have had many anyway) I had motorbikes, famous riders coming in and out of our home and a race track in which to run and play instead of the vast garden that richer kids might have had.

Motorbikes, not motorcars.

Bikes, bikes and nothing but bikes.

Why motorbikes?

My father taught me that motorcycles are as natural and instinctive as they are technological, something between the beauty of enthusiasm and the pain of grief. A car always offers almost maternal protection and is constraining compared to the overwhelming freedom of expression you get with a motorcycle. Moreover, a motorcycle is often the tool with which an adolescent expresses his first dissent: in asking his parents for a scooter, he engages his first battle, sparks the first family conflicts; once that battle is won his bike is the means by which he flees from everyday ordinariness, life's rules, everything that has been denied him. Finally, he feels free – and is. Free to conquer limitless kingdoms against that most beautiful and romantic of enemies, the wind.

Do you think there's a greater human component in motorcycles than there is in cars?

Undoubtedly. Because the motorcycle becomes part of the rider and the rider becomes the centaur of antiquity. The most beautiful of these fascinating creatures was Chiron, teacher of medicine to Asclepius, the first human doctor, later symbolised by Hippocrates. Hence it can be said that medicine itself derived from a centaur; now that medicine helps the centaurs of motorcycling I'd say that we're simply paying antiquity's debt.

As a youth did you dream of becoming a rider?

It was forbidden for me to become a rider. Not only was I not allowed to ride a motorcycle, I wasn't even allowed to dream of becoming World Champion – although I do admit I got round that particular prohibition.

And yet your father loved motorcycles and motorcycling!

He was categorical: if I wanted to follow in his footsteps actually riding a motorcycle was out of the question. Sounds absurd, doesn't it?. But bear in mind that my father also loved the classics: he told me that Homer was blind when he saw and sang the praises of the greatest Greek heroes and, analogously, nothing would stop me living a full life in motorcycling just because I didn't know how to ride a motorcycle. By forbidding me to sit in the saddle he did, in a sense, blind me, yet at the same time said that I would consequently see everything more intensely with the aid of love and imagination. The comparison with Homer, for a youth who was then studying the classics, was small recompense. But it worked because I've never ridden a motorcycle.

Don't you think, in the light of everything you've built up over the years and everything you've done for the riders, that, rather than passion, it would be more appropriate to speak of a devotion to motorcycling.

Yes, because I wasn't born a doctor. First I learnt to love the world and only afterwards dedicated myself to the medical profession. When I realised that a lot of the results, recoveries and healings were triggered by the forces hidden inside all of us, I became even more enthusiastic and I began to think that if human beings harbour such riches then I and all those that have never even touched a motorcycle might have them too! So motorcycling became not only one of life's lessons but also proof of how life can be great even in the presence of that one thing that modern society abhors: risk. Yet in embracing this abhorrence society has forgotten the central message in one of childhood's fairy tales, The Ugly Duckling. To become the beautiful swan the ugly duckling has to throw himself into the pond. Not that I'm saying there's anything wrong with safety and self-preservation, it's just that what's good for the species is often lethal for the individual. Because an individual sometimes needs risk and danger to find his own identity, individuality and the inner beauty that'll turn him into a swan.

So you believe that people should put themselves to the test, even aggressively?

Can you think of any better way? You only get better and find yourself by taking risks. When you find out who you are you complete one of the most important tasks that life assigns you, because when you're given life you know that at some point it'll be taken from you and that you only have so much time to find the essential truth about yourself. I think finding that truth is life's most beautiful reward and motorcyclists teach us that even a calculated risk can grant you the stature, calibre, harmony and colour that an anonymous life, without jolts or dangers will never be able to give.

Do you think motorcycling's a sport where, even today, despite technology's dominance, risk and suffering still play a huge part?

Yes, it's that ambivalence I was talking about before: a motorcycle is a means with which to project oneself towards unlimited, almost marvellous freedom while the flip side is that the rider runs the risk of fractures, injuries, illness and suffering. However, the riders have shown us that in recovering from those injuries they offer a message of hope not only to themselves or their loved ones but a message of hope to all other sportsmen and all those that suffer in the world: it is nothing less than the promise that paradise has not been lost.

You mean that paradise is the world we inhabit?

Yes.

How would you define a rider?

First and foremost, a human being. In facing risk, in lowering his visor at the start of a qualifying session or a race, he becomes a man, a truly alive man. When the race is over he again has to face life, his own merits and defects, because, believe me, even the greatest champions have their defects.

I've spoken to a lot of riders: some are aware of the risks they're running, others no. Why do you think that is?

Well, I'd say they're only apparently blasé, because danger and death are constantly at hand, whether the riders say they think about it or not:

when a rider gives the impression that he doesn't think about death it means the Death is standing there right next to him.

So the less they speak about it the better?

Yes, at an unconscious level. Remember that death has a presence. No-one speaks of funerals, death, misfortune: all those things seem far-off, hidden in the fog, but in truth these are sensations the rider carries in his core all the time.

Does this mean we can say motorcycle riders are courageous?

You bet they are. Because courage isn't just a willingness to put yourself at risk of injury. It's having the nerve to play the game of life. It's a courage that anyone can have: in deciding to play a bigger role in your family, school or profession you show courage – and courage goes hand-in-hand with fear. Courage-plus-fear is the mix which makes a human being. I would never trust anyone who vaunts fearlessness.

But I've found so very few riders who have admitted – even just once – to being afraid.

True enough. Courage and fear are banished from conversation, yet they co-exist inside every rider: the courage is there and is demonstrated every time he gets on his bike – but the fear's in there too: when fear gains the upper hand the rider will hesitate an instant and stop racing. Riders usually stop motorcycling when they get to the end of their career, but there are plenty of other occasions, and I've witnessed them, where the rider has stopped racing just like that; to stop in an instant means that all the ingredients of renunciation were already inside him. So you see, all that fear and the presence of death were not so far away after all: they were just hidden from view.

Do you consider motorcycle riders to be stronger than the average man?

Yes. I'm not trying to be complimentary, but I do believe that motorcycle riders have an above average psychological toughness because when the race begins, he knows what he's risking. He puts on his helmet and leathers to protect himself and in so doing almost admits that he's limited, that he is, far from being immortal and invulnerable, just a man preparing to write his own brief page of history. But in tugging down his visor he is free to challenge all the laws of nature and seek the elation that comes from living on the edge.

How do riders generally react to the pain caused by a fall?

Their reaction is the most beautiful human beings are allowed: to change the meaning of something. They somehow manage to shift, to transfigure and sublimate the pain's meaning the same way Dante sublimated love and knowledge to justify life's briefness. By mutating the dimension of pain, he can even make it his friend, and carry it into the race with him to complete his enterprise. If pain overcomes and invades you you're crushed, paralysed, obliterated. If, instead, pain is considered to be something normal, human, the presence of which still allows you to do what you want to do, then all those questions like "Will I get better? Will I be all right? Will I be an invalid when I'm old?" disappear as the rider is galvanised by his desire to do the thing he loves most (and in doing the thing he loves he becomes a psychologically stronger man). At this point pain becomes his friend. And if pain is your ally the ensuing feats can prove incredible. Believe me, we've witnessed plenty of such feats. All I can do is bow to such greatness, because it's not me or the medicines that count. Or, rather, there's only one medicine capable of triggering that psychological transformation of pain: the love demonstrated by those who stick with you and help you.

Said like that, it's almost as if the riders enjoy their pain, as if it were both an essential part of the test and proof that it has been surmounted.

I can't really say that, but it's certainly an exultant experience. It's an experience that guides men onto the path of mysticism and greatness, allowing them to live without fear of dying.

Fear of dying: do you honestly believe that anybody's ever ready to die?

No, I believe not. I think death is the most frightening thing of all for everyone. Yet there are those who can convert this limit into a victory. The first stage of that victory is to form an alliance with pain, and with pain still manage to do just what it is you want. That's what these riders do almost daily, in testing, qualifying and racing. That's why I love them and that's why I think they're heroes – and, perhaps, envy them a bit. Not because they ride motorcycles, but because their minds carry that potential, that marvellously magical capacity to transform fear into a feat and a feat into victory.

Modern-day samurai, then.

They exist today just as samurais and knights existed in other epochs.

Nothing ever really changes: these value are always with us. It's the world which throws a pall of fog over them.

Boxers also have to dominate their fear and dig deep to find courage. They often show pride in injuries received in the ring: is there a similar attitude amongst motorcyclists?

Injuries mental and physical are man's calling cards: they're both the promise and the confirmation that he is a man.

So these riders, then, often physically perfect and in tip-top condition, race and win with their heads?

Yes, they're starting point is that of the athlete, healthy and fighting fit (but not always: we've seen some world champions who would have been berated at school as weaklings and even champions who have needed corrective therapy). In the end they end up riding injured, with bones that have yet to mend so, yes, their real strength is drawn from their minds.

Do you find that riders are more ambitious than the average person?

The ambition certainly has to be there: ambition mixed with a touch of narcissism can be a pretty healthy thing.

You've spoken of champions who race when injured: the most glaringly obvious case among those you've treated is Doohan, a rider you got back on his bike after an appalling accident.

Or Loris Capirossi, who raced in Holland with a double fracture of the hand sustained the morning before the race. He said "I think I've broken my hand, Claudio. I want to race the Dutch Grand Prix today". The mindset that allows you to utter phrases like that can make the impossible possible.

He didn't ask if it was possible to race. He said he would race that afternoon.

Yes, he wanted to race that GP. One of the fractures was displaced and the Dutch doctors wanted to keep him off the starting grid. He asked for an official medical examination at 1 p.m. and prepared himself for it. It was a cruel examination, the sort of thing specifically intended to make you cry out in agony so that they can say "Understand now? There's no way you can race". He responded to every bend of the hand with a smile, and a smile is one of the most disarming strategies in the book, the weapon with which a mother soothes a weeping child. In the end they gave him the green light. We helped Capirossi along with medicines, anaesthetics, painkillers, drip feeds and what have you, but his own conviction that he could do it was what pushed him over the finish line.

And Mick Doohan?

All right, let's take Doohan as a representative of those that have achieved similar things. First, he risks losing his life and not just his leg. Next, we spirit him away from the Dutch hospital from which he sent his request for help: we fly in with an air ambulance we were able to rent thanks to a Dutch friend, practically kidnap him from the hospital, load him onto the plane and bring him to Italy. Here he battles to hang on to life and then leg. Unbelievably, 40 days later, his wounds still bleeding, he gets out of bed to race the last two Grand Prix events of the season in an attempt to win the World Championship, and when he failed in that attempt I thought, well, there's just no justice in the world. Well, I, mere mortal that I am, was wrong about that. Justice had something much better lined up for Doohan: five World Championship titles.

Has there been a rider who you see as being more rider than all the others?

If I were to say I don't have my preferences, I'd be lying. I have had and will continue to have those preferences, and the sincere answer to your question is this: I'm not telling you.

You've had an amazing career: what's the achievement you're proudest of?

The Clinica Mobile. I almost envy it because it's become a legend while I've remained a person. You should be interviewing the Clinic, not me! The Clinica Mobile is the world hospital of motorcycling. Not only does this hospital look after the riders, it's also the workplace of three highly qualified female doctors that, unfortunately , are not to be found in any other hospital: their names are Love, Hope and Trust.

I've heard that before the advent of the Clinica Mobile the riders were pretty much left to fend for themselves.

Yes, the Clinica Mobile came into being exactly because of this shortcoming. Even today, now that all the tracks have their Medical Centres, the Clinica Mobile carries on because it offers the riders those three doctors I mentioned earlier, because it provides fast help after an on-track accident, because it's something the riders need to be able to count on.

You meet the riders when they're at the peak of their careers,

when their lives are most vibrant but you also see them afterwards when they stop racing. What happens to riders when they become ex-racers? Do they find the switch difficult?

The change is an intensely emotional one: when they stop racing they lose their divinity to become human. And when they conquer that humanity they gain a great advantage: after their retirement their eyes shine with serenity, calm and the most beautiful of emotions life has given us since we were chased, tearful and afraid to look back, from the garden of Eden: nostalgia. The fabric of our lives is woven with nostalgia for events that, for a moment, have given us happiness; nostalgia is the hope that such happiness might come our way again. When it comes to hope, I think ex-riders have a pretty good life.

Do you believe in God?

Yes.

Is this a help in life? Does a rider who believes in God have any advantage over one who doesn't?

Faith is an aspect that's never really discussed in racing circles, for the simple reason that, regardless of whether one believes in God or not, motorcycling is something of a sacred altar in itself, so there's no real need to trouble divinity. However, that's the first question I'm really not quite sure how to answer. I've never asked riders whether they believe in God, and they've never asked me either. I don't know. I've never asked anyone and they've never told me. No, there's no talk of God on the trackside, and we've never asked ourselves what you want to know. Since the question is an intelligent one all I can do is promise I'll get back to you on that one in a year's time.

One year has now gone by, and I'll answer as promised.

In motorcycling irrational willpower is the precious patrimony of almost all the riders; they employ that willpower as they attempt to recover from injury or transcend the limits imposed by pain. On the path of courage, desires and impossible dreams are the rider's constant companions. It is on the altar of motorcycling that this irrational trust creates faith: that marvellous faith that helps the knights of risk ride on even when injured. In attempting the impossible they work the miracle that leads to the epiphany of the divine and the awareness that God lives in all of us.

Faith is a gift. Those without faith often forget just how close this gift is to their own hearts. Pain and torment have no meaning for those poor beings lost behind the illusion of richness and wealth, but one day the wistful sound of bells tolling in the world's churches will help them remember where God truly lives – in us. The bells of motorcycling have already reminded all those who race or ride that God exists and lives in their hearts.

PART FIVE
The Riders' Home

As the riders travel all over the world to race on tracks that are so far from their homes, they have a place which follows them in their wanderings, which they see as a home from home: the Clinica Mobile. The riders are its guests and they are always welcome, at any time of day or night, whatever their problems.

Yet the Clinica is not just "home" to the riders. There are also its "servants", that is, those who have built it up, run it and transport it around the world to alleviate the riders' sufferings. There are quite a few of them, and in the following pages you'll have the opportunity to meet some of them.

The riders that I have treated over the years also have other homes. First and foremost comes the Feudino, which, before it became my home, was that of my father and his father before him. Today, when riders come to visit, they find my mother Silvana ready and waiting to welcome and feed them. Mick Doohan lived here for forty days. Today, in the room in which he battled against his pain, there hovers the presence of some indefinable ghost that disturbs whomsoever sleeps there.

Then, twelve miles from Imola, there is the Riva, in the village of Fontanelice in the splendid Santerno valley. The riders come here as friends, eat the locally grown foods, season them with olive oil produced in the surrounding hills, drink the wine made from our own grapes. The Riva is a place that I see as wholly mine: consequently, it belongs to all those that I love.

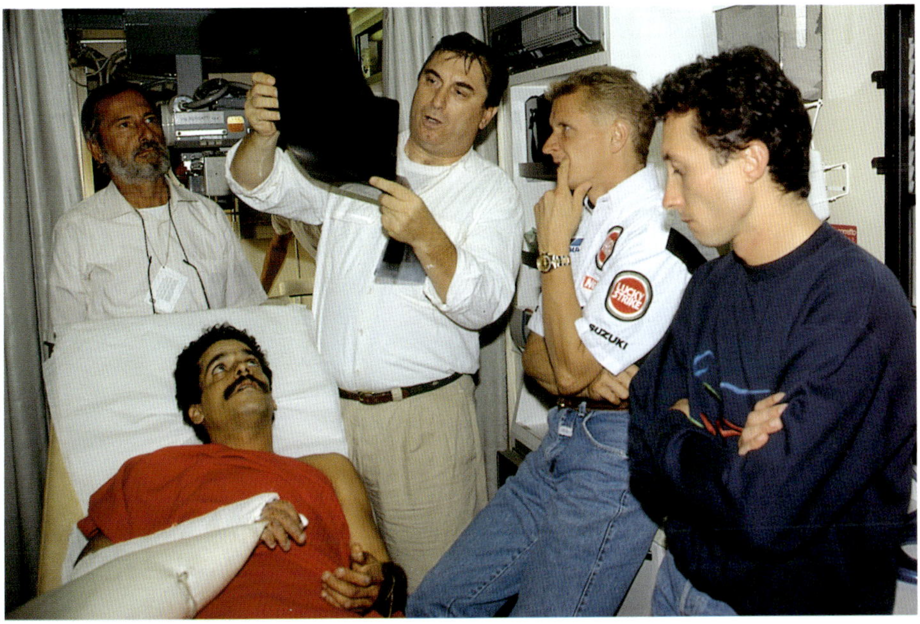

From left: Giancarlo Caroli, Carlos Levado, Dr. Costa, Kevin Schwantz, Loris Reggiani.

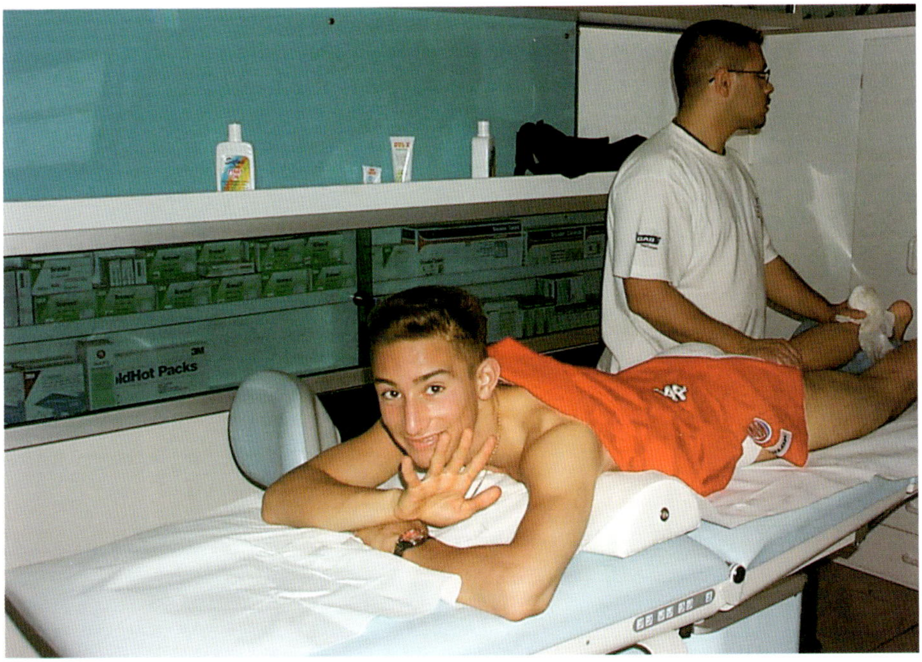

Manuel Poggiali, an unchained Titan.

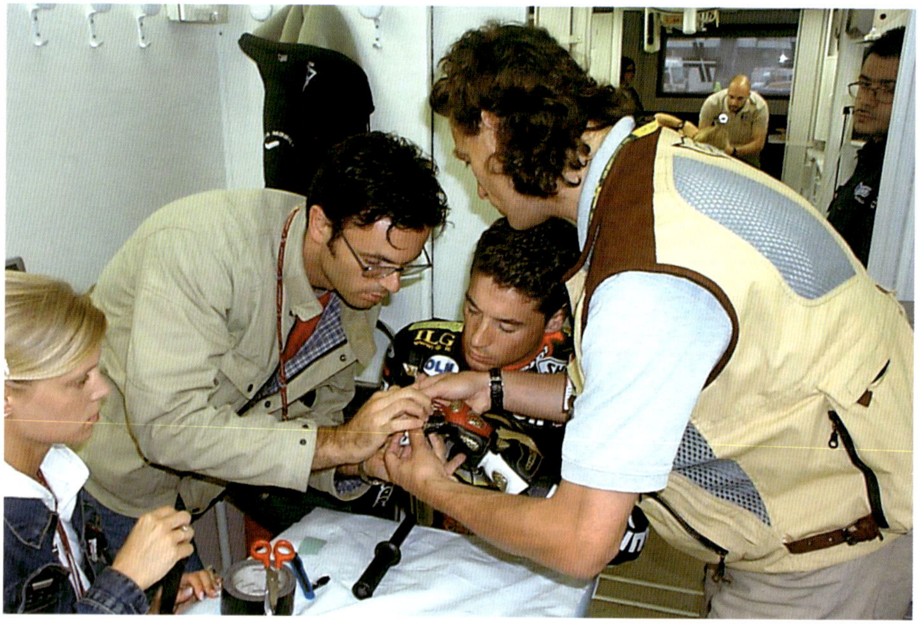

Four helping hands for Lucio Cecchinello's injured one.

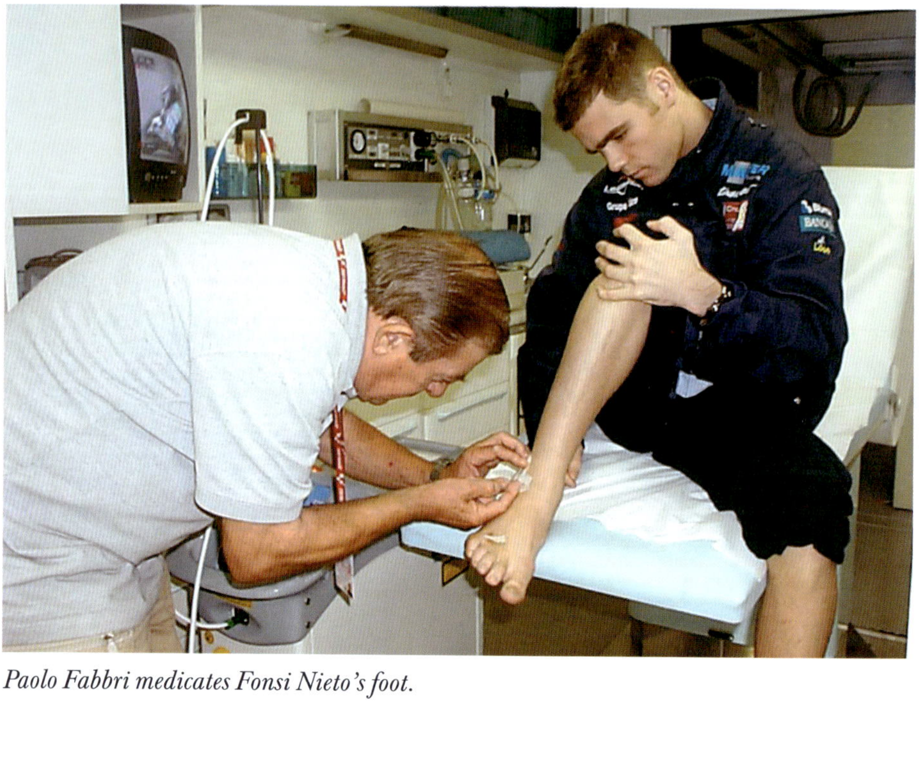

Paolo Fabbri medicates Fonsi Nieto's foot.

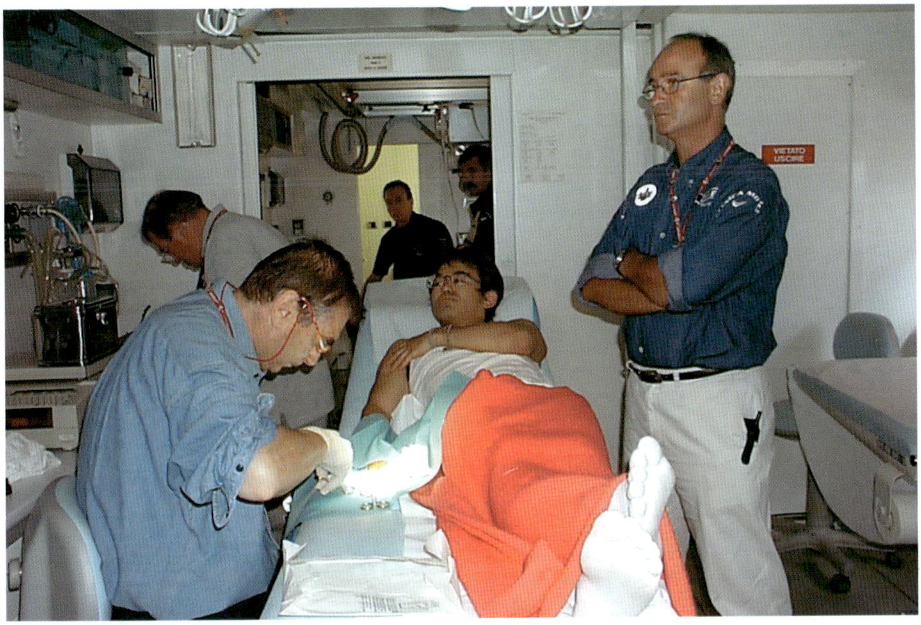

Ueda calmly watches TV as Dr. Costa stitches his hand.

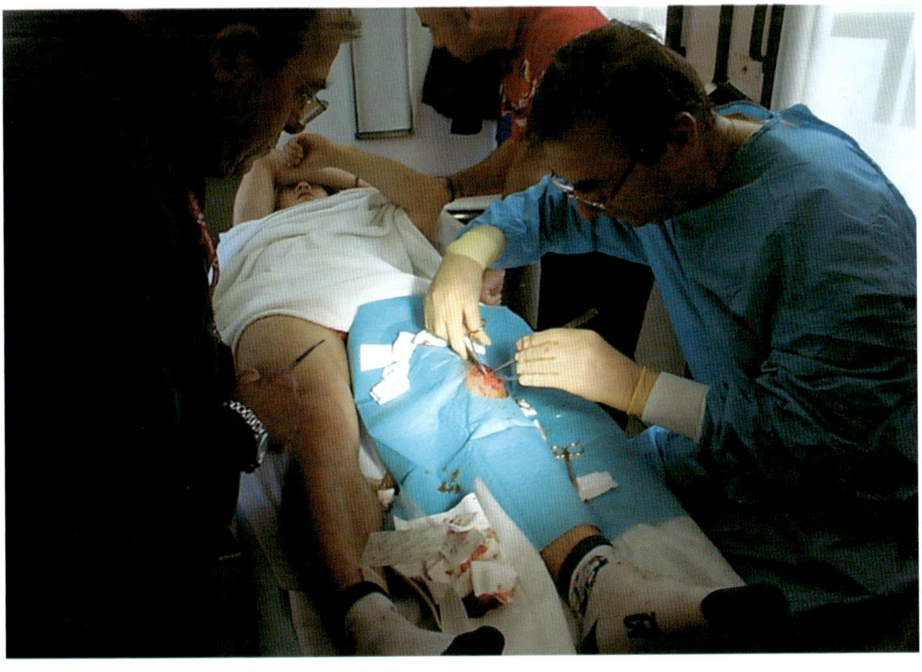

Stitching up Norifumi Abe's wounded knee.

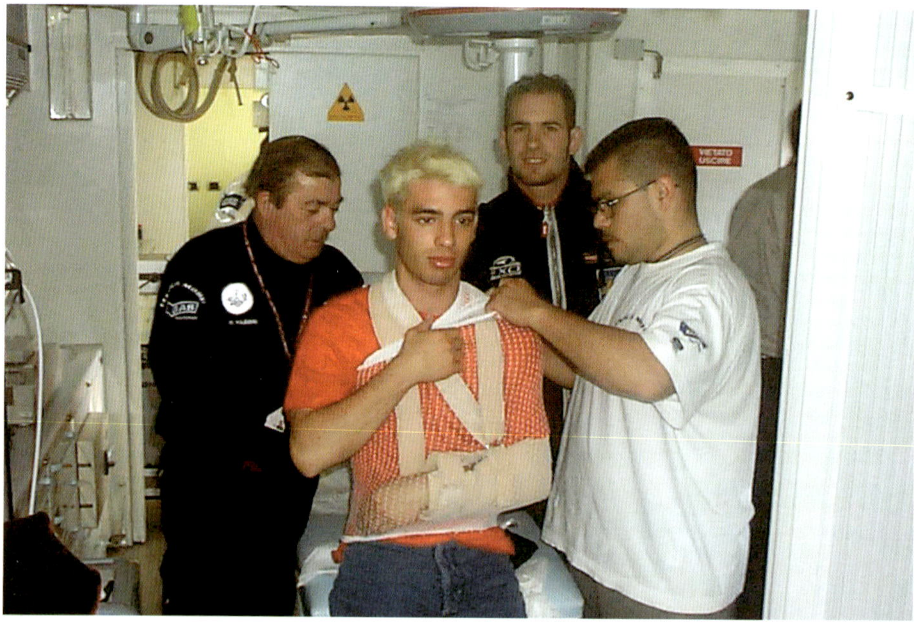

Paolo Fabbri and Marco Montanari "gift-wrap" Marco Melandri.

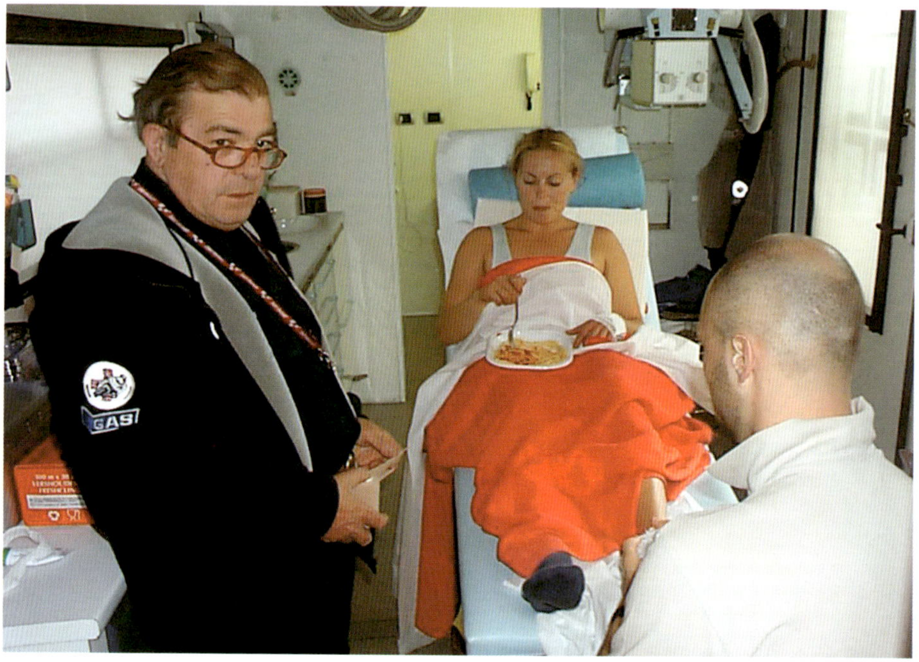

Katja Poensgen takes the best medicine going: a plate of spaghetti.

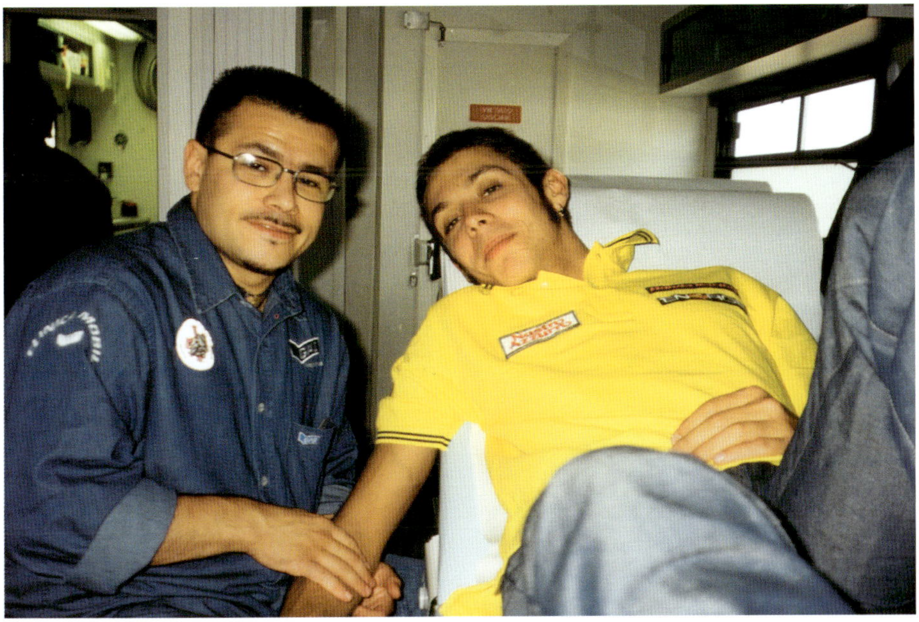

Valentino Rossi with his trusted physiotherapist Marco Montanari.

Claudio Costa and Leon Haslam. His father, Ron, was a Clinica Mobile customer too.

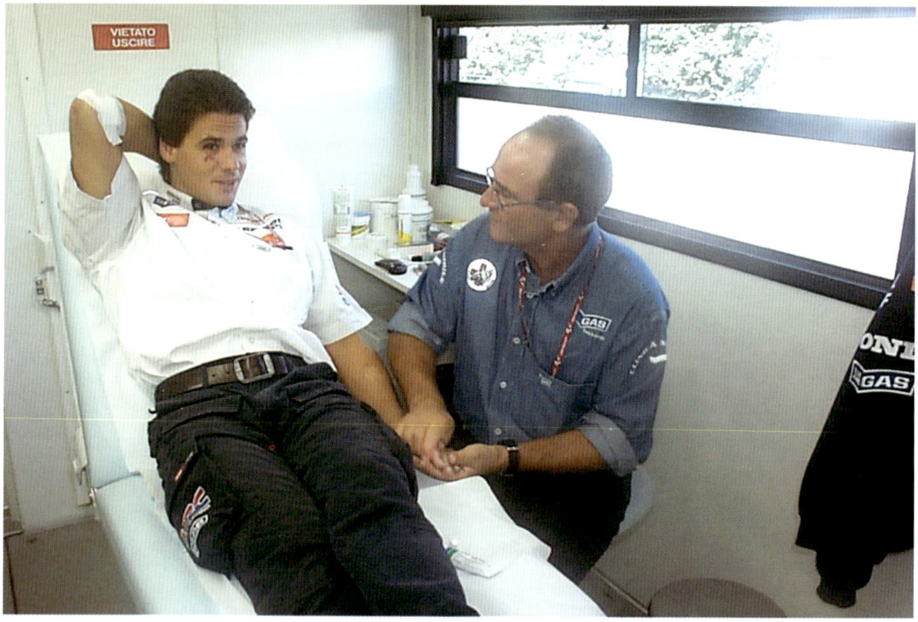

Bernard Achou "repairs" Alex Criville's battered body.

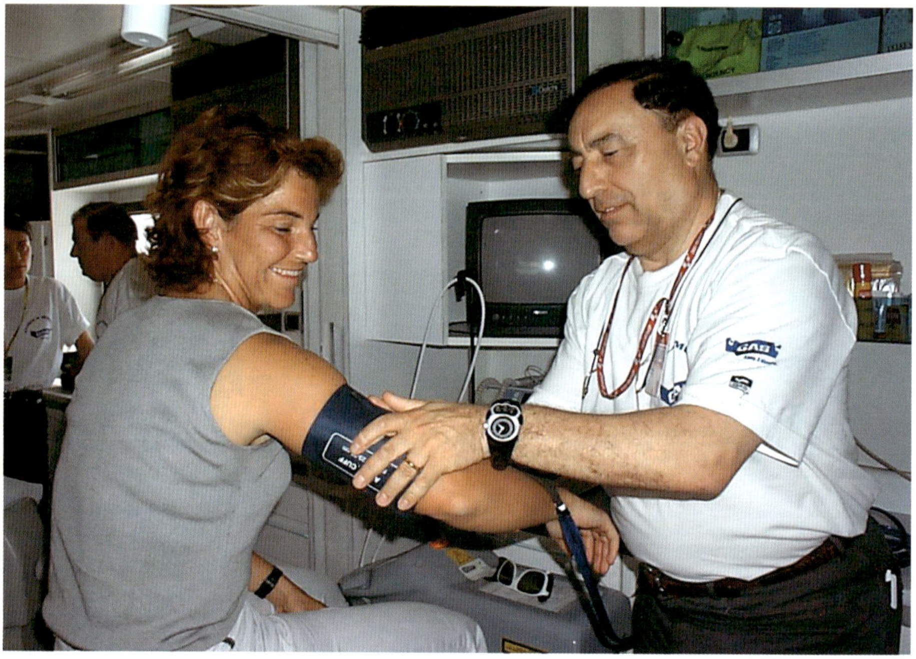

Dr. Salvatore Marrone checks Arancia Sanchez's blood pressure.

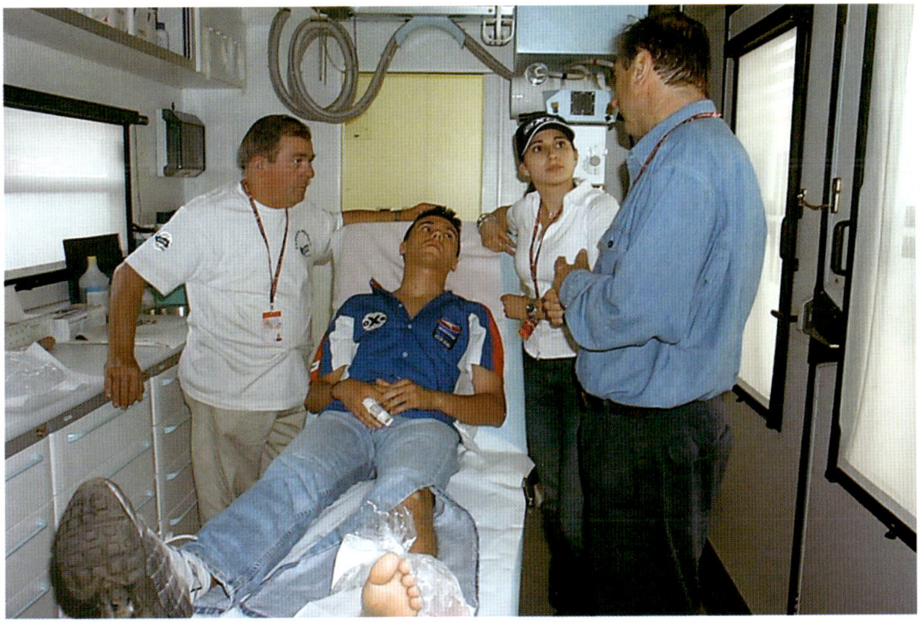

Mirko Giansanti listens to the sentence after his fall.

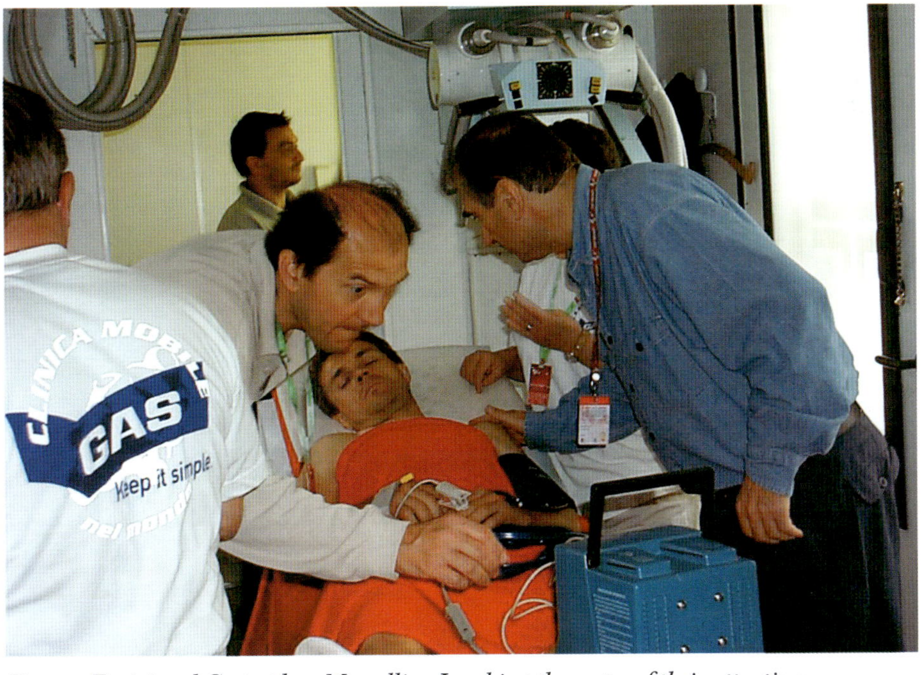

Doctors Enrici and Costa place Marcellino Lucchi at the centre of their attentions.

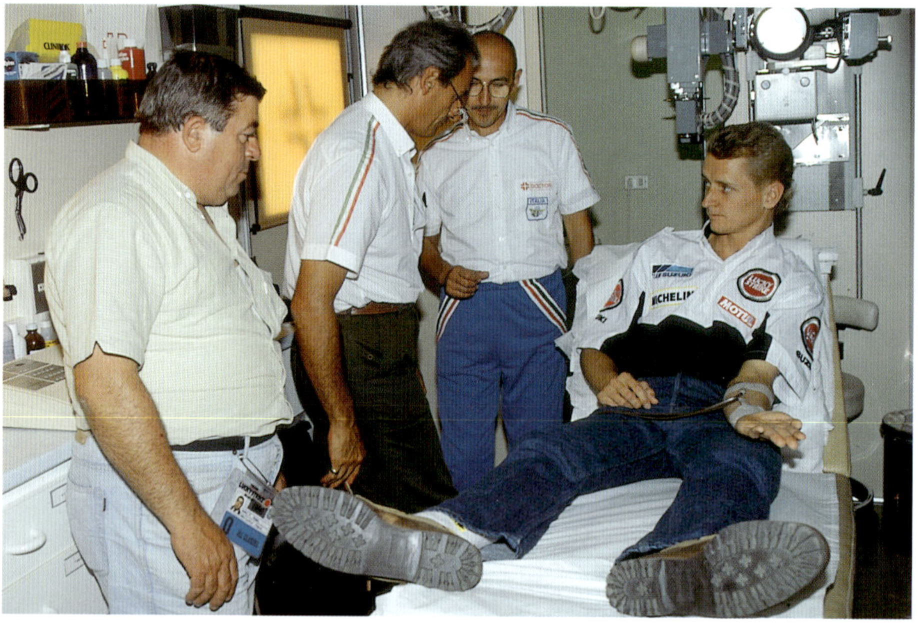

Paolo Fabbri, Lello Rubbini, Ruggero Mattioli, Kevin Schwantz.

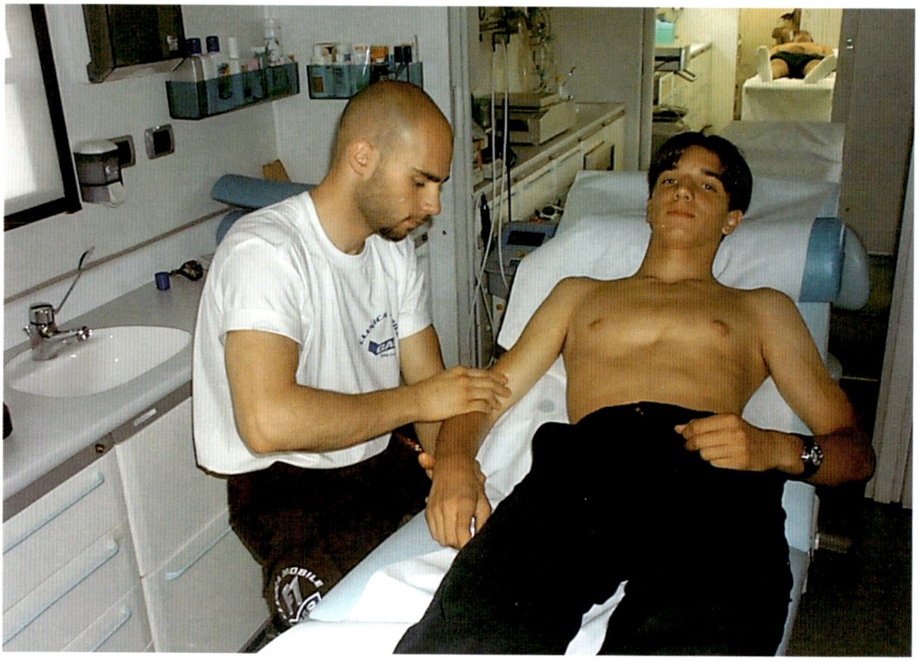

Francesco Chionne massages Alex De Angelis.

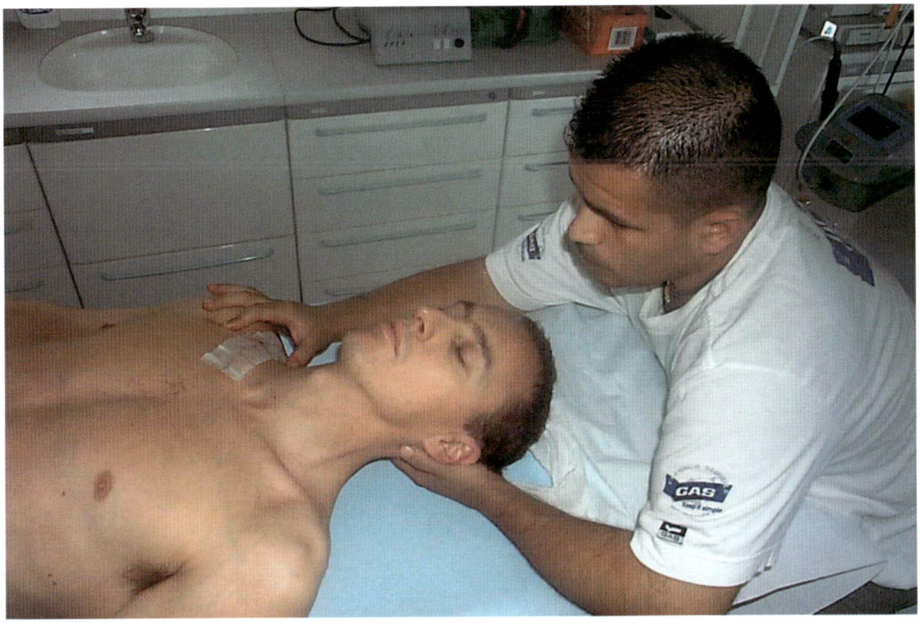

Twelve days after the operation on his collar bone McWilliams is "prepared" by Montanari.

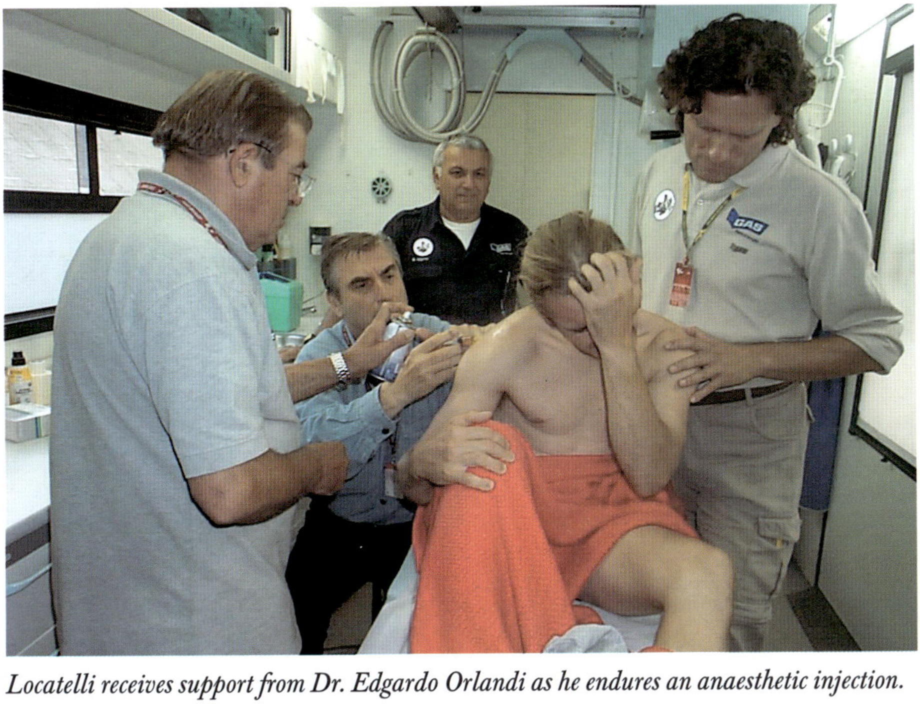

Locatelli receives support from Dr. Edgardo Orlandi as he endures an anaesthetic injection.

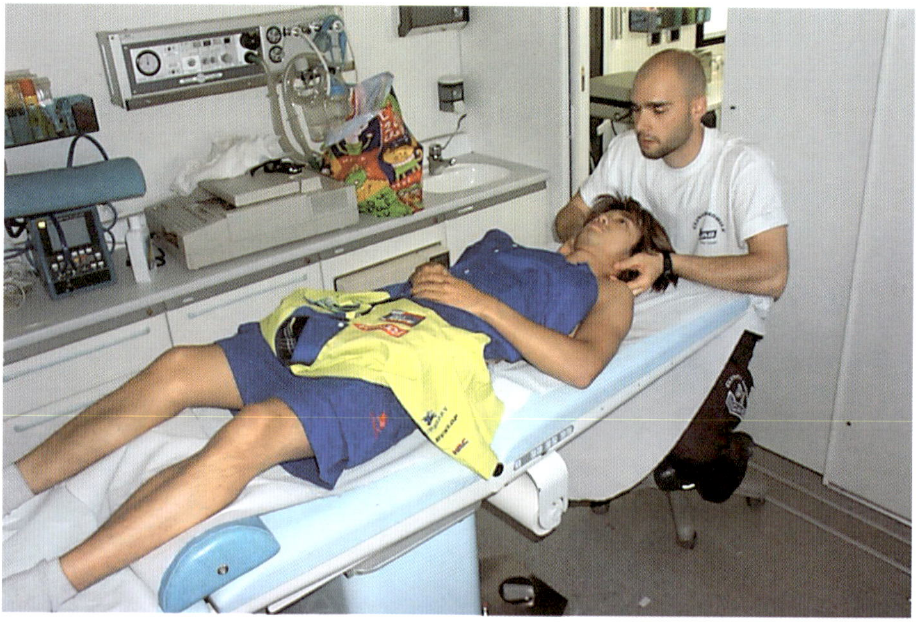

Daijiro Katoh gets a neck massage.

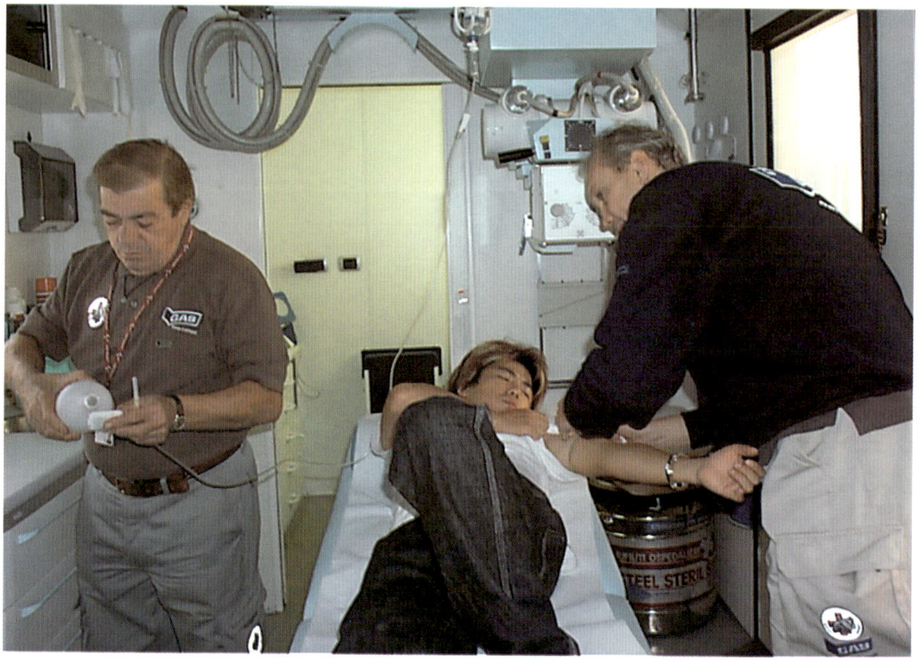

Dr. Guerra prepares a mineral salt, sugar and vitamin drip-feed for Ui prior to the race.

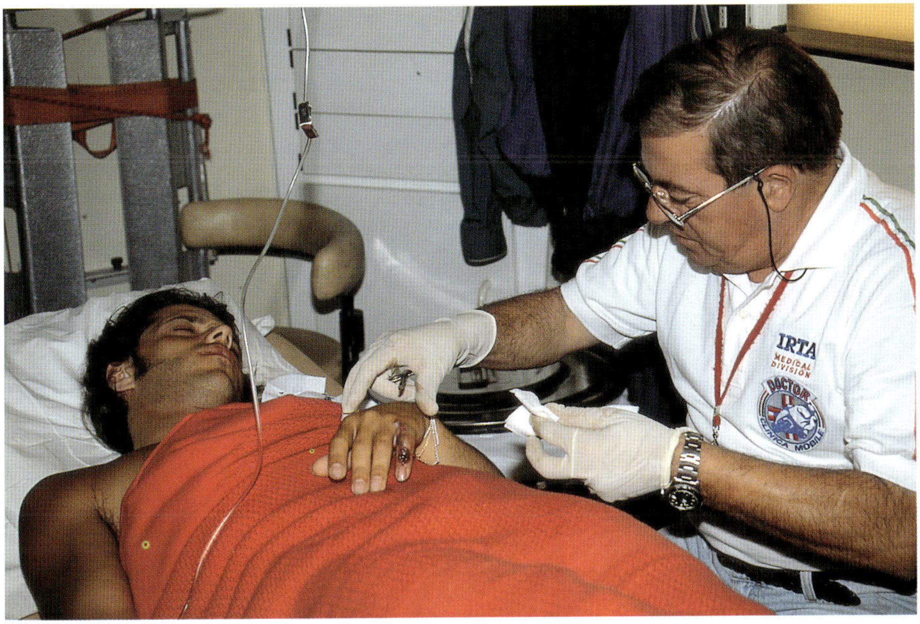

Paolo Fabbri medicates Loris Capirossi's injured little finger.

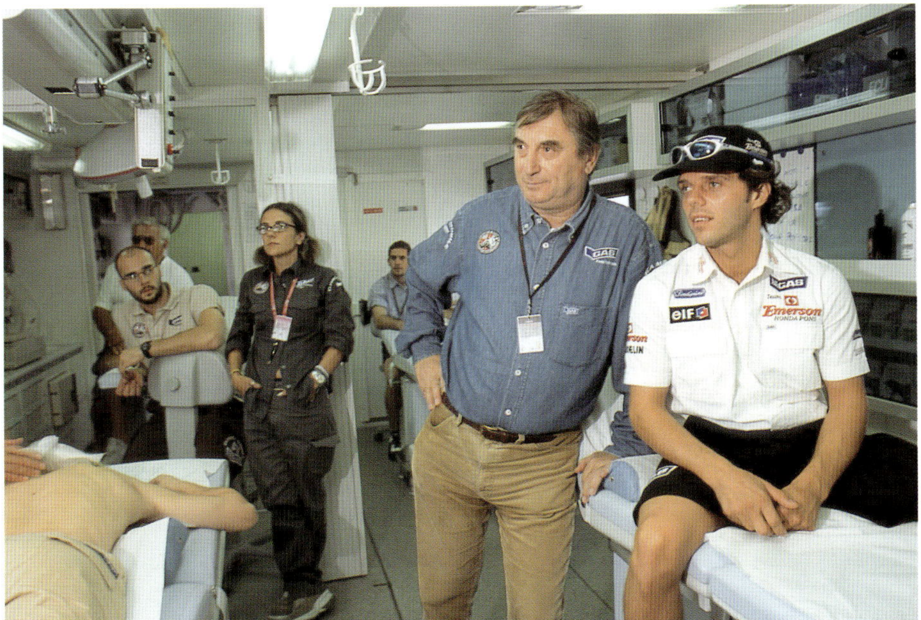

Doctors, staff and riders follow the 125 cc race on the Clinica's TV.

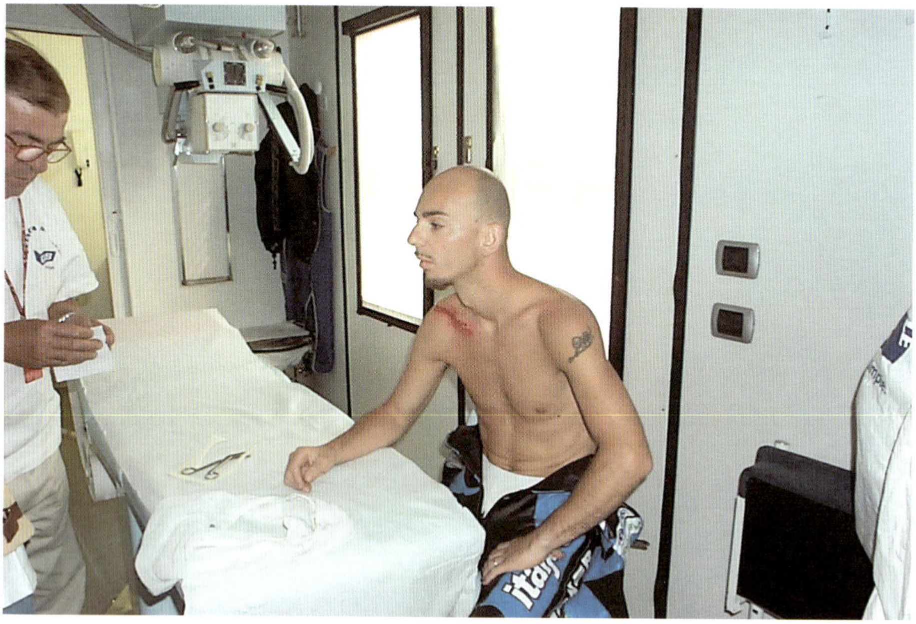

Gianluigi Scalvini 12 days after his collar bone operation.

Max Sabbatani smiles from his Clinica Mobile bed.

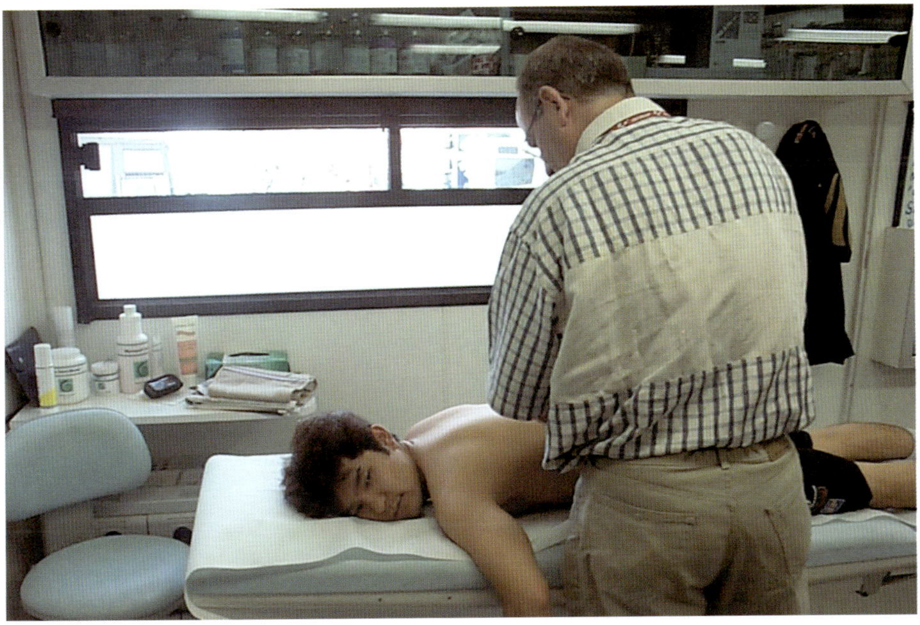

Tetsuya Harada warms up his muscles with a pre-race massage.

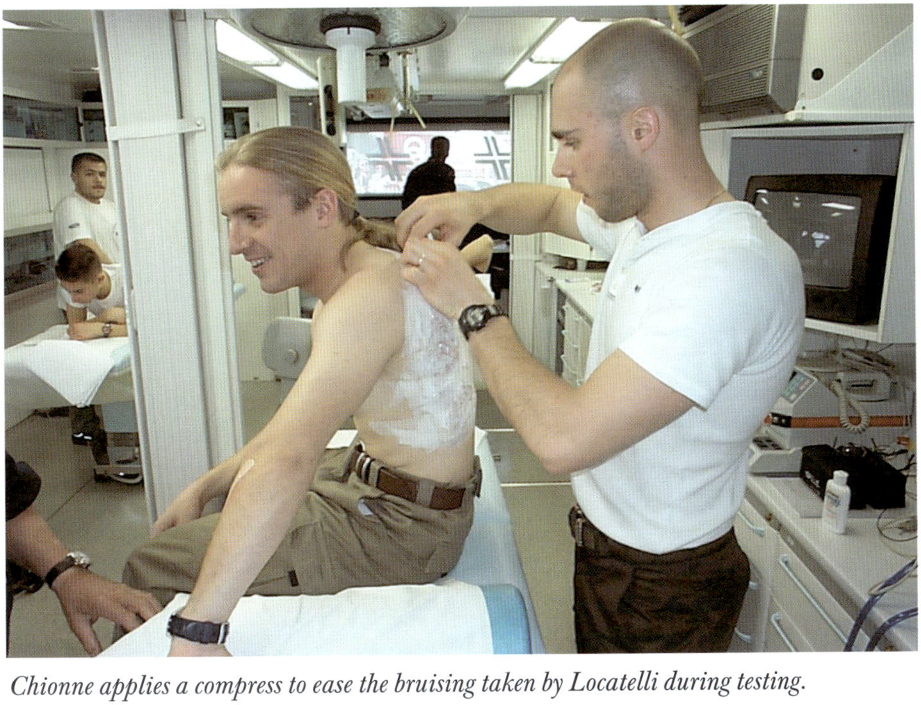

Chionne applies a compress to ease the bruising taken by Locatelli during testing.

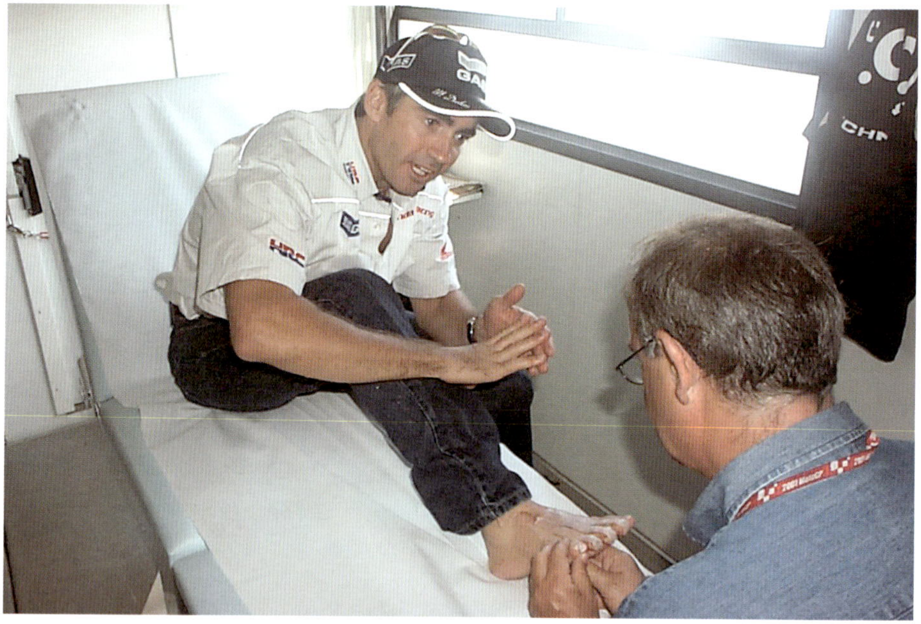

Mick Doohan in the Clinica Mobile: there can be no champion, nor man, without injury.

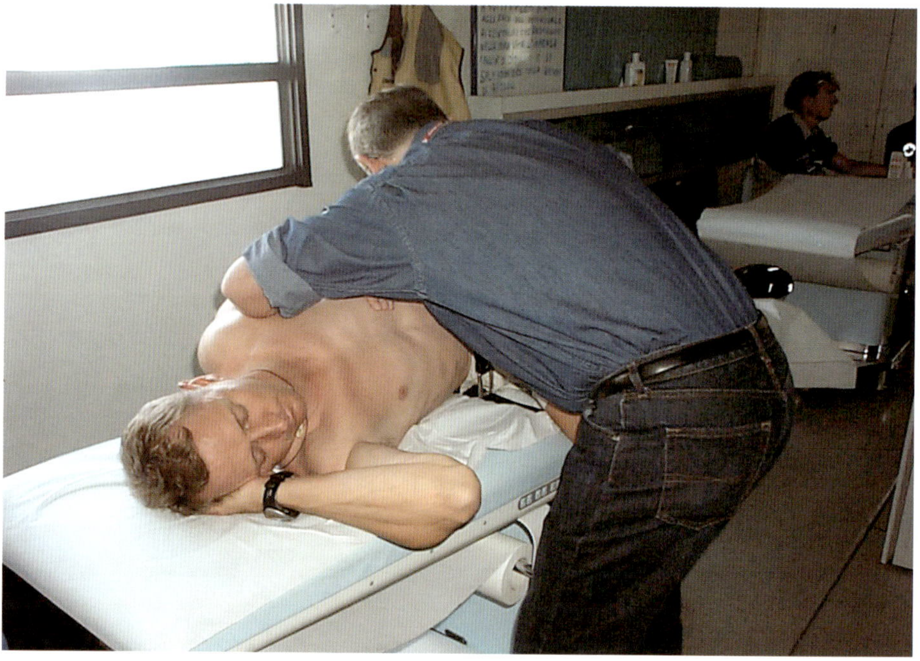

Kevin Schwantz: human contact, a sure begetter of happiness.

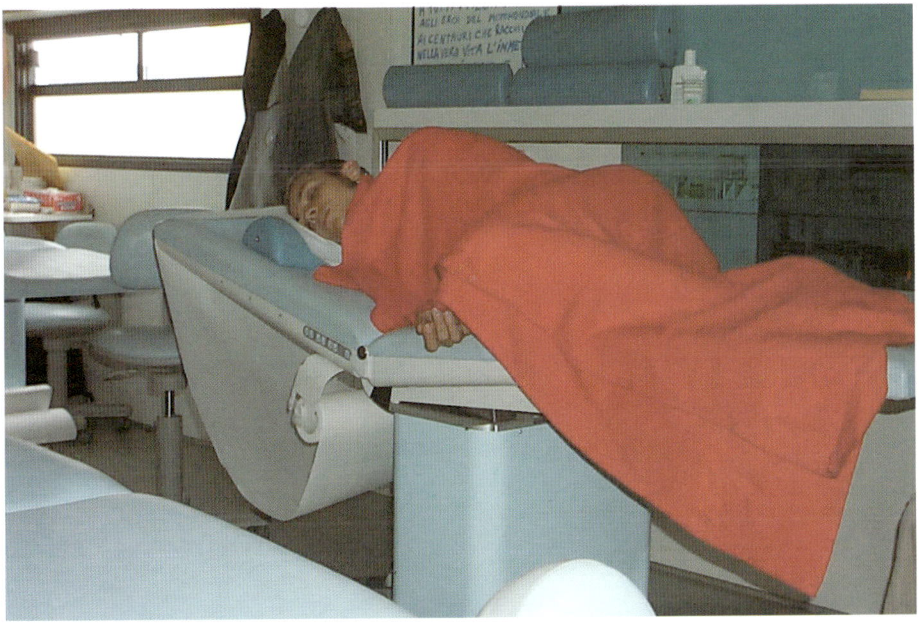

"Generals always sleep serenely before battle" (A. Manzoni). Rossi proves his point.

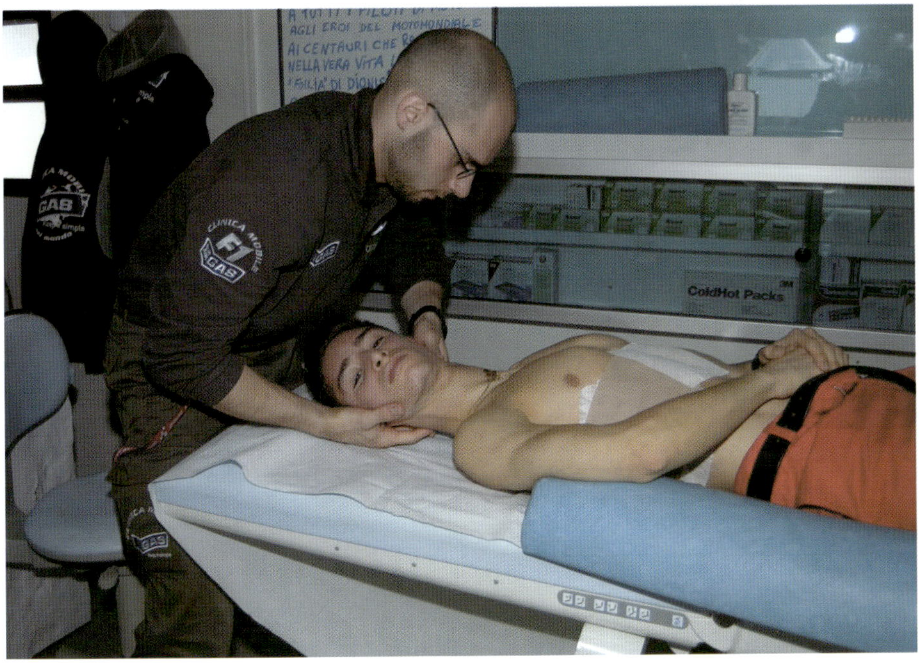

Manuel Poggiali in the hands of Francesco Chionne following a torso injury.

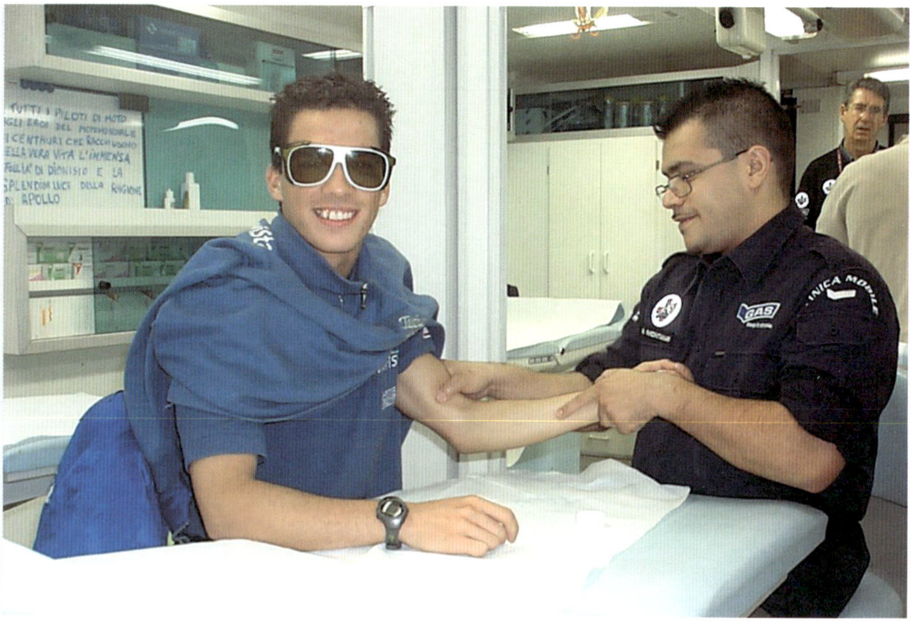

Toni Elias: the delight of a boy who knows playtime is not far off.

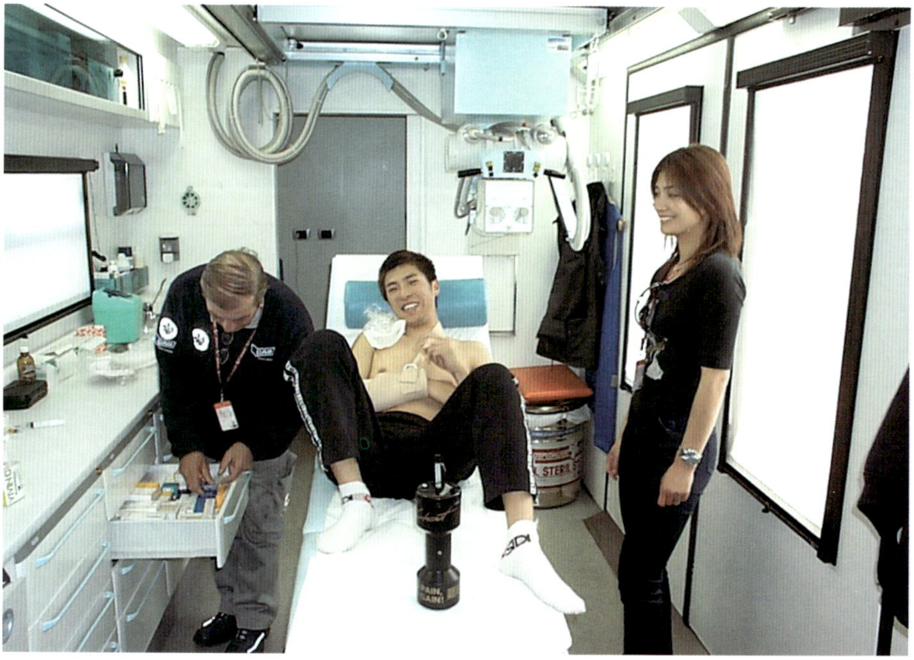

Aoki and his actress girlfriend smile away the pain: they know his clavicle will soon heal.

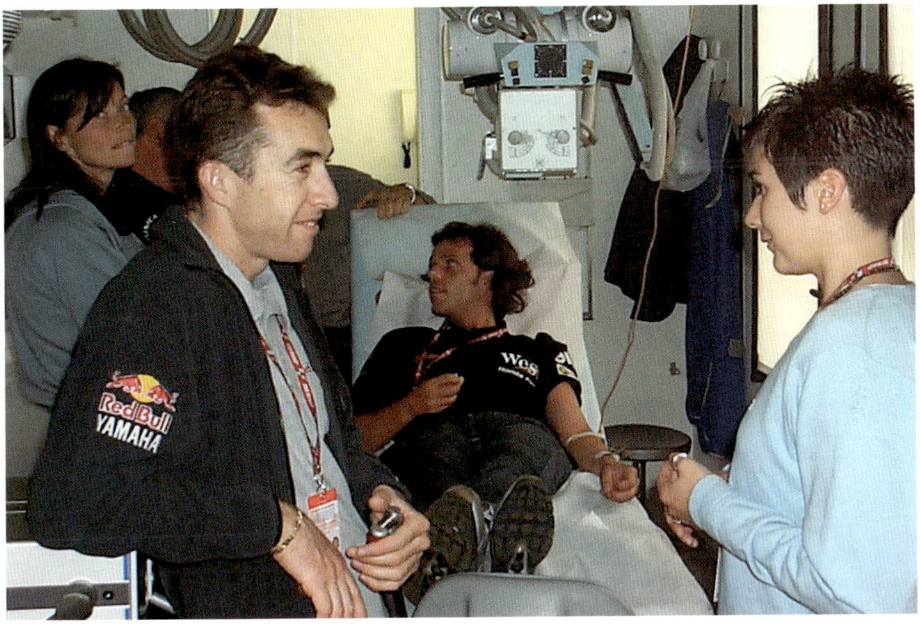

Garry McCoy waits his turn on the Clinica Mobile bed.

A jokey Ueda in the Clinica's hospitality tent, which feeds some 270 people at every GP.

Claudio Costa embraces his "encyclopaedia" of fractures: Barry Sheene.

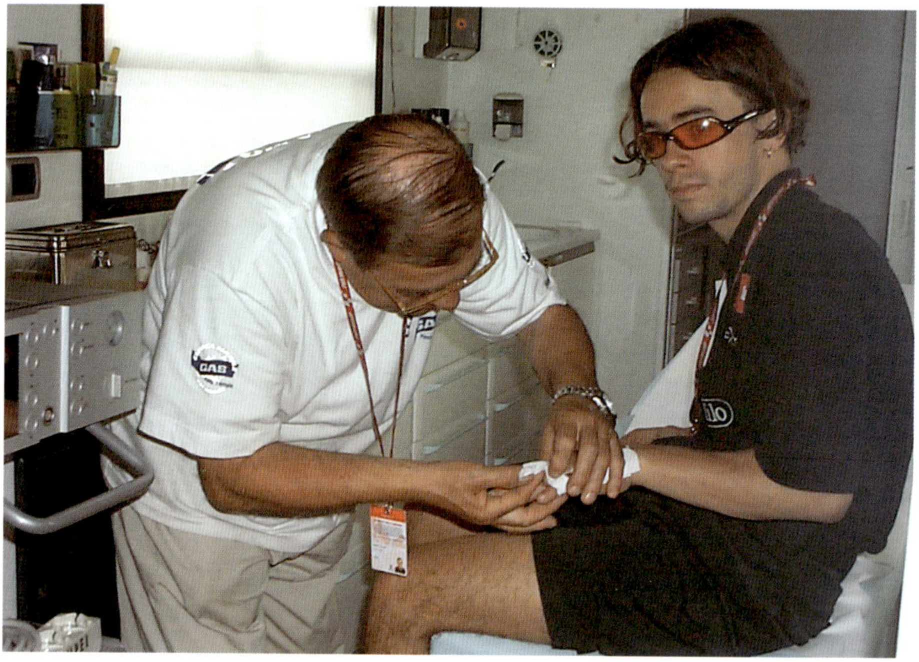

Paolo Fabbri medicates Simone Sanna with his usual devotion.

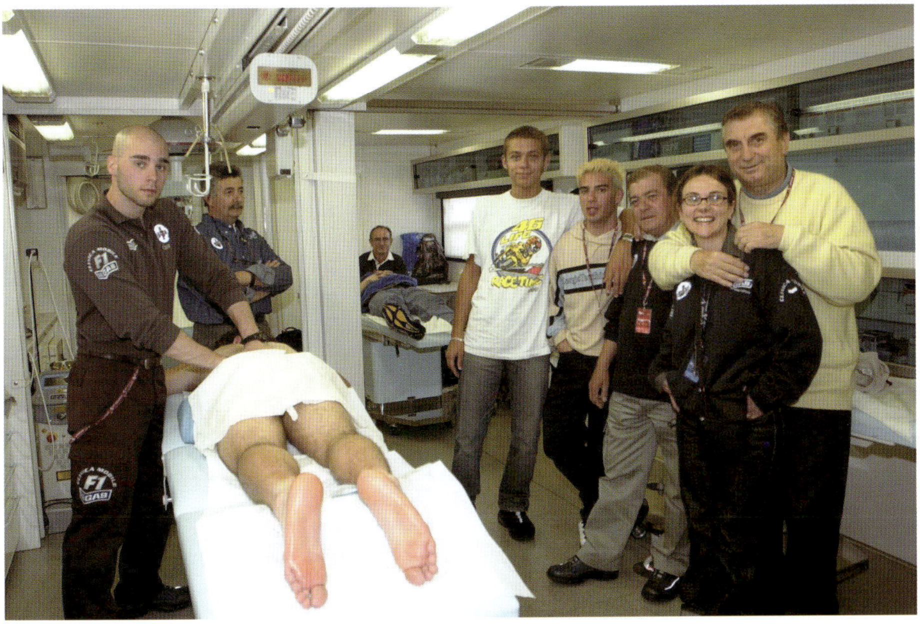

Jerez 2001: inside the Clinica Mobile with Valentino Rossi and Marco Melandri.

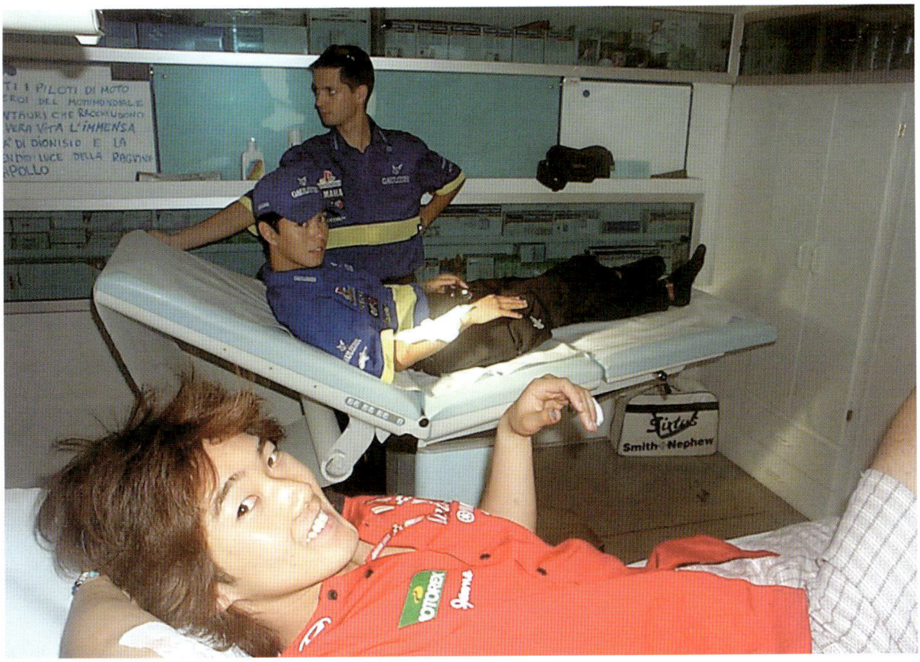

Abe and Nakano: two battered samurai.

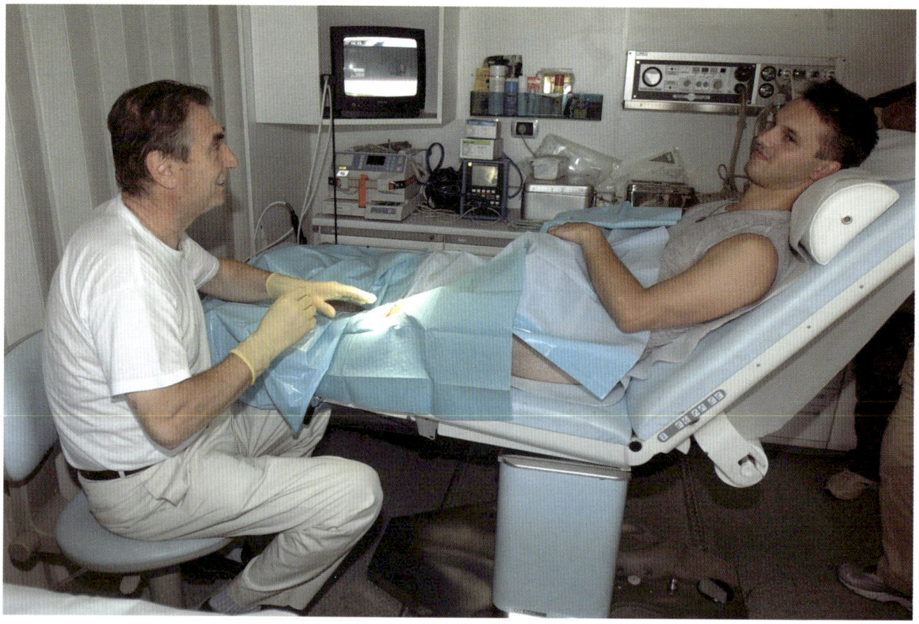

Claudio Costa promises to fix Borsoi's knee: the next day he was back racing.

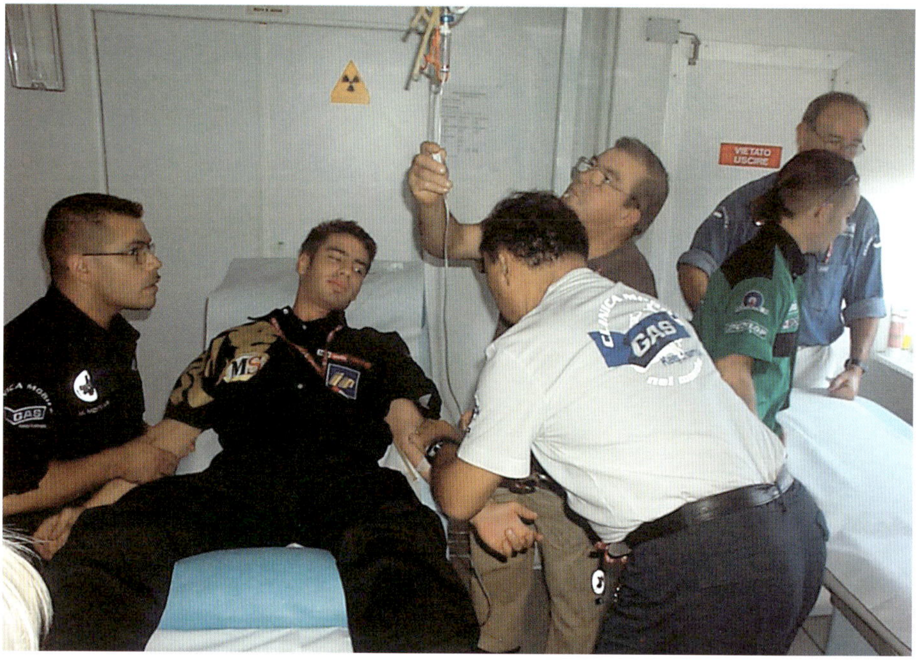

Drip-feed, massage and loving care for Marco Melandri.

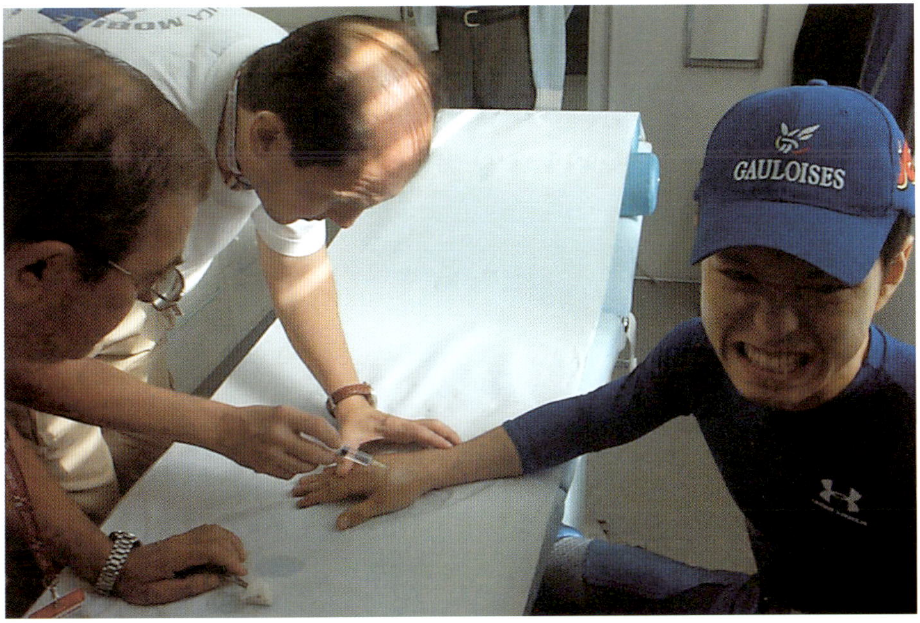

Nakano winces as Dr. Alberto Enrici injects his broken hand with anaesthetic.

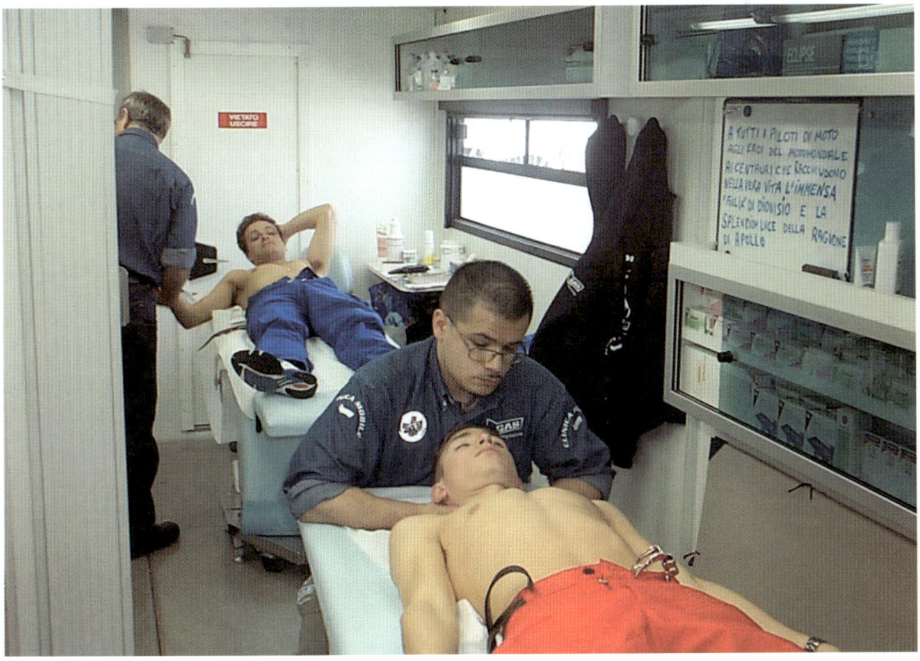

The physiotherapists get to grips with Manuel Poggiali and Emilio Alzamora.

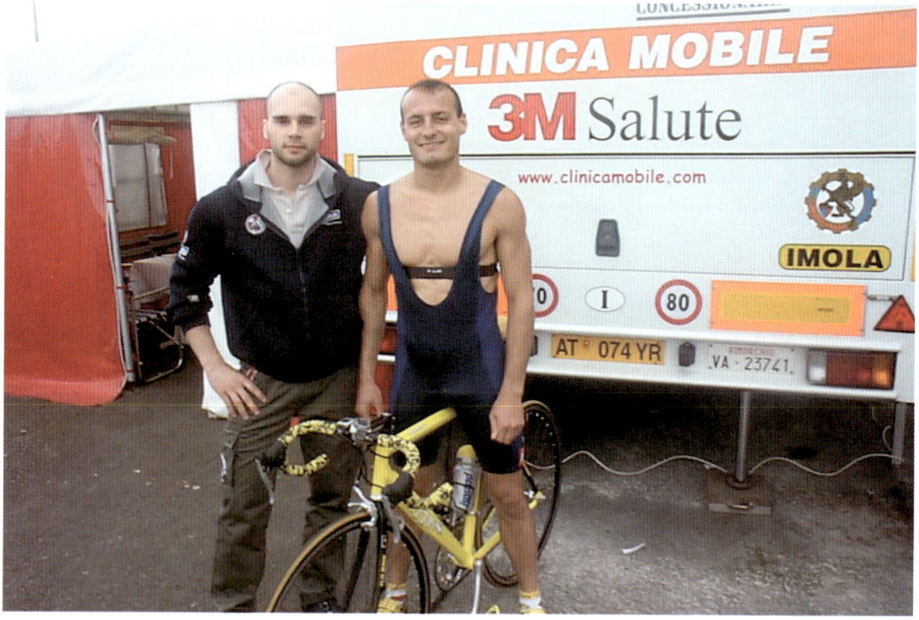

Franco Battaini tests out a heartbeat monitor.

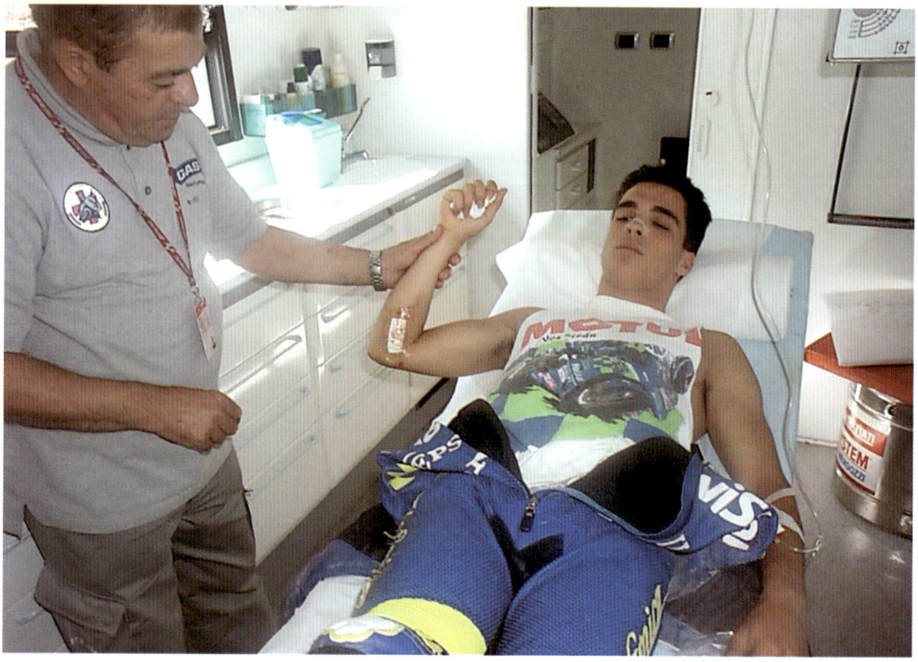

Toni Elias has his injured elbow photographed.

Lello Rubbini, Bernie Ecclestone, Claudio Costa.

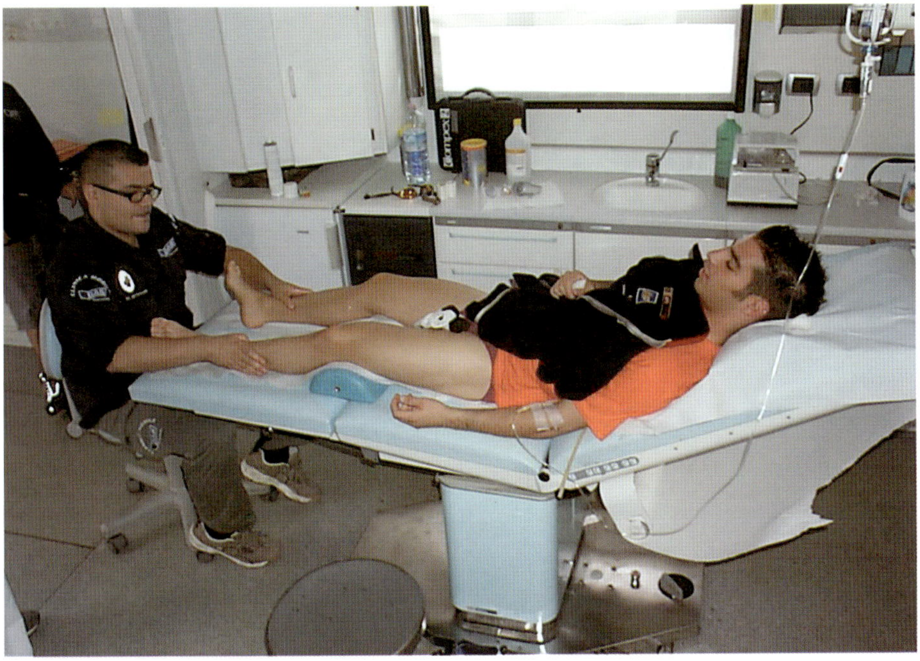

Marco Montanari at the feet of Marco Melandri.

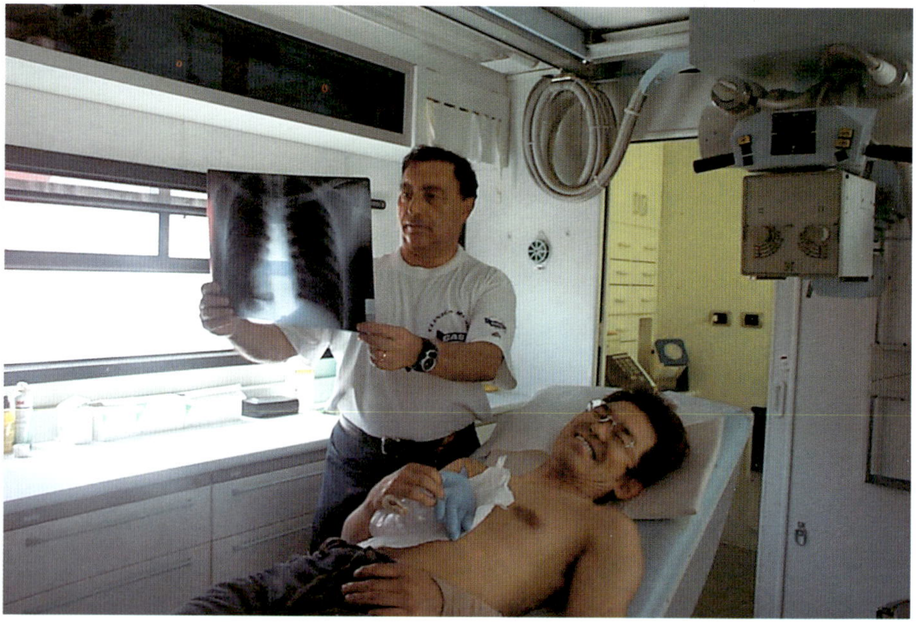

Dr. Salvatore Marrone examines Ueda's chest X-ray as the rider smiles happily.

Doriano Romboni and Claudio Costa.

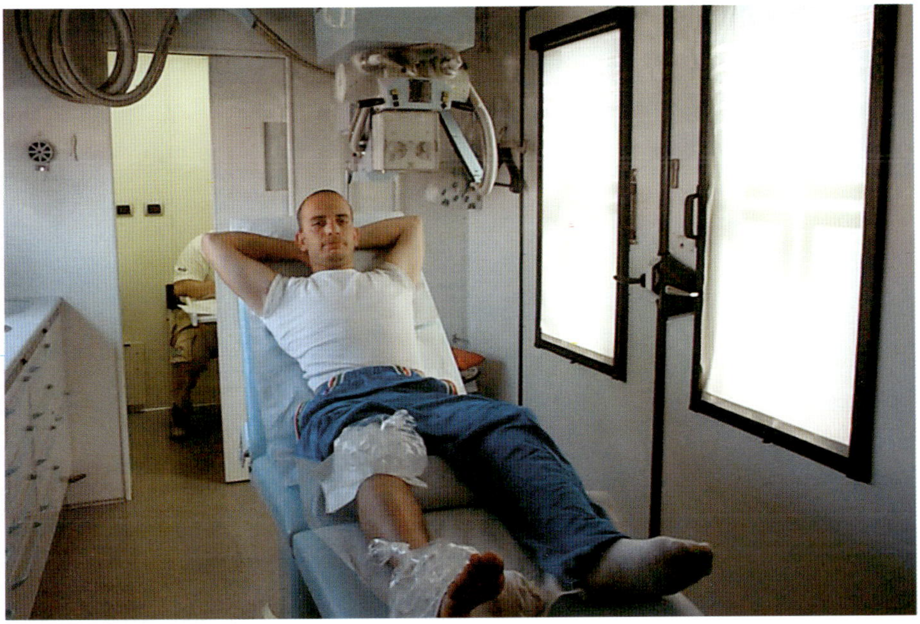

Stefano Perugini cools it with some Clinica Mobile ice.

Carlos Checa with Kenny Roberts Jr and the Clinica Mobile Staff.

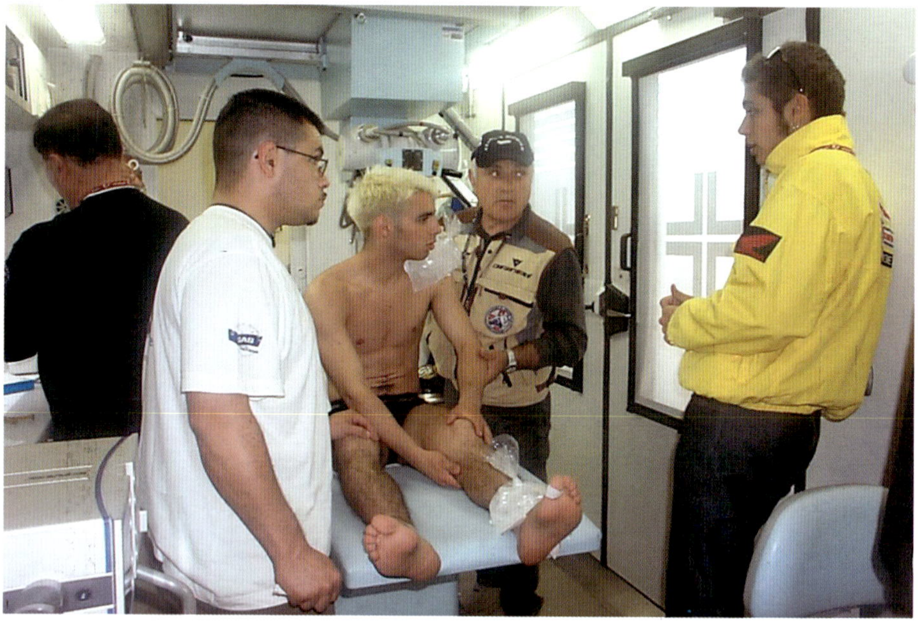

From right: Valentino Rossi, Franco Fontana, Marco Melandri and the physio Montanari.

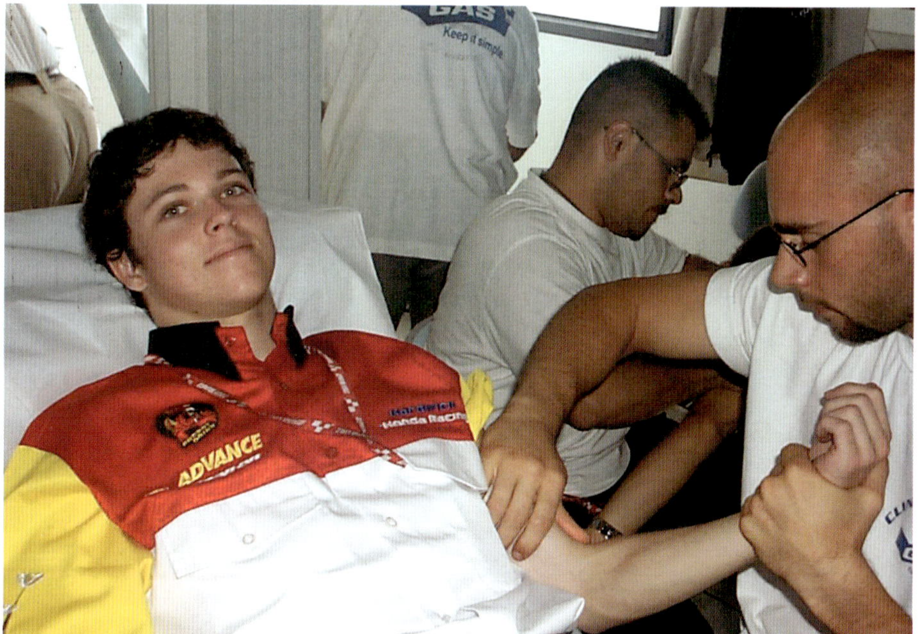

Brendan Clarke: even angels need physiotherapy.

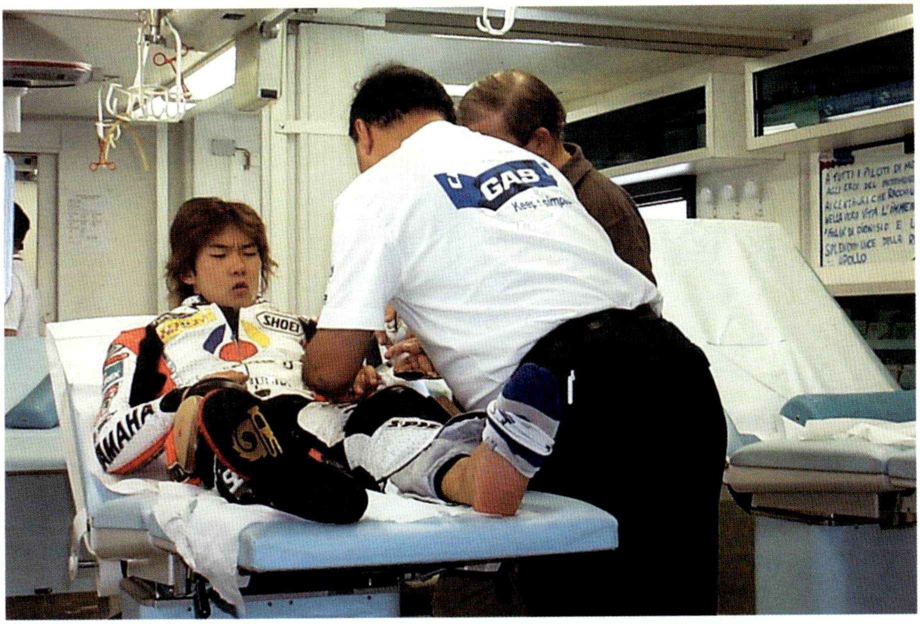

Norifumi Abe winces with the pain.

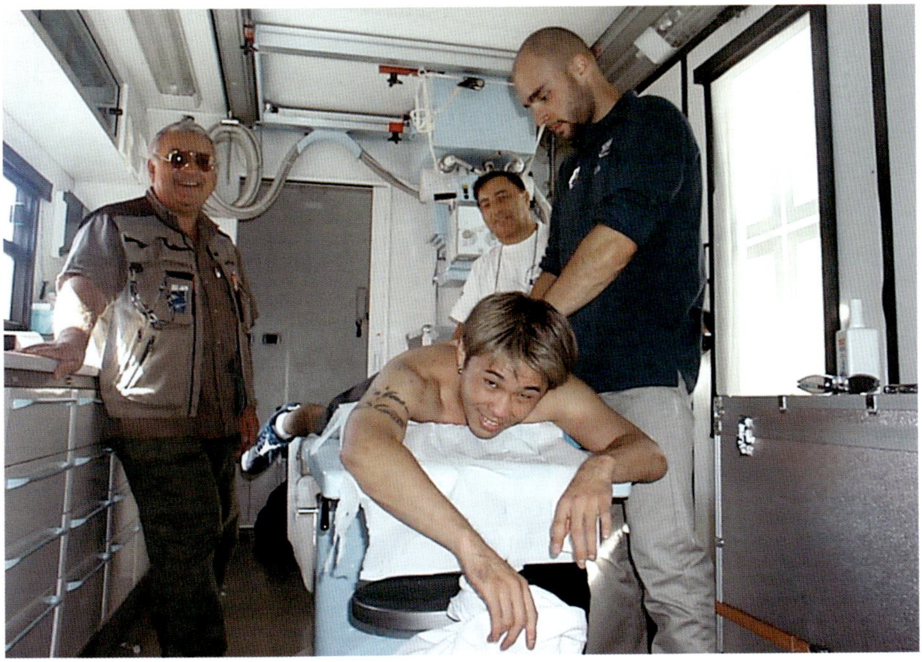

After the Portuguese race: Noriyuki Haga relaxes with a massage.

AVANTI, C'È POSTO!!!
LOURDES SUCCURSALE
CLINICA MOBILE
CAROLI & Matitaccia 95

ALMENO URLASSE COME TUTTI DURANTE LE MEDICAZIONI... MACCHÈ, LUI SOLO SI LAMENTA, MA DELLE GOMME!!!
Matitaccia 94

I PILOTI VEDONO ORMAI CLAUDIO COSTA COME UN GURU, UN SANTONE, UN DIO...
MA VA!..
CLINICA MOBILE
DOTTORE, IO NON SON DEGNO DI ENTRARE NELLA TUA CLINICA, MA DI' SOLTANTO UNA PAROLA E LA MANO MIA SARA' GUARITA!
Matitaccia 96

CHI CUCI, CLAUDIO?
CUCIO KIKUCHI.!!
Matitaccia 98

Claudio Costa flanked by Medical Directors Claudio Macchiagodena and Ruggero Mattioli.

Massimo Corbascio, Claudio Costa, Mauro Vivoli.

From left: Michele Macchiagodena, Luca Pini, Romano Guerra, Paolo Fabbri, Alberto Enrici.

One of the many Clinica Mobile 3 teams.

One of the many Clinica Mobile 4 teams.

From left: Chionne, Tassinari, Filippin, Montanari, Achou.

From left: Franco Sgubbi, Pietro Castaldi, Bruno Orazi, Franco Fontana.

Claudio Costa in front of the Feudino in a photo portrait by Carlo Orsi.

Dr. Costa in Mick Doohan's second home: the Feudino.

Aldo Drudi, Claudio Costa and Kevin Schwantz around the Feudino dining table.

From his portrait, Checco Costa keeps watch over the Feudino's many guests.

Costa and Melandri at the Feudino, where riders go to forget their injuries.

The Riva: Alessandro Zanardi promises Dr. Costa he'll be back as one of life's winners…

...and, on 15th December 2001, at the Autosprint Caschi d'Oro awards, he keeps that promi-

APPENDICES

BIBLIOGRAPHY

This is not the standard collection of sources consulted by the author. It is a list of the works that have inspired me and guided my hand in the writing of this book. To tell the truth, it should also include the names of every rider I've ever met, including all those I have not mentioned in these pages: without them this book would never have been written.

Agostino di Tagaste, *Confessioni*, Mondadori, Milano 1992-1997.
Alighieri Dante, *La Divina Commedia*, La Nuova Italia, Firenze 1985.
Aristotele, *Opere*, Laterza, Bari 1973.
Battista Ivan, *Kentauros*, Pieraldo, Roma 1996.
Bergson Henri, *L'evoluzione creatrice*, Laterza, Bari 1957.
Bettelheim Bruno, *Il mondo incantato*, Feltrinelli, Milano 1995.
Bolen Jean Shinoda, *Gli dei dentro l'uomo*, Astrolabio, Roma 1994.
Bousquet Joë, *Tradotto dal silenzio*, Marietti, Genova 1987.
Campbell Joseph, *L'eroe dai mille volti*, Guanda, Parma 2000.
Camus Albert, *Il mito di Sisifo*, Bompiani, Milano 1942.
Canetti Elias, *Massa e potere*, Adelphi, Milano 1995.
Carotenuto Aldo, *Amare tradire*, Bompiani, Milano 1991.
Carotenuto Aldo, *Attraversare la vita*, Bompiani, Milano 1991.
Carotenuto Aldo, *I sotterranei dell'anima*, Bompiani, Milano 1993.
Carotenuto Aldo, *Il fondamento della personalità*, Bompiani, Milano 2000.
Carotenuto Aldo, *Integrazione della personalità*, Bompiani, Milano 1992.
Carotenuto Aldo, *La chiamata del Daimon*, Bompiani, Milano 1999.
Carotenuto Aldo, *La strategia di Peter Pan*, Bompiani, Milano 1995.
Carotenuto Aldo, *Le lacrime del male*, Bompiani, Milano 1996.
Carotenuto Aldo, *Le rose nella mangiatoia*, Raffaello Cortina, Milano 1990.
Carotenuto Aldo, *Trattato di psicologia analitica*, voll. 1 e 2, UTET, Torino 1992.
Cicerone Marco Tullio, *La natura divina*, Rizzoli, Milano 1992.
Coehlo Paulo, *Manuale del guerriero della luce*, Bompiani, Milano 2001.
Costa Claudio Marcello – Caroli Giancarlo, *Esperienze di traumatologia nello sport motociclistico*, Grafiche Galeati, Imola 1983.

De Rougemont Denis, *L'amore e l'occidente*, Rizzoli, Milano 1993.
Delli Carri Luca, *Gli indisciplinati*, Fucina, Milano 2001.
Dickinson Emily, *Poesie*, Bompiani, Milano 1978.
Donnini Mario, *Tourist Trophy*, Apex, Gualdo Tadino (PG) 1999.
Dostoevskij Fëdor Michajlovic, *Il giocatore*, Demetra, Verona 1993.
Dostoevskij Fëdor Michajlovic, *Memorie dal sottosuolo*, Newton Compton, Roma 1998.
Eraclito, *I presocratici – testimonianze e frammenti*, Laterza, Bari 1983.
Freud Sigmund, *Al di là del principio del piacere*, Boringhieri, Torino 1977.
Freud Sigmund, *Totem e tabù*, Boringhieri, Torino 1975.
Freud Sigmund, *Il disagio della civiltà*, Boringhieri, Torino 1973.
Fromm Erich, *Avere o essere*, Mondadori, Milano 1977.
Galilei Galileo, *Dialogo sopra i due massimi sistemi del mondo*, Barbera, Firenze 1929-1934.
Galimberti Umberto, *Psiche e techne*, Feltrinelli, Milano 2000.
Gehlen Arnold, *L'uomo – La sua natura e posto nel mondo*, Feltrinelli, Milano 1983.
Gibran Kahlil, *Il profeta*, Tea, Milano 2000.
Goethe Johann Wolfgang, *Faust*, Mondadori, Milano 1997.
Goethe Johann Wolfgang, *Romanzi*, Mondadori, Milano 1991.
Graves Robert, *I miti greci*, Longanesi, Milano 1980.
Hesse Hermann, *Religione e mito*, Mondadori, Milano 1988.
Hesse Hermann, *Siddharta*, Adelphi, Milano 2000.
Hilmann James, *Le ferite del puer e la cicatrice di Ulisse*, Raffaello Cortina, Milano 1988.
Ippocrate, *Male sacro*, UTET, Torino 1976.
Jamison Kay Redfield, *Toccato dal fuoco*, Longanesi, Milano 1993.
Jung Carl Gustav, *Tipi psicologici*, Boringhieri, Torino 1981.
Jung Carl Gustav, *Ricordi, sogni e riflessioni*, a cura di Daniela Jaffe, Rizzoli, Milano 1990.
Jung Carl Gustav, *L'uomo e i suoi simboli*, TEA, Milano 1967.
Jung Carl Gustav, *La dinamica dell'inconscio*, Boringhieri, Torino 1989.
Kafka Franz, *Il processo*, Mondadori, Milano 1982.
Kafka Franz, *Prometeo*, Mondadori, Milano 1983.
Kafka Franz, *Il castello*, Mondadori, Milano 1985.
Kafka Franz, *La metamorfosi*, Mondadori, Milano 1983.
Kierkegaard Søren, *Diario di un seduttore*, Demetra, Verona 1995.

Kierkegaard Søren, *Il concetto dell'angoscia*, Paravia, Torino 1956.
Kleist Heinrich von, *Lettere*, Vallevecchi, Firenze 1962.
Kleist Heinrich von, *Sul teatro delle marionette*, Sansoni, Firenze 1959.
Kristeva Julia, *Sole nero*, Feltrinelli, Milano 1988.
Leopardi Giacomo, *Tutte le opere*, Sansoni, Firenze 1976.
Leopardi Giacomo, *Operette morali*, Garzanti, Milano 1982.
Masters Edgar Lee, *Antologia di Spoon River*, Einaudi, Torino 1971.
Milton John, *Paradiso perduto*, Mondadori, Milano 1990.
Natoli Salvatore, *La felicità*, Feltrinelli, Milano 1994.
Nietzsche Friedrich, *Al di là del bene e del male*, Demetra, Verona 2000.
Nietzsche Friedrich, *Così parlò Zarathustra*, Rizzoli, Milano 1985.
Nietzsche Friedrich, *Ecce homo*, Libritalia, Cerbara (PG) 1997.
Nietzsche Friedrich, *La filosofia nell'epoca tragica dei greci*, Adelphi, Milano 1991.
Nietzsche Friedrich, *La volontà di potenza*, Bompiani, Milano 1992.
Nietzsche Friedrich, *La nascita della tragedia*, Adelphi, Milano 1972.
Novalis (Friedrich von Hardenberg), *Frammenti*, Rizzoli, Milano 1991.
Omero, *Iliade*, Einaudi, Torino 1974.
Ovidio, *Le metamorfosi*, Einaudi, Torino 1979.
Pascoli Giovanni, *Poesie*, Garzanti, Milano, 1981.
Pavese Cesare, *Il mestiere di vivere*, Einaudi, Torino 1990.
Perls Fritz, *Qui e ora piscoterapia autobiografica*, Sovera, Roma 1991.
Pirandello Luigi, *Una, nessuno e centomila*, Orsa Maggiore, Forlì 1995.
Pirazzini Ezio, *I giorni del coraggio*, Calderini, Bologna 1975.
Pirazzini Ezio, *Addio campione*, Calderini, Bologna 1977.
Pirazzini Ezio, *I giorni dell'ira e del dolore*, Calderini, Bologna 1976.
Pirsig Robert M., *Lo zen e l'arte della manutenzione della motocicletta*, Adelphi, Milano 1992.
Platone, *Tutte le opere*, Sansoni, Firenze 1974.
Rank Otto, *Il doppio*, Sugarco, Milano 1979.
Rank Otto, *Il mito della nascita dell'eroe*, Sugarco, Milano 1987.
Rank Otto, *Trauma della nascita*, Sugarco, Milano 1990.
Rilke Rainer Maria, *I sonetti a Orfeo*, Feltrinelli, Milano 1991.
Rilke Rainer Maria, *Il testamento*, Guanda, Milano 1974.
Saint-Exupéry Antoine de, *Il piccolo principe*, Bompiani, Milano 2001.
Schellenbaum Peter, *La ferita dei non amati*, Demetra, Verona 1995.
Schopenhauer Arthur, *Il mondo come volontà e rappresentazione*, Mondadori, Milano 1989.

Schopenhauer Arthur, *La volontà della natura*, Laterza, Bari 1989.
Sgarbi Vittorio – Goldoni Luca – Poltronieri Mario, *Il circuito di Imola*, Rizzoli, Milano 2000.
Shakespeare William, *Tutte le opere*, Sansoni, Firenze 1982.
Sofocle – Eschilo – Euripide, *Tragedie greche*, Orsa maggiore, Forlì 1994.
Wilde Oscar, *De profundis*, Feltrinelli, Milano 1982.
Winicott Donald W., *Gioco e realtà*, Armando, Roma 1986.
Wolf Christa, *Cassandra*, E/O, Roma 1999.
Yourcenar Marguerite, *Le memorie di Adriano*, Einaudi, Torino 1998.

FILMOGRAPHY

Bergman Ingmar, *The Seventh Seal*, Sweden 1956.
Brest Martin, *Scent of a Woman*, USA 1992.
Daldry Stephen, *Billy Elliot*, GB 2000.
Kubrick Stanley, *A Clockwork Orange*, GB 1971.
Scott Ridley, *White Squall*, USA 1996.
Scott Ridley, *Thelma and Louise*, USA 1991.
Spielberg Steven, *E.T.*, USA 1982.
Spielberg Steven, *Saving Private Ryan*, USA 1998.
Van Sant Gus, *Finding Forrester*, GB – USA 2000.
Weir Peter, *Dead Poets' Society*, USA 1989.
Wolfgang Petersen, *The Never Ending Story*, Germany 1984.

PHOTOGRAPHIC SOURCES

The author would like to thank all the photographers and archive owners who have allowed me use of their material.

Photographers.
Barbanti Alessio
Oscar Bergamaschi
Dario Ferlini
Jan Hnizdo
Giacomo Gardi
Marco Guidetti
Marco Isola
Tino Martino
Angelo Orsi
Carlo Orsi
Fabrizio Porrozzi
Gianni Sanna
Giorgio Serra (disegni)
Gigi Soldano
Taglioni Stefano
Guido Zucchi
Archives.
Archivio Autosprint
Archivio Daniele Amaduzzi
Archivio Cassa di Risparmio di Imola
Archivio Clinica Mobile
Archivio Claudio Costa
Archivio Ducati
Archivio Gamberini
Archivio Motosprint
Archivio Giovanni Perrone
Archivio Franco Villani

INDEX OF NAMES

Printed in Italy
April 2002
by Arti Grafiche Passoni, Milan